AN IMPORTANT MESSAGE TO OUR READERS

This product provides information and general advice about the law. But laws and procedures change frequently, and they can be interpreted differently by different people. For specific advice geared to your specific situation, consult an expert. No book, software or other published material is a substitute for personalized advice from a knowledgeable lawyer licensed to practice law in your state.

1st edition

Nolo's Quick LLC

by Attorney Anthony Mancuso

KEEPING UP-TO-DATE

To keep its books up-to-date, Nolo issues new printings and new editions periodically. New printings reflect minor legal changes and technical corrections. New editions contain major legal changes, major text additions or major reorganizations. To find out if a later printing or edition of any Nolo book is available, call Nolo at 510-549-1976 or check our website at http://www.nolo.com.

To stay current, follow the "Update" service at our website at http://www.nolo.com/update. In another effort to help you use Nolo's latest materials, we offer a 35% discount off the purchase of the new edition of your Nolo book when you turn in the cover of an earlier edition. (See the "Special Upgrade Offer" in the back of the book.) This book was last revised in: June 2001.

FIRST EDITION	**June 2001**
EDITOR	Beth Laurence
PRODUCTION	Sarah Hinman
COVER	Toni Ihara
PROOFREADER	Robert Wells
INDEX	Sayre Van Young
PRINTING	Bertelsmann Services, Inc.

Mancuso, Anthony.

   Nolo's Quick LLC / by Anthony Mancuso

      p. cm.

   Includes index.

   ISBN 0-87337-573-4

   1. Limited partnership--United States--Popular works. 2. Private Companies--United States--popular Works I. Title.

KF1380.Z9 m363 2000

346.73'0668--dc21   00-020580

ACKNOWLEDGMENTS

A special thanks to Bethany Laurence and Jake Warner for help reworking and editing this material, and to all the Noloids at Nolo for their continued assistance in helping me produce and publish another self-help law business resource.

CONTENTS

INTRODUCTION

CHAPTER 1

AN OVERVIEW OF LLCS

CHAPTER 2

THE LLC VS. OTHER BUSINESS STRUCTURES

CHAPTER 3

MEMBERS' CAPITAL AND PROFITS INTERESTS

CHAPTER 4

TAXATION OF LLC PROFITS

CHAPTER 5

LLC MANAGEMENT

CHAPTER 6

STARTING AND RUNNING YOUR LLC: THE PAPERWORK

CHAPTER 7

GETTING LEGAL AND TAX HELP FOR YOUR LLC

APPENDIXES

INDEX

Introduction

In the business world, limited liability companies are hot, really hot! That's because, as you may already know, a limited liability company (LLC) is a relatively new business ownership structure that combines the best features of the corporation and the partnership. In short, an LLC gives small business owners corporate-style protection from personal liability while retaining the pass-through income tax treatment enjoyed by sole proprietorships (the legal term for one-person businesses) and partnerships.

Protection from personal liability—often referred to by the legal jargon "limited liability"—means that creditors of the business cannot normally go after the owners' personal assets to pay for LLC debts and claims arising from lawsuits; pass-through tax treatment means that business profits are reported and taxed on the individual income tax returns of the business owners. I'll discuss limited liability and pass-through taxation in much more depth in Chapter 1.

All 50 states and the District of Columbia now allow the formation of this unique type of legal and tax entity, and most make it easy, convenient and even relatively economical for small businesspeople to create and register an LLC. For these reasons, more and more entrepreneurs are choosing to organize their businesses as LLCs. And there have been two recent developments that have added additional fuel to the LLC fire:

- Unlike the situation just a few years ago, when an LLC had to have two or more owners, all states save Massachusetts and the District of Columbia now permit the formation of single-owner LLCs. This means that a person who has done business in the past as a sole proprietor (or is just starting out) can now protect her personal assets from business debts and claims by making a simple LLC filing with the state—thus forming an LLC.

- The IRS has recently started to allow LLCs (including single-owner LLCs) to choose between pass-through taxation and corporate tax treatment. Although in most instances LLC owners will decide to stick with pass-through tax status (being taxed on their individual income tax returns), electing to be taxed as a corporation allows LLC owners the option of splitting business income between the business and their own personal income tax returns, which can lower overall business income taxes. As you'll see in Chapter 4, Section C, income splitting can make sense for LLCs if the business makes more than the owners want to take out of the business or if the owners need to keep substantial profits in the business on a regular basis.

There are many ways to gauge the big increase in LLC popularity. You can look at increased filing activity in the state LLC filing offices throughout the country—from 1993 to 1997 the number of LLC filings increased by more than tenfold. Or you can point to the greatly increased coverage of the legal and tax aspects of the LLC in the business media. But for me, the most convincing evidence that the LLC has indeed caught on as a popular small business legal entity is the fact that, almost every day, I notice more small businesses with the telltale "LLC" tag at the end of their business names. If you doubt this, just enter any big office building and look at the directory of tenants and you're bound to notice a good sprinkling of LLC business names along with the traditional "Inc." and "Corp." designators you have been accustomed to seeing.

A. Should You Seriously Consider Forming an LLC?

Okay, now you know that forming a new business as an LLC is an easy, quick and relatively inexpensive way for new business owners to operate a business with limited liability while paying taxes on their individual income tax returns. Likewise, converting an existing sole proprietorship or partnership to an LLC is an easy way for sole proprietors and partners to protect their personal assets without changing the income tax treatment of their business.

But this doesn't address the larger question: Does it make sense for you to form your new business as an LLC, or, if you're already in business, to convert your existing business into an LLC? Unless you run a micro-business that has little chance of incurring debts or liabilities, or unless your business is already a corporation, my answer is simple: Yes, you probably should form an LLC. Here's why I am so pro-LLC. Forming an LLC is very easy to do—you just fill in a standard articles form provided by most state LLC filing offices and file it, for a usually modest filing fee. And in exchange for your small efforts, you receive a big legal present—your personal assets will be protected from business debts and claims, and you'll get this personal liability protection without needing to make your business into a more complicated taxable entity (like an incorporation).

A few examples help to illustrate when it does and doesn't make sense to form an LLC:

Example 1: Sam sets up a music store to sell guitars, keyboards and musical accessories. Because members of the public will enter his retail space, Sam has opened himself up to various types of liability exposure (to slip-and-fall lawsuits, to name one). In addition, he knows that it's easy to become enmeshed in contract disputes with suppliers and customers (for example, buyer's remorse can often set in shortly after the purchase of a pricey guitar or synthesizer). Even though Sam will carry a reasonable amount of commercial liability insurance and do his best to keep his customers satisfied, he sensibly decides that it makes sense to file LLC articles of organization with his state for a $125 fee—so he can take advantage of the extra personal security that limited liability protection affords. Sam's state, like many others, also charges a $50 annual report fee each year, but aside from this small amount and the few minutes it takes to complete the simple one-page annual filing form, there are very few added costs or burdens associated with his doing business as an LLC. And Sam knows that by forming an LLC instead of operating as a sole proprietor, he won't get a different tax status, as he would if he elected to form a corporation (the other legal entity that provides all of its owners with limited personal liability for business debts).

Example 2: Stella and Vera have operated a pet grooming business from rented quarters in a strip mall for several years. Their partnership has been successful, and they've managed to increase their profits every year. Of course, there have been small problems with an occasional fussy pet owner—and they were sued once in small claims court for a poodle dye-job that went slightly awry—but no big lawsuits or other major legal hassles. However, as profits have grown, so too has Stella's and Vera's anxiety about their business. They are a lot busier than they used to be, and have had to hire several employees. They know that although most of their employees are well trained, expensive mistakes can happen, especially when new people are hired. Stella and Vera have also begun to worry about employee lawsuits. If the owners have to fire an employee, will he go quietly or will he hire a lawyer and make their lives miserable for a while?

Because of these issues, and because both of them are getting sore knuckles from knocking wood every time one of them gets anxious, Stella and Vera decide to convert their partnership to an LLC. They do this by filing a one-page "Conversion of Partnership to an LLC" form, provided by their state. The filing fee is small, and they still retain their partnership tax status (each owner continues to report and pay taxes on her share of business profits on her 1040 individual income tax return, and the business continues to file IRS Form 1065, an informational tax return). Now both Stella and Vera rest a little easier at the end of each pet-grooming day, knowing that whatever legal problems they face in the future of their business, they cannot be held personally liable for them. Of course, because the assets of their business remain at stake (as opposed to their personal assets), Stella and Vera need to remain vigilant when it comes to heading off legal problems.

⚠️ **Not all states provide a form for converting from a partnership to an LLC.** In states that don't provide a conversion form, partners file regular articles of organization to create their LLC. In some states they also have to publish a notice in a local newspaper that they are terminating their partnership. I discuss this in Chapter 6, Section, A4.

Example 3: Winston is a graphic artist, sitting 40 hours per week in his well-lit cubicle, churning out computer art for a software publishing firm. He yearns for the day when he can work for, and answer only to, himself in his own computer-graphics business. Rather than just quit his day job cold-turkey, Winston starts his new business by working from home in the evenings and on weekends doing 3-D animation. Winston does most of his work on a work-for-hire basis for Bill, a good friend of Winston's and an entrepreneur who recently started a video game software company. Winston not only likes the fact that his animation work is fun, but he loves the fact that he can bill his services at an hourly rate that is twice what he makes at his day job.

Winston has heard about the advantages of forming an LLC, but he decides not to form one for his moonlighting business, at least for the time being. His reasons are:

- *He doesn't feel that his sideline business exposes him to personal liability since he works at home, under the terms of a very basic work-for-hire agreement with Bill, who pays Winston's invoices on time every time.*

- *He is too busy with his regular job and his new business to concentrate on the legal end of his business.*

- *Even if he had more time, he's not yet making enough money—or subjecting himself to enough legal liability—to change his legal status from that of a sole proprietor to an LLC.*

Winston's decision is a sensible one. Even though converting a sole proprietorship to an LLC isn't difficult—you just fill in an LLC articles form, write a check, and mail off the form for filing with the Secretary of

State—Winston doesn't need to take this step yet. If Winston continues to operate as a sole proprietor (as most freelancers do), he doesn't need to keep his personal funds and business funds separate, and, if he decides to stop moonlighting, he need do nothing except stop working. Forming an LLC, no matter how easy, will make Winston's business life a little more formal, and if he goes on to something else, he will have to officially dissolve his LLC entity. Specifically, if Winston were to form an LLC, he would need to keep his personal funds separate from his business funds (to be sure that a court will respect the separate legal existence of his LLC, and its limited liability protection). In other words, Winston would have to deposit all of his business income into, and write all business checks (including Winston's own "salary") out of, a separate LLC checking account. No question, this is a little more trouble than just doing business as a sole proprietorship.

Example 4: Bill, Winston's only client, has just started his own video game software venture, as I mentioned in the above example. Bill knows that forming an LLC is a modern legal strategy, and he is definitely a cutting-edge kind of guy. His plans are big—he hopes to hire a crew of talented C++ programmers from the local college, then turn them loose to create the latest in 3-D video game software. He can't pay his software team much to start, but he is sure he can convince them of the profit-making potential of the enterprise, particularly if one of the company's software offerings gets licensed by one of the big video game companies. He's sure his company has a good chance of success, but he also wants to limit his personal liability in case something goes wrong (for instance, if his company folds while owing money to creditors).

Bill considers forming an LLC, but decides to form a corporation instead. The corporation will give him the same limited liability protection an LLC affords, but it offers Bill some special advantages that suit his business plan better. With a corporation, Bill can attract employees by offering them stock options—these are the rage among Internet workers these days, considered so desirable that, in companies that have the potential to go public or be acquired

*for big bucks, they can be as attractive as big salaries. Also, after reading
Chapter 2 of this book, Bill understands that forming a corporation is often the
best approach for attracting outside investors. This is important to Bill, since
he plans to do a lot of networking to find a venture capital firm to help fund
the growth of his business. With a corporation, Bill can offer investors stock
ownership and a seat on the board of directors.*

Even though a corporation requires much more work to maintain—
holding annual and special director and shareholder meetings, plus
keeping a more complicated set of accounting records for the business
and preparing a separate income tax return—incorporating makes sense
for Bill. While an LLC is great at insulating the personal assets of owners
of a small, privately held business venture, sometimes it's not as good a
vehicle for outside investors like venture capitalists. Let's take a look at
the reasons.

It's true that an LLC can be set up with a management structure that
has the same centralized features as a board-managed corporation—for
example, the LLC can select a management team consisting of owners
who are active in the business and possibly an outside investor (see
Chapters 1 and 5 for a discussion of manager-managed LLCs). But
precisely because LLCs are more flexible and informal business entities,
they can be less disciplined and less responsive to the interests of
outside investors. Specifically, they don't provide as many management
protections and controls as do corporations, such as shareholder inspec-
tion rights and annual disclosure requirements, which makes it more
difficult for investors to hold management accountable.

In addition, it's more difficult to set up different classes of ownership in an LLC to cater to the special concerns of investors. By contrast,
in a corporation, the founders can adopt an off-the-shelf capitalization
structure of nonpreferred and preferred shares—which are usually
immediately attractive to venture capital investors. And forget about
taking an LLC public with an IPO (initial public offering of stock)—if

this is your short-term dream, you'll definitely want to incorporate to take advantage of the long-established statutory procedures that address the interests of attracting and maintaining a large group of investors (shareholders).

⚠ Most small businesses don't want to incorporate. Because a corporation limits its owners' personal liability for business debts, and because, unlike LLCs, corporations have been around for well over 100 years, people often ask if it makes more sense to incorporate. The answer is most often "No" unless, as discussed just above, there is a really good reason to incorporate, such as wanting to sell stock to investors or to distribute stock options to employees. For most other small businesses—those that are owned by just a few people and have no plans to "go public"—forming an LLC is usually the best approach. That's because corporations are considerably harder to maintain. For example, state corporate statutes have specific rules for holding meetings of directors and shareholders, issuing stock, distributing profits, and much more. Also, unlike creating an LLC, setting up a corporation means the creation of a separate tax entity that calculates profits according to a lot of special corporate tax rules and then reports and pays taxes on these profits separately from its owners. While LLCs have the option to elect this added income tax complexity, they can wait until the owners decide if and when it makes tax sense to do so. (I discuss electing corporate tax treatment in Chapter 4, Section C.)

Don't worry if you still have no idea whether an LLC is right for you. By reading the rest of this book, you'll understand better the features of an LLC and how it can work for you. Also, in Appendix C, I've provided a checklist that includes a list of questions to ask yourself before deciding whether it makes sense to run your business as an LLC.

There are some types of businesses that cannot form an LLC. For example, businesses that engage in the banking, trust or insurance business typically are prohibited from forming LLCs. In addition, some states also prohibit certain professionals from forming an LLC, or at least subject them to special rules when forming one. If you fall into one of these categories, take a minute to skip ahead to Chapter 1, Section C1, to see if you'll be eligible to form an LLC.

B. What This Book Does and How to Use It

In this book I provide basic legal and tax information that applies to LLCs. My purpose is to help you fully appreciate exactly where LLCs fit into the larger picture of business ownership structures and to help you decide whether it makes sense for you to form an LLC to conduct your business.

Because many busy people won't have time to read this book from end to end (although this is always a good idea), I do my best provide this information in a well-organized, easy-to-access format. First, I suggest you read Chapter 1 to get a good overview of how LLCs work. Then, to find the exact material you're interested in, one good approach is to look at the chapter subheadings in the table of contents. (These are repeated at the start of each chapter.) Each time you pick up the book to read a different section, your "LLC IQ" will increase and, within a short time, you'll know enough to decide if the LLC business structure might be a good fit for you and your business. Another reason why I take this practical approach is philosophical. A major attraction of the LLC is that you can form one simply, quickly, and with a lot of flexibility. It follows that a book like this one that provides an overview of LLCs should fit this same model. The idea is to use it quickly to get the information you need and then get back to business. And, let's be honest—if you are going to spend leisure time curled up with a book, I'm sure you can think of more than a few with better plot lines and character development.

C. What This Book Doesn't Do

You can't form an LLC using this book alone. Its goal is to provide a good overview of the subject, no more. So if you already know a good deal about LLC legalities and tax issues, including how LLCs are formed and operated, you may want to get right to the task of forming one. If so, my other Nolo books and products can help you do the job. These Nolo LLC resources are listed in Section E, below.

D. Legal and Tax Experts

In this book, I provide basic legal and tax information. As in any other specialized field, LLC legal and tax information constantly changes. If you decide you want to form an LLC, you will probably benefit by discussing your specific situation with a small business lawyer and/or a small business tax advisor. Not only can professional advisors make sure you have the most current information on forming an LLC in your state, but they can also serve as great sounding boards that you can check your legal, tax and practical conclusions with. In Chapter 7, I provide several recommendations on how to find knowledgeable and helpful legal and tax advisors.

E. Other Nolo LLC Resources

Below is a list of Nolo resources that can help you actually form and operate an LLC. Of course, these are not the only helpful products on the market—they're just the ones I know best (since I wrote or created most of them!).

- *Nolo WebForms*. Check out Nolo's new WebForms at http://www.nolo.com/product/webforms_home.html to see if we have a WebForm for creating the LLC organizational document (articles of organization, certificate of organization or certificate of formation) in your state. After answering a few simple questions in an online interview, guided by clear online help, you'll be able to print out your LLC articles or certificate, which you can then file with your state LLC filing office to create your LLC.
- *Form Your Own Limited Liability Company*, by Anthony Mancuso. This book contains step-by step instructions for preparing articles of organization (the main organizational document for LLCs) and an operating agreement (similar to corporate bylaws) to form an LLC in your state. It also provides a full treatment of state LLC laws and legalities. Comes with tear-out and computer disk forms.
- *LLC Maker*™, by Anthony Mancuso. This Windows 95 software assembles articles of organization for you, plus an operating agreement and other LLC formation paperwork, all according to your state's legal requirements. It includes extensive help, plus state-by-state information screens. *LLC Maker*™ also launches your web browser to go to your state's LLC filing office website and LLC act automatically. Available in May 2000.

- *Your Limited Liability Company: An Operating Manual*, by Anthony Mancuso. This post-startup book provides guidance and information on how to best operate your LLC on an ongoing basis. It provides ready-to-use minutes forms and instructions for holding formal LLC meetings, as well as information for formally approving legal, tax and other important business decisions that arise in the course of operating an LLC, along with resolution forms to record these decisions. All forms come as tear-outs and on disk.
- *How to Create a Buy-Sell Agreement*, by Anthony Mancuso and Bethany K. Laurence. This book shows you how to adopt comprehensive provisions to handle the purchase and sale of ownership interests in an LLC when an owner withdraws, dies, becomes disabled or wishes to sell her interest to an outsider. Comes with an easy-to-use agreement on disk and as a tear-out form—you simply check the appropriate options, then fill in the blanks.
- *Tax Savvy for Small Business*, by Frederick Daily. This book gives LLC owners information about federal taxes and explains how to make the best tax decisions for your business, how to maximize profits and how to stay out of trouble with the IRS.

NOTES AND ICONS

Throughout the text, I have included the following icons to help organize the material and underscore particular points:

 A commonsense tip to help you understand or comply with legal requirements.

 A caution to slow down and consider potential problems.

 A suggestion to seek the advice of an attorney or tax expert.

 An indication that you may be able to skip some material that may not be relevant to your situation.

 A suggestion to consult another legal or tax resource.

A suggestion to check out a helpful website.

 An indication that further discussion of the topic can be found elsewhere in the book.

CHAPTER 1

An Overview of LLCs

The LLC is a relatively new and highly popular alternative to the five traditional ways of doing business: as a sole proprietor, a general partnership, a limited partnership, a C (regular) corporation and an S corporation. In this book I'll not only explain how LLCs work and why so many small business people are forming them, but I'll also discuss the advantages and disadvantages of each of these other business forms, comparing them to the LLC (see Chapter 2 for these comparisons).

By and large, the business media have heralded the arrival of the LLC with unabated enthusiasm. Is this fanfare justified? Yes. The LLC is the first business ownership structure that allows all owners of the business to quickly and easily achieve the dual goals of "pass-through" tax treatment (the same tax treatment sole proprietors and partnerships receive) and limited personal liability protection (which means owners aren't personally liable for business debts and claims). I'll explain how each of these LLC attributes work in Section A.

A VERY SHORT HISTORY OF THE LLC

The LLC is the U.S. version of a type of business organization that has existed for years in other countries. Specifically, it closely resembles the German *GmbH*, the French *SARL* and the South American *Limitada* forms of doing business, all of which allow small groups of individuals to enjoy limited personal liability while operating under partnership-type rules rather than the more complex tax rules that apply to corporations.

In the U.S., the Wyoming legislature enacted the first LLC legislation in 1977, followed by Florida in 1982. In those days, doing business as one of these new-type business entities was risky, in part because the IRS had not yet made it clear whether it would tax an LLC as a partnership or a corporation. In fact, because the central promise of the LLC—to enjoy the tax status of a partnership with the personal liability protection of a corporation—seemed almost too good to be true, few business owners were brave enough to avail themselves of this new business model. Similarly, most other states were unwilling to pass legislation authorizing LLCs until the IRS gave its approval.

The first big break in the LLC stalemate came in 1988, when the IRS ruled that an LLC formed under the Wyoming statute was eligible for pass-through tax status. This nod of approval from the IRS created an immediate national wave of enthusiasm for LLCs in the business press, with the result that all 50 states plus the District of Columbia quickly adopted LLC legislation.

But it wasn't until January 1, 1997, that LLCs really went mainstream. That's when the IRS threw out its old and unnecessarily complicated tax classification regulations, agreeing that multi-owner LLCs could henceforth enjoy partnership tax status (and that one-owner LLCs could be taxed as sole proprietors) without the need to jump through a bunch of previously required technical hoops. And even better, the IRS decided to give LLC owners the flexibility to change their tax status by electing corporate tax treatment if they decided this would save money on taxes. (I'll have more to say on this special and important corporate tax election in Chapter 4, Section C.)

A. The Elements of an LLC

Now let's look more closely at the specific legal and tax characteristics that make the LLC so attractive and set it apart from the other business ownership structures. As you'll see in Chapter 2, most of the LLC's characteristics are shared by at least some of the other business structures. What makes the LLC unique is that it's the only business entity with its particular mix of legal and tax attributes—most importantly, limited personal liability for LLC owners (the same legal protection that owners of a corporation enjoy) and, unless they elect otherwise, the ability of owners to be taxed as individuals (like sole proprietors, or the owners of a partnership). Another way to say this is that the legislators who thought up the LLC business structure were smart enough to realize that there was no need to reinvent the wheel—all they needed to do was combine the best legal and tax aspects of the corporation and the partnership.

1. Number of Owners (Members)

Contrary to what you may have read just a few years ago, you can now form an LLC with just one person almost everywhere in the U.S. Only Massachusetts and the District of Columbia still require an LLC to have two owners, who, incidentally, are referred to as "members." And even these sluggish jurisdictions are almost sure to climb on the bandwagon and allow the formation of one-member LLCs soon. Incidentally, if you want to form a one-owner LLC in Massachusetts or the District of Columbia right now, and you are married, you can come pretty close by making your spouse the LLC's second member.

While there's no maximum number of owners (called members, remember) that an LLC can have, for practical reasons you'll probably want to keep the group reasonably small. There's no magic number here, but my feeling is that any business that's actively owned and operated by more than about five people risks serious problems maintaining good communication and reaching consensus among the owners.

Of course, if some of your co-owners will be passive investors only—and you'll have a small management group call the day-to-day shots—you can sensibly have more owners. (See the discussion of manager-managed LLCs in Section 6, below.) But I still think there is a commonsense limit to the number of members (including active owners and inactive investors). In my experience, once you get more than about ten investors, you'll find that accounting and communication issues are likely to use up too much of your time (outside investors will want to stay informed and may make your business life more complicated if your management choices do not result in increasing profits in future years). Not to mention the fact that the larger your investor group grows, the more likely you are to run into securities law complexities (see Chapter 6, Section C).

2. Limited Personal Liability Protection

In an LLC, the owners are not personally liable for the debts of their business or claims made against it (with a few exceptions, discussed in Section B, below). This legal protection, called "limited liability" in legal slang, is written into each state's LLC law. It should be obvious why most small business owners are so attracted by this feature. But just in case it isn't, consider that almost every business will accumulate debts and be at some risk of being sued. Without limited personal liability, all business owners are 100% legally responsible to repay these debts, even if it means using personal assets. With limited liability, their personal assets should remain untouched, even if the business fails under a heavy weight of debts and judgments.

HOW A BUSINESS CAN GO INTO DEBT

Businesses accumulate debt as a routine part of their activities. For example, when sales or net profits are low, employees, suppliers and other routine business expenses must still be paid. In times like these, a business might take out a loan or use a line of credit with a bank to handle cash flow fluctuations so that these expenses may be paid. Many businesses also defer payment of expenses by buying needed materials and supplies from vendors on account (usually with a 30- to 90-day grace period to pay these balances). In short, there are innumerable ways for a company, even a successful one, to get into and stay in debt as it transacts business.

Example 1: George and Vera quit their day jobs, deciding to go into business for themselves selling a new brand of wireless modem under an exclusive distributorship license with the modem manufacturer. They believe they can ultimately develop a large repeat-customer base of consumers who are looking for the latest, easiest way to connect their computers to the Internet. George and Vera realize, however, that it will be slow going at the start of their new venture, which makes them worry about what will happen if they are not able to resell all the modems they have to buy upfront to qualify for their distribu- torship license. In a worst case scenario, they might even have to fold up their new business. While they are ready to accept the risk of their business failing, they are frightened that they could be left with a mountain of personal debt so high they will have to liquidate most of their personal assets to pay off the debts and maybe even declare bankruptcy.

If George and Vera operated their business as a partnership, they would be right to be worried, since any debts of their business would automatically become their personal debts. But if George and Vera instead form an LLC, they'll have a lot less to worry about. If their business idea does not succeed, any debts owed by their business will not become their personal debts. Or put more directly, as long as George and Vera do not personally guarantee (cosign) any debts of their LLC, they are simply not on the hook for any unpaid business debts. They'll be able to go back to their unforeclosed-upon houses, reapply for their day jobs and start building their dreams and fortunes again.

⚠ Commercial insurance doesn't cover business debts. While commercial insurance can protect a business and its owners from some types of liability (for instance, slip-and-fall lawsuits), insurance never covers business debts. The only way to limit your personal liability on business debts is to use a limited liability business structure such as an LLC, a corporation, a limited partnership or an RLLP (which I discuss in Chapter 2).

Example 2: *Zena forms her own one-person mail-order business, "Personal Goddess Boutiques," consisting of a specialty catalog she plans to distribute to women with lots of disposable income. Her catalog will include inexpensive as well as high-priced items, such as luxury cruises, spa accommodations and even resort-area luxury condos. Zena, who has an MBA and has built up an impressive resume of past experience in service businesses including travel agencies, luxury resorts and retail sales, knows she will have to use most of her $250,000 in savings to buy mailing lists, establish a cool website and do other things to reach her projected customer base. She hopes to buy or arrange for the purchase of much of her catalog inventory on a consignment or commission basis, thus minimizing her risk of overstocking inventory, but she realizes that inevitably she will have to buy a significant portion of her sales inventory, and that many of these luxury items will be non-returnable if they can't be sold. Another area of financial exposure is the service package part of her business. She knows from experience that disgruntled clients can refuse to pay for packages (or demand a refund) for all sorts of good and bad reasons. In addition, while Zena is excited about the prospects for her new business, she also realizes that at least for the first few years before she builds up a solid* *base of repeat customers, her business will be extremely vulnerable to all sorts of problems, not the least of which is a recession that causes even wealthy people to cut back on their spending. While she is willing to risk her $250,000 investment to pursue her dream, she is worried that if Personal Goddess fails, she will be buried under a pile of debt. Zena decides to form an LLC, with herself as the only owner. She feels a lot better going into business knowing that even under the worst possible scenario she can walk away without risking any personal assets.*

An LLC is a good choice for Zena because she'll get the benefits of limited liability protection without having the hassles of forming and running a one-person corporation.

3. Flexible LLC Capital Structure

In addition to limited personal liability, LLC owners (members) enjoy the benefits of a structure that allows great ownership flexibility. Let's start with the basics. Owners of an LLC invest money or property in the LLC and in return receive a capital interest in the form of an undivided percentage of the assets of the company. Often a member's capital interest is represented by a certain amount of "membership units," much like shares in a corporation. For instance, a member who owns one half of an LLC may own 500,000 out of a total one million membership units. In other instances, an LLC won't break down a capital interest into membership units, but will just say a one-half owner has a 50% capital interest. Either way, each owner's ownership percentage (capital interest) is used to divide LLC assets among the members if the LLC is sold or liquidated, or when a member wishes to sell a membership interest. The owners' relative percentages of ownership also can be used—but do not have to be—to calculate how to split up profits and losses of the LLC, and for other purposes; for example, to divide up LLC management voting power.

Example 1: *Three people form an LLC. Two contribute half the cash and property used to set up the LLC, the third invests the other half. Under a typical ownership scenario, the first two members would each get a 25% capital interest in the LLC; the third member gets a 50% interest. Under standard provisions of an LLC operating agreement, each member would be allocated a percentage of LLC profits and losses that corresponds to their relative capital interests. That is, each 25% member would be allocated 25% of the LLC's profits and losses, and the 50% member would be allocated 50%. Also, if one of the members wishes to leave the LLC and sell her interest to the other members, she can expect to receive a percentage of the current value of the LLC that corresponds to her capital interest percentage—a 25% member can expect to be paid 25% of the current value of the LLC if she sells her interest to the remaining two members.*

Example 2: *Tasty Treats, LLC is a neighborhood bakery owned by Ned and Sylvia and four of their relatives. Only Ned and Sylvia work in the bakery. The LLC issues a total of 600,000 membership units to the initial investors. Under their LLC agreement, Ned and Sylvia, who contribute their know-how plus an investment of cash and property, get 200,000 membership units each; their relatives, each of whom makes a small cash investment, get 50,000 units each. If Ned were to resign from the LLC, he would get one-third of the value of the LLC (200,000/600,000). Likewise, if Ned and Sylvia were to decide to buy out their relatives, they could expect to pay one-third of the value of the LLC for all of their relatives' capital interests.*

Assuming other members agree, LLC members can contribute cash, property or services, or a promise to deliver any of the above, in exchange for capital interests in the LLC. While it's most common for all LLC members to contribute cash, it's not unusual for a member to also contribute a vehicle or a piece of equipment to the LLC. I discuss these various types of contributions and the tax ramifications of each in Chapter 3, Section B.

4. Flexible Distribution of LLC Profits and Losses

Many LLCs divide up profits and losses according to how much of the LLC each member owns. But rather than being restricted to dividing up profits this way (as is the case when paying out dividends in a corporation), LLC owners may choose to divide profits and losses any way they wish (subject to special IRS rules, which I discuss in Chapter 3, Section E). For example, if three equal LLC owners decide to divide profits 40%, 40% and 20%, that's fine with the IRS, as long as the special rules are followed and each pays taxes on what he receives.

Example: Steve and Frankie form an educational seminar business, with each getting a one-half capital interest in the LLC. Steve puts up all the cash necessary to purchase a computer with graphics and multimedia presentation capabilities, to rent out initial seminar sites, to send out mass mailings and to purchase advertising. As the traveling lecturer and student pied piper, cash-poor Frankie will only contribute services to the LLC. Although the two owners could agree to split profits and losses equally (in proportion to their ownership interests), they decide that it's fair for Steve to get 65% of LLC profits for the first three years as a way of paying him back for putting liquid assets (cash) into the LLC. After that, profits will be divided 50–50.

Again, in Chapter 3, Section E, I cover the IRS rules that apply when you want to make a special split of LLC profits and losses.

When it comes to actually paying out profits to the members, LLCs do have to pay attention to a few legal rules—in many states, there are financial standards that dictate when distributions can legally be made. I'll discuss these standards in Chapter 4, Section A3.

5. Pass-Through Income Taxation of LLC Profits and Losses

As mentioned earlier, the other huge benefit of the LLC has to do with its tax status. Like partnerships and sole proprietorships, an LLC is automatically recognized by the IRS as what is called a "pass-through" tax entity. This jargon refers to the fact that all of the business's profits and losses "pass through" the business and are reflected and taxed on the owners' individual tax returns. (I discuss the pass-through taxation of profits fully in Chapter 4.) By contrast, the profits and losses of a corporation must be reported and taxed on a separate, corporate tax return, at special corporate income tax rates. And, of course, money paid to corporate owners by way of salaries, bonuses and dividends are taxed on the owners' individual returns.

Why do many small business owners prefer pass-through taxation? For one, it's what most business owners who have previously done business as sole proprietors or partners are used to. And, of course, this is also how every individual wage earner's salary is taxed. So when a business owner considers starting an LLC, it's natural to be attracted to the fact that the individual tax rates will still apply to income earned from the business.

Here's another reason. The alternative to pass-through taxation—corporate taxation—is too complicated for most small business, at least when the business is in its start-up phase. A corporation is treated as a separate taxable entity by the IRS, so it doesn't just pass its profits through to its owners. Without going into the details, it's safe to say this means more bookkeeping, more accounting and more complexity. (I explain corporate taxation in detail in Chapter 2, Section E3.)

An LLC can elect to be taxed as a corporation. While most new LLCs will not choose to do so, a few will find that being taxed as a corporation actually reduces their tax bill. Generally, this occurs in a situation where an LLC earns enough profits that it wants or needs to keep some in the business, rather than paying all of the profits out to the owners. The savings occur because corporate tax rates are initially lower than the individual rates that apply to most LLC owners. I'll have more to say on this in Chapter 4, Section C. For now, I simply want you to understand that, because the LLC is a highly flexible business structure, if LLC owners find they will pay less taxes, they can very easily elect to have their business taxed as a corporation.

Lastly, since new businesses often lose money the first year or two, they usually want the ability to pass business losses along to the owners to deduct against their other income (usually salary earned working for another company or income earned from investments). Fortunately, LLC members (like owners of partnerships) can deduct their LLC losses against other income.

6. Flexible LLC Management Structure

LLCs are managed by their members (known as *member-management*) unless they choose to elect management by a manager or management group (known as *manager-management*). LLCs with only a few members are almost always managed by all members—after all, most small business owners want to have an active hand in management. Undoubtedly over 95% of new business LLCs fall into this category. And fortunately for those LLCs, member-management is simple and straightforward.

But member-management isn't the best choice for all LLCs. Under the other option, manager-management, an LLC is managed by a single manager or a small group of managers consisting of one or more selected

LLC members, one or more nonmembers, or a mixture of the two. Manager-management may make sense for an LLC if:

- one of the LLC members (actually, usually more than one) wants to invest in the LLC only, not help run it or take part in the management decisions

- the LLC members wish to give an outsider (a nonmember) a vote in management (for instance, an outsider wishes to lend money to the LLC, but only on the condition that he be given a say in management decisions). To give the nonmember management authority, the LLC must select manager-management and create a management group made up of the members of the LLC and the outsider.

- the sole member of an LLC wants to manage the business but gift membership interests to nonmanaging family members, who will step into a management role only when the current owner-manager steps down.

Fortunately, an LLC can easily choose manager-management to handle any of these situations. In most states, a short clause is included in the articles of organization (which are filed with the state to form the LLC) that specifies that the LLC is managed by a manager or a group of managers. (A few states such as Minnesota and North Dakota refer to managers as "governors.") In the other states, the management structure of the LLC must be spelled out in the LLC operating agreement. I discuss creating operating agreements, which play a similar role to bylaws for corporations, in Chapter 6, Section A2.

Let's look at some management options for Ned and Sylvia's LLC, Tasty Treats, which I introduced in the example in the Section 3, above.

Example 1: If Tasty Treats is set up with member-management, all of the members, including Ned and Sylvia's investing relatives, manage the LLC. This may initially seem like an overly worky management structure since, after all, Ned and Sylvia are the only two owners who work in the bakery. In practice, it usually isn't. The LLC operating agreement requires a full member vote only for major decisions, such as the admission of a new member, the sale of a membership interest, the incurring of LLC debt outside the normal course of LLC operations, the sale of major LLC assets, a dissolution of the LLC, and the like. And, after all, these are exactly the types of big decisions these relatives want to be consulted on. Ned and Sylvia alone handle the day-to-day management of the bakery and are allocated an extra percentage of LLC profits for their management duties, over and above their workaday salaries.

Example 2: *Now let's look at how things would work if Tasty Treats were organized as a manager-managed LLC. Now assume Ned and Sylvia's relatives want no say in LLC business, which they primarily invested in to help out Ned and Sylvia. The relatives just want their share of annual LLC profits (after Ned and Sylvia are paid their salaries and their extra share for running the bakery), and a proportionate percentage of the proceeds if it is later sold at a profit. The LLC elects manager-management in its articles, and Ned and Sylvia are named as the LLC's two managers. In this operating scenario, only Ned and Sylvia's votes are required to reach a decision when any of the major decisions specified in the operating agreement come up for a management vote.*

Of course, these examples only outline two broad management styles. When it gets down to fine-print management provisions, there are numerous ways to set up the management of your LLC, whether you opt for a member-run or manager-run LLC. I discuss LLC management, decisionmaking and recordkeeping in more detail in Chapter 6, Section C.

B. Exceptions to Owners' Limited Liability

While LLC owners enjoy limited personal liability for many of their business transactions, it is important to realize that this protection is not quite absolute. Or put another way, in several situations that I discuss below, an LLC owner may become personally liable for business debts or claims. Understand, however, that this drawback is not unique to

LLCs—these same exceptions apply to all limited liability business structures, including corporations. The limited liability protection held by LLC members is just as strong if not stronger than that enjoyed by the corporate shareholders of small corporations (to see why, see Section 4, below).

That said, let's look at the most common areas where an owner will not be able to use his limited liability status to protect his personal assets.

1. Members' and Managers' Personal Liability for Personally Guaranteed Business Debts

No matter how a small business is organized, whether as an LLC, a partnership or a corporation, its owners may be asked to sign bank loan obligations or to guarantee to pay business debts in their personal as well as their business capacity. If this is done, the owners voluntarily give up their limited liability protection as to the personally "co-signed" loans.

Example: A married couple owns and operates Books & Bagels, a coffee shop cum bookstore. In need of dough (the green kind) to expand into a larger location, the owners ask a bank for a smallish loan. The bank grants the loan to the LLC on the condition that the two owners personally pledge their equity in their house as security for the loan. Because the owners personally guarantee the loan, if the LLC goes broke, the bank can seek repayment from the owners personally. If they can't come up with the cash, the bank could even foreclose on their house. No type of business ownership structure—an LLC, a corporation or a limited partnership—can insulate owners from this voluntary choice to assume personal liability.

But don't worry: Even if you have to personally co-sign a business loan from time to time, there are plenty of other situations where your LLCs limited liability protection remains intact. That's because, as I pointed out in previous examples, most of your business debts—and possibly even loans you negotiate with individuals—will not also be personal debts. For instance, your LLC's lines of credit with vendors and other suppliers and all its routine bills are debts of the LLC only, not personal debts of the LLC owners. In short, unless you go out of your way to pledge personal assets for business debts, you'll have no personal liability for them, meaning that if the business folds up, no one will grab your personal bank account or the roof over your head.

2. Members' and Managers' Personal Liability for Injuries to Others (Torts)

Like it or not, members and managers of an LLC, like corporate directors and shareholders, partners and all other business owners, can be held personally liable for financial loss caused by their own careless behavior. Called "torts" in legalese, negligent acts such as those that result in car crashes are the everyday stuff of American litigation. For example, carelessly running a red light, which causes an accident and damages another automobile, is a tort. But while an LLC member or manager is personally responsible for her own negligence if the LLC can't pay, the good news is that personal liability for torts does not normally extend to the other LLC members. Or put another way, in a two-member LLC, Member One is personally liable for his own negligent acts, but not for those of Member Two.

Example: Otto, one of the two members of Otto's Auto Parts Supply LLC, gets in the LLC's Mazda Miata to pick up a throw-out bearing for a customer's Mercedes SUV. On the way, he negligently sideswipes a slow-moving Geo, a stunt that results in a $5,000 repair bill to the Geo owner and a $25,000 medical claim for whiplash to George, the Geo driver. If insurance doesn't cover George's damages, Otto can be held personally liable for the $30,000 (the LLC entity can be liable too if the accident happened on company time). But Mike, the other owner of the LLC, shouldn't be held personally liable for Otto's tort, nor should he be held personally liable if the Geo driver obtains a legal judgment against the LLC itself.

Although LLC law does not protect members and managers from the consequence of their own torts, insurance can. Commercial, automotive, workers' compensation or in some instances even the individual's homeowner's policy may cover some or all of the damage caused by an LLC manager's or member's tort. But don't rely on personal policies to provide business-related protection. It's essential to get a reasonable amount of appropriate liability insurance to cover potential personal and business liabilities arising from LLC operations. Typically, a commercial general liability insurance policy will cover the following:

- torts caused by business owners and employees in the course of business or on the business premises (a policy for bodily injury and property damage—so-called "slip-and-fall" coverage), and

- fire, theft and a long list of catastrophes.

Professionals should take special considerations into account. If an LLC is organized to render licensed professional services such as health care, law, accounting, architecture, engineering and similar services, state law normally says that each individual professional remains personally liable for her own malpractice, even if the business is organized as a corporation, LLC or RLLP, so it's essential for each person to purchase adequate malpractice insurance to cover this additional professional tort liability.

More importantly, professionals who are considering forming an LLC need to be mindful of another point: in many states, the LLC statutes do not *specifically* protect a professional in a multi-member LLC from personal liability for the malpractice of other professionals in the firm, so it is yet to be seen whether professional LLCs will protect their owners from this sort of "vicarious liability." However, all states have enacted statutes that allow certain professionals to form registered limited liability partnerships (RLLPs) instead of LLCs. (I discuss RLLPs further in Chapter 2, Section G.)

3. Members' and Managers' Personal Liability for Breach of Duty to the LLC

In a co-owned LLC, the managers (either its members in the case of a member-managed LLC or its specially appointed managers in the case of a manager-managed LLC) have a legal obligation to manage the LLC in good faith and in the best interests of the LLC and its members. In legal jargon, this duty is known as their "duty of care," and is similar to corporate directors' and officers' duty to their corporation. If a member or manager of an LLC does violate this duty of care, she can be held personally liable for any money damages that result from her action or inaction.

Although it sounds as threatening as it does portentous, as interpreted by courts this duty of care is a fairly relaxed legal standard. Managers have been held to violate it only if they do something intentionally fraudulent, illegal, or so clearly wrong-headed that a fair-minded person would conclude they were taking a grossly negligent risk. In short, LLC members and managers are not normally personally responsible to outsiders for any honest mistakes or acts of poor judgment they commit in the execution of their job-related duties.

Example: A customer of Jen & Len's Computers LLC sues the company, as well as each owner personally, for not fixing a problem with his two-gigabyte hard drive, resulting in 40 hours of extra work for her to get the data back. Assuming Jen and Lee conscientiously did their best to fix the customer's hard drive, they are not personally liable to the customer. The limited liability afforded to them by their LLC protects them.

LLC members and managers in smaller LLCs often rely primarily on commercial liability insurance to protect them in the event of lawsuits brought by outsiders, at least at the beginning of LLC operations (see the above subsection for a discussion of commercial insurance). Later, if they can afford to, they may decide to back up this basic coverage with appropriate personal liability policies covering members or nonmember managers. Policies of this sort specifically protect LLC members and managers from personal liability for their management decisions (these policies should be distinguished from commercial liability insurance policies, which insure the LLC against catastrophic damage and injuries to employees and outsiders).

It's important to realize that the duty of care applies not only to managers' treatment of the LLC's customers, but managers' actions toward all members of the LLC. For example, in a manager-managed LLC, the nonmanaging LLC members can sue a manager who knowingly entered a fraudulent transaction that hurt the LLC financially for a breach of her duty of care. And in member-managed LLCs, a member who violates the duty of care opens himself up to personal liability in a lawsuit by the other members.

Example: Robert, Juliet and Greg are the three owners of the Lucky Lock Company LLC, a member-managed LLC. They vote at a management meeting about whether to use one-quarter of the company's cash reserves to market and sell the Neon Big-Lock Clock, a unique, three-by-five-foot lock plate with a neon clock display, which Robert invented. Greg is against the idea of committing company funds to promote a device that he believes no one will buy. But Robert and Juliet disagree with Greg, believing that the big clock will find a market. The neon clock idea does not catch on and Lucky Lock goes broke. Greg sues Robert and Juliet in their personal capacity. The judge finds that, although they made what turned out to be a bad business decision, Robert and Juliet did so armed with all the facts and in good faith, and did not breach their duty of care.

But now let's change a few facts and assume Bob and Juliet have researched the availability of certain key parts and know that because several would have to be custom-made, the Neon Big-Lock Clock will be very difficult and expensive to produce. Instead of telling Greg these facts, they keep their knowledge secret and vote to go ahead with the project. This time when Greg sues, the judge supports his claim and finds that Juliet and Robert have breached their duty of care. Greg is awarded a significant judgment.

To better understand why Robert and Juliet were liable in the second situation in the above example, but not in the first, it helps to understand that courts have interpreted a business owner's duty of care by creating a "business judgment rule" that should be followed by a company's management. This rule says that in making management decisions, managers will not be personally liable for honest business mistakes. Another way of saying this is that decisions made with some rational basis (based upon facts known to managers or reported to them from someone with superior knowledge) should not give rise to personal liability even if they turn out to be mistaken and result in financial loss to the business and its owners. Let's go back to the Lucky Lock Company and change the scenario one more time.

Example: *Again, Robert, Juliet and Greg discuss at a management meeting whether to use one-quarter of the company's cash reserves to market and sell the Neon Big-Lock Clock. This time, Robert and Juliet do disclose to Greg that certain essential parts would be very difficult and expensive to produce. Based on this disclosure, Greg is even more against the idea of committing company funds to promote a device that he is strongly convinced will not appeal to many customers. Greg's opinion, along the information that casts doubt on the profitability of the Neon Big-Lock Clock, is fully discussed at the membership meeting. Nevertheless, based on their experience in the clock business and the fact that many offbeat designs (for example, the cuckoo clock) have been extremely profitable, Robert and Juliet vote to proceed (and Greg is outvoted two to one).*

Again, the Neon Big-Lock Clock is a disaster. Can Greg successfully sue the other owners personally for their bad business judgment? No, according to the business judgment rule. Robert and Juliet made an informed business decision without underhandedness, concealment or misrepresentation of facts, or other fraud or illegality. The fact that they guessed wrong does not make them personally liable to Greg.

Disclose, Disclose, Disclose! The above example highlights a basic LLC management rule: Full and fair disclosure of all material facts is part and parcel of LLC managers' and members' duty of care to the LLC. As long as this duty is met, the business judgment rule will normally protect members and managers from personal liability for their management decisions.

But what if an LLC member or manager is sued based on a claim that she breached her duty to the LLC? Even if the member or manager who was sued ultimately wins, can't the costs of suit alone be disastrous to the defending member or manager? Not necessarily. When a member or manager is sued for breach of duty of care to the LLC but prevails, the laws of many states permit or require "indemnification" by the LLC. This means that the LLC must pay any legal expenses, fines, fees and other liabilities owed by the LLC member or manager for ill-advised management decisions or other liability-causing events. But again, state rules say that the person to be indemnified must have acted in good faith and in the best interests of the LLC before he can receive indemnification. And, as you might guess, intentional misconduct, fraud and illegal acts normally can't be covered under these rules.

Financially irresponsible acts can also lead to a loss of limited liability. As I mentioned in Section A4, above, an LLC must satisfy certain financial standards before a managing member or a manager can approve a distribution of profit. In short, these standards mean that an LLC shouldn't pay out profits if it can't afford it. If these standards are ignored and the company is later sued, the member or manager who approved the distribution may be personally on the line for the amount of the invalid distribution. I'll talk about this again in Chapter 4, Section A3, but for now, just know that this is another way an LLC member or manager can be held personally liable.

4. Losing Your LLC's Limited Liability Status

In Section 3, just above, I discussed situations where LLC members can be held personally liable for acts that occur in the course of their business. Here I change the focus to examine whether and under what circumstances the limited liability status of an LLC itself can be disregarded.

Because the LLC is a relatively new business form, state courts have not had much time to flesh out all the legal implications of doing business in this legal structure. The result is that there are not a lot of court decisions dealing with the issue of when an LLC should be treated as a sham entity and its members held liable in their personal capacities.

On the other hand, state courts have had plenty of time to discuss and interpret the limited liability protection that *corporations* provide to their owners, and to carve out exceptions to a corporation's limited liability status under extreme circumstances. Most legal commentators believe that state courts will follow the guidelines set out in these corporate cases when the limited liability protection offered by LLCs starts to get challenged in state courts. Because I agree that this is likely to happen, it makes sense to briefly look at instances where courts are likely to disregard a corporation's separate legal status and hold its owners personally liable (in legal slang, called "piercing the corporate veil").

Generally, the courts say that corporate limited liability protection will be disregarded—that is, the corporate owners will be held personally liable for business debts and claims—only in extreme cases. Most typically this occurs when owners fail to failed to respect the separate legal existence of their corporation, but instead treated it as an extension of their personal affairs. For example, if owners fail to follow routine corporate formalities, such as adequately investing in or capitalizing the corporation, issuing stock, holding meetings of directors and shareholders, and keeping business records and transactions of the business separate from those of the owners, a court is likely to say the corporation doesn't really exist and that its owners are really doing business as individuals who are personally liable for their acts.

What does all of this mean for an LLC? Well, for starters, because many states' statutes specifically allow LLCs to act more informally than corporations (for example, not hold regular meetings), the failure to adhere to annual-meeting-type formalities should not be a problem. But several areas of concern remain, as follows:

- *Act fairly and legally.* Do not conceal or misrepresent material facts or the state of your finances to vendors, creditors or other outsiders. Or put more bluntly, don't engage in fraud.

- *Fund your LLC adequately.* You don't have to invest a lot of money in your LLC, but do try to put enough cash or other liquid assets in at the beginning so your LLC will be able to meet foreseeable expenses and liabilities. If you fail to do this, it is possible that a court faced with a balance sheet that shows a very minimal investment may disregard your LLC's limited liability protection. This is particularly likely if you engage in a risky business that everyone knows needs a large investment.

- *Keep LLC and personal business separate.* Nothing will encourage a court to disrespect your LLC entity more than your own failure to respect its status as an entity separate from its owners. This means you'll want to immediately get a federal Employer Identification Number for your LLC and open up a separate LLC checking account. As a routine business practice, write all checks for LLC expenses or payouts of profits out of this account, and deposit all LLC revenue into it. Do all of this even if you set up a single-member LLC. And of course, you will want to keep separate accounting books for your LLC—these can consist of a simple single-entry system, such as your LLC check register and deposit slips, but a double-entry system will serve you better when it comes time to prepare your end-of-year income tax returns, especially if yours is a multi-member company, which will have to prepare and file an IRS Form 1065, the informational return for partnerships (see Chapter 4, Section B). Lastly, you should keep written records of all major LLC decisions.

C. Basics of Forming an LLC

In Chapter 6, Section A, I discuss in detail what you'll need to do to form an LLC. Here I just want to give you a flavor of what to expect.

1. What Types of Businesses Can Form LLCs?

With few exceptions, LLCs may be formed for all types of businesses. You may even form one LLC to engage in several businesses—for example, furniture sales, trucking and redecorating can all be operated under one legal, if not physical, roof. But certain special kinds of businesses, mostly financial in nature, may either be restricted or prohibited from setting up an LLC in your state. For example, businesses that engage in the banking, trust or insurance business are typically prohibited from forming LLCs.

Certain professionals may also be prohibited from forming an LLC in some states, or at least be subject to special rules when forming one. For example, the initial LLC members may need to obtain a statement from their state licensing board, certifying that they all have current state licenses, and file it with their LLC articles. State restrictions for professionals apply mostly to doctors and other licensed health care workers, lawyers, accountants and, in some states, engineers and architects. In a few states, including California and Rhode Island, these professionals may not be able to form an LLC at all. In other states, these professionals may have to form a "professional LLC" or at least follow special procedures if they choose to form an LLC—typically they must comply with one or more of the following rules:

- Only licensed professionals in one profession—or in a group of related professions—may own a membership interest in a professional LLC.

- The LLC must use a special LLC designator in its name—typically the words "Professional Limited Liability Company" or the abbreviation "PLLC."

- Each member must carry a specified amount of malpractice insurance—the LLC's shield of limited liability does not protect a professional from personal liability for his own malpractice. This is the rule in all states.

Note that some professionals may be better off forming a professional corporation or a registered limited liability partnership (RLLP), both of which I discuss in Chapter 2. Corporations and RLLPs are often specifically designed to limit the personal liability of professionals to the maximum extent possible. For example, in many states, these entities specifically protect a professional from personal liability for business debts and contracts (like an LLC), as well as from personal liability for the malpractice of another professional in the practice. (In most states, the LLC statutes do not specifically say that an LLC protects a professional from this sort of "vicarious liability" for another practitioner's malpractice.)

⚠ Call your state LLC filing office if you are a licensed professional. If you have a vocational or professional license, before spending any more time reading about LLCs, it makes sense to call your state LLC filing office to check if you can form an LLC in your state, and if so, whether there are special rules or restrictions. You may have to form a professional corporation or an RLLP instead. If your state LLC filing office can't help you, you can read your state's LLC act yourself. I discuss how to get a copy just below.

2. State LLC Laws

LLCs are regulated by the specific statutes of the state where they are formed. Each state, plus the District of Columbia, has an LLC act in place. And, since state legislators are not beyond a little legal plagiarism, it is common to see a remarkable degree of similarity between a state's LLC act and the acts of adjoining states.

Although state LLC statutes do not make for the most scintillating reading, there are many instances when you can save yourself a bundle in legal fees by doing you own LLC research. For example, you may want your LLC operating agreement to set out procedures for buying out the membership interest of a departing member. While state LLC law usually gives you great latitude in drafting your LLC operating agreement, it often provides mandatory rules for certain major LLC matters, such as the purchase of the interest of a departing member. Specifically, some states require that a departing member receive payment of the fair value of the membership interest within a reasonable time after his departure. And, of course, the statute may go on to say what the minimum fair value of the interest can be, or how it must be determined, or the maximum time a departing member must wait to receive payment.

Resource for state-by-state LLC laws. For a discussion of special LLC statutory rules that apply to the admission of LLC members and the transferring of membership interests to a new member, see the state information in the appendix of *Your Limited Liability Company: An Operating Manual*, by Anthony Mancuso (Nolo).

LLC statutes are generally not lengthy, and LLC acts, as a whole, are not massive. In just a few minutes you should be able to find the section of law you are interested in. In Chapter 7, Section A5, I discuss in depth how to find and research your state's statutes. Of course, once you have read the statutes yourself, you may want to check your conclusions with a lawyer. But this should cost less than it would if you relied on the lawyer to do the basic statutory research and explain to you what the law says.

NATIONAL MODEL LLC ACT

A bit belatedly, efforts are being made to adopt a national "Model LLC Act" that can be used by individual state legislatures to pass future LLC legislation. One model is the Prototype Limited Liability Company Act, sponsored by the American Bar Association's Section of Business Law. Another is the Uniform Limited Liability Company Act, developed by the National Conference of Commissioners on Uniform State Laws. Both of these acts are still in development, and there is justified skepticism as to whether states will replace their current LLC laws with either model act. More likely, states will adopt portions of the model acts to supplement their current LLC statutes. In short, while LLC laws are fairly similar now and may become more so soon, important state-by-state differences are likely to remain.

3. What Does It Take to Form an LLC?

The basic legal step normally required to create an LLC in most states is to prepare and file LLC "articles of organization" with your state's LLC filing office. (Some states call this document a "certificate of organization" or a "certificate of formation." See Appendix A for your state's preferred jargon.) Many states supply a blank one-page form for the articles of organization—you'll simply need to fill it out and send it in with a filing fee. Typically, you need only specify a few basic details about your LLC, such as its name, principal office address, agent and office for receiving legal papers, and the names of its initial members (or managers, if you're designating a special management team to run the

LLC). I'll discuss articles of organization in more detail in Chapter 6, Section A.

One disadvantage to forming an LLC over a partnership or a sole proprietorship is that you'll have to pay a filing fee when you send in your articles to create your LLC. But in most states, the fees are modest (although the business unfriendly states of California, Massachusetts and Illinois, among a few others, sock it to new LLCs). See the chart "State LLC Formation Fees," below; for your state's filing fee. Also, this filing fee is a one-time-only fee in most states and, for most LLC owners, is a small price to pay for the peace of mind they get by having limited liability. Some states do, however, have recurring annual fees, including California, Delaware, Illinois, Massachusetts, New Hampshire, Pennsylvania and Wyoming, which charge between $100 and $500 each year. In the chart "State LLC Formation Fees," I note the states that have an annual fee of $100 or more.

STATE LLC FORMATION FEES*

Alabama	$40, payable to the "Secretary of State," plus a separate check for $35 for the "Probate Court Judge," who receives and records the original Articles.
Alaska	$250 fee (includes $100 biennial license fee due every two years), payable to the "State of Alaska."
Arizona	$50, payable to the "Arizona Corporation Commission."
Arkansas	$50 fee, payable to the "Arkansas Secretary of State."
California	$70, payable to the "Secretary of State." Plus $800 to the California Franchise Tax Board as an initial LLC fee.

California (cont'd): Annual fee: $800 to the Franchise Tax Board. Plus, LLCs with total annual incomes of $250,000 or more must pay the following additional annual fee amounts (the proposed fees effective for 2000):

$250,000-$499,999	$1,042
$500,000-$999,999	$3,126
$1,000,000-$4,999,999	$6,251
$5,000,000 or more	$9,377

Colorado	$50, payable to "Secretary of State."
Connecticut	$60, payable to "Secretary of State."
Delaware	$70, payable to the "Delaware Department of State." The Department of State, Division of Corporations, also accepts major credit cards. Annual Fee: $100 to the Franchise Tax Office of the Division of Corporations.

District of Columbia	$100, payable to the "D.C. Treasurer."
Florida	$250 for filing Articles, plus $35 for filing the Designation of Registered Agent form, for a total of $285, payable to the "Department of State."
Georgia	$75, payable to "Secretary of State." Attach the check to a completed "Transmittal Form."
Hawaii	$100 fee, payable to the "Department of Commerce and Consumer Affairs."
Idaho	$100 fee, payable to the "Idaho Secretary of State." If the Articles are not typed or if attachments are included, the filing fee is $120.00
Illinois	$400, payable to the "Secretary of State." Payment must be made by certified check, cashier's check, money order or Illinois attorney's or CPA's check (do not send a personal check). Annual Fee: LLCs must pay an annual LLC renewal fee of $300.
Indiana	$90, payable to "Secretary of State" (staple check to Articles).
Iowa	$50, payable to the "Iowa Secretary of State."
Kansas	$150 fee, payable to the "Kansas Secretary of State."
Kentucky	$40, payable to the "Secretary of State."
Louisiana	$60, payable to "Secretary of State."
Maine	$250, payable to the "Secretary of State."
Maryland	$50, payable to "SDAT" (this is the acronym for the State Department of Assessments & Taxation).

Massachussetts	$500 fee, payable to the "Commonwealth of Massachusetts." Annual Fee: You must file an annual report and pay a fee of $500 per year.
Michigan	$50 nonrefundable fee, payable to the "State of Michigan."
Minnesota	$135, payable to the "Minnesota Secretary of State."
Mississippi	$50, payable to the "Secretary of State."
Missouri	$105, payable to the "Director of Revenue."
Montana	$70 fee, payable to the "Montana Secretary of State."
Nebraska	$100, plus $5 per page of Articles, plus $10 for a "certificate of organization," payable to the "Secretary of State."
Nevada	$125, plus $10 for the certification of one copy of the Articles, payable to the "Secretary of State."
New Hampshire	$85, payable to the "Secretary of State." (This fee includes $50 for filing an Addendum form.) Annual Fee: LLCs must pay an annual report fee of $100.
New Jersey	Check or money order for $100, payable to "Secretary of State."
New Mexico	$50, payable to the "State Corporation Commission."
New York	$200, payable to the "Department of State." Fee must be paid by postal money order, certified check or attorney's check (do not send a personal check).
North Carolina	$125, payable to "Secretary of State."
North Dakota	$135 (includes $10 for filing Registered Agent Consent to Serve form), payable to the "Secretary of State."

Ohio	$85 fee, payable to the "Ohio Secretary of State."
Oklahoma	$100, payable to the "Secretary of State."
Oregon	$40, payable to the "Corporation Division." (Credit card orders can also be submitted; the card number and expiration date should be submitted on a separate sheet of paper.)
Pennsylvania	$100 fee, payable to the "Department of State." Annual Fee: An annual registration fee of at least $330 is payable to the Department of State.
Rhode Island	$150, payable to the "Secretary of State."
South Carolina	$110 fee, payable to the "South Carolina Secretary of State."
South Dakota	Payable to the "Secretary of State," as follows: LLCs with less than $50,000 of capital $90 LLCs with $50, 001 to $100,000 of capital $150 LLCs with more than $100,000 of capital $150 plus 50 cents for each additional $1,000 of capital over the first $100,000.
Tennessee	Minimum fee is $300, payable to the "Tennessee Secretary of State." (Actual fee is $50 per LLC member, so the fee will go up for LLCs with more than six initial members.)
Texas	$200, payable to the "Secretary of State."
Utah	$50, payable to "State of Utah."
Vermont	$75, payable to "Vermont Secretary of State."
Virginia	$100, payable to "State Corporation Commission."
Washington	$175, payable to "Secretary of State."

West Virginia	$100, payable to the "Secretary of State."	
Wisconsin	$130, payable to the "Department of Financial Institutions."	
Wyoming	Payable to the "Secretary of State," as follows:	
	LLCs with less than $50,000 of capital	$100
	LLCs with $50,001 to $100,000 of capital	$200
	LLCs with more than $100,000 of capital	Contact the Secretary of State.
	Annual Fee: Annual LLC tax of $100.	

* All states fees were current as of spring 2000. Check with your state LLC filing office to see if they have changed.

A few states require an additional step before your LLC will be official: the publication in a local newspaper of a simple notice of your intention to form an LLC. See your state's entry in Appendix A to see if this additional step is required.

Once your articles of organization are on file and any publication requirement is met, your LLC is "official." But even though it is not required by state law, it is essential that you also create an "LLC operating agreement." This is the document where you set out your rules for the ownership of the business (much like a partnership agreement or the bylaws of a corporation). A typical operating agreement includes:

- the members' capital interests

- the rights and responsibilities of members

- how profits and losses will be allocated

- how the LLC will be managed

- the voting power of all the members (and any managers)

- rules for holding meetings and taking votes

- "buy-sell" provisions, which lay down a framework for what happens when a member wants to sell his interest, dies or becomes disabled.

Creating an operating agreement should be done even if your LLC has just one or two members. The main reason is as simple as it is important. An operating agreement is essential to make sure a state court will respect the LLC's limited personal liability protection for its owners. This is particularly key in a one-person LLC, where without the formality of an agreement, the LLC will look a lot like a sole proprietorship. Once your paperwork is completed and filed, you're ready to do business! See the Checklist for Forming an LLC in Appendix C for some more practical details.

Practical Information on Starting and Running a Business. Nolo offers several helpful resources that explain the steps involved in opening any new business. First check out Nolo's Small Business Center at www.nolo.com/category/sb_home.html. Here you'll find Encyclopedia articles and FAQs full of free tips for starting your business. For more, read Nolo's bestselling book, the *Legal Guide to Starting and Running a Small Business*, by Fred Steingold. It offers a comprehensive, two-volume treatment for entrepreneurs on how to start and operate a business. *The Small Business Start-Up Kit: A Step-by-Step Legal Guide*, by Peri Pakroo, gives you a quick lowdown on how to open the doors of your new business quickly, from choosing a name, to finding a location, to getting a business license.

■

CHAPTER 2

The LLC vs. Other Business Structures

Your decision as to whether forming an LLC makes sense for your business should include a good understanding of the principal legal ways you can organize your business. After all, your larger goal is to decide which type of business ownership structure ("business entity," in legal jargon) is right for you. I've already said that the LLC mixes and matches a number of the best attributes of other business forms. Now it's time for me to back up this assertion.

A. Business Structures Other Than the LLC

To begin with, there are three traditional ways of doing business:

- sole proprietorships
- partnerships, and
- C (regular) corporations.

In addition, to fully understand the pros and cons of LLC life, you'll need to compare the LLC to two variants of these traditional business forms:

- limited partnerships, and
- S corporations.

These last two types of business structures are particularly interesting because they come closest to resembling the LLC in its legal and tax characteristics. And just to make matters more complicated, all 50 states have also recently added another type of business entity that's even newer than the LLC. Its called the:

- registered limited liability partnership (RLLP).

Let's briefly look at each one of these business structures.

B. Sole Proprietorship: Advantages and Disadvantages

The simplest way of being in business for yourself is as a "sole proprietor." This is just a fancy way of saying that you are the owner of a one-person business. There's almost no cost or bureaucratic red tape to forming a sole proprietorship—other than the usual business license, sales tax permit and local and state regulations that any business must face. As a practical matter, most one-person businesses start out as sole proprietorships just to keep things simple.

Example: *Remember Winston, the graphic artist we introduced at the beginning of this book (see the Introduction, Section A, Example 3) who started moonlighting in his own home-based computer graphics business? Because Winston only works in his business part-time and has no employees, just a couple of clients and no pressing personal liability issues, he chooses to operate as a sole proprietor (his other choices would be to form an LLC or a corporation). Outside of normal business license, fictitious name and tax permit issues, which apply to all businesses, Winston does not need to file any legal paperwork. Like all other one-person business owners, unless Winston takes steps to change the legal structure of his business—such as forming a one-person LLC or corporation—his one-person business will be automatically classified and treated as a sole proprietorship.*

1. Number of Owners

By definition, a sole proprietorship has only one owner, so if your one-person business grows and you wish to include other owners, you will need to move to a more complicated type of business structure. The minute you begin to own and split profits with another person, you automatically have a partnership on your hands. Or you can choose instead to form an LLC or a corporation by filing papers with the state.

If you'll work with your spouse, consider a "husband-wife sole proprietorship." You can create a sole proprietorship and have your spouse do "volunteer" work (without pay) for your business. Technically, there will only be one owner—you. But this setup allows your spouse to provide services for the business without being classified as an employee, freeing the business from having to pay payroll tax. This way, you can retain the simple tax status of a sole proprietorship and avoid being treated as a partnership. Of course, your spouse will not be a legal owner of the business, although in many states, marital property laws will give your spouse a share in your business (so it may not be significant that your spouse won't technically be an owner). But if your spouse wants an official say in management, you'll have to form a partnership, an LLC or a corporation.

2. Personal Liability for Business Debts

Unfortunately, although a sole proprietorship is legally very simple, it can also be a risky way to operate. That's because, as explained in Chapter 1, the sole proprietor is 100% personally liable for all business debts and legal claims. For example, if someone slips and falls in a sole proprietor's business and sues, the owner is responsible for paying any resulting court award (unless commercial liability insurance covers it). Similarly, if the business fails to pay suppliers, banks or other businesses' bills, the owner is personally liable for the unpaid debts. This means the owner's personal assets, such as his bank accounts, his equity in his house or car and other personal assets can be grabbed (attached) and sold to provide funds to repay business debts and judgments.

Of course, some businesses are much more vulnerable to debts and lawsuits than others. If yours is a part-time micro-business that does not operate on credit and is highly unlikely to engender lawsuits, you needn't lie awake worrying about these issues.

3. Sole Proprietorship Income Taxation

A sole proprietor reports her business profits or losses on IRS Schedule C, *Profit and Loss From Business (Sole Proprietorship)*, which she files with her 1040 individual federal tax return. The owner's profits are taxed at her individual income tax rates. This is called "pass through" taxation because the income passes through the business to the owner's individual tax return. In other words, like a partnership, a sole proprietorship is not a taxable "business entity" under the federal tax scheme. Instead, the tax law says a sole proprietorship is "disregarded as an entity separate from its owner."

Most startup business owners prefer pass-through taxation of their business income, at least in the beginning. Why? Reporting and paying individual income taxes by preparing a Schedule C (and a Schedule SE for self-employment tax) is a lot less complicated than preparing other types of income tax returns (partnership or corporate returns). In fact, many small business owners can do the Schedule C and Schedule SE work themselves.

Because a sole proprietor is self-employed, it seems at first glance that her business income will be subject to an increased self-employment (Social Security and Medicare) tax rate—about twice the rate a corporate employee would personally pay. But if you take a longer look, you'll see the actual amount of self-employment taxes that a sole proprietor pays turns out to be the same as what she would pay if her business was organized as a one-person corporation and taxed separately. That's because the owner-employee of a corporation personally pays half the total self-employment tax, and her corporation pays the other half, whereas the sole proprietor simply pays the total amount of self-employment tax in one lump sum (when she prepares the Schedule SE, *Self-Employment Tax Return*, which she attaches to her Schedule C and 1040 tax return each year).

4. Taxation of Benefits

During the years 2000 through 2001, a sole proprietor—as compared to the owner of a one-person LLC who has elected corporate tax treatment—faces a small tax disadvantage when it comes to deducting his family's health insurance premiums. He can only deduct 60% of those premiums on his Schedule C. He can deduct the remaining portion of the premiums as an itemized deduction if that amount plus other uncovered medical expenses is more than 7.5% of his adjusted gross income for the year. But deducting health insurance costs won't remain a disadvantage for sole proprietors for long—in the year 2002, a sole proprietor will be able to deduct 70% of his family's premiums, and by the year 2003, he'll be able to deduct the full cost of health insurance premiums.

5. Sole Proprietorships Compared to LLCs

As mentioned, no organizational fees or paperwork are required to start a sole proprietorship. By contrast, forming an LLC does require payment of some state filing fees (see Chapter 1, Section C3, for a list of state filing fees). And, of course, as you should now know, starting an LLC does require that you draw up organizational papers, including articles of organization and an operating agreement. Finally, operating an LLC may require more ongoing recordkeeping than running a sole proprietorship. To make sure your LLC will be respected as a separate entity in any subsequent court action, you'll want to keep written records of all major LLC decisions. In addition, all LLC financial transactions will have to be kept on the LLC books, separate from the finances of the LLC owners. This means you'll need to get a federal Employer ID from the IRS (by submitting IRS Form SS-4) and set up a separate LLC bank account, making sure to pay all expenses and payouts of profits from this account.

This extra work and money is the trade-off you make in exchange for the LLC's biggest advantage: the fact that it provides all of its owners with personal liability protection (see Chapter 1, Sections A and B, for more on the limited liability an LLC provides). While a commercial insurance policy can lessen a sole proprietor's liability for business mistakes and accidents, most affordable commercial policies contain high deductibles, meaning that even if it's available, most smaller businesses can't afford to buy full coverage for all foreseeable risks. And, of course, no insurance policy will provide owners protection from their failure to pay ordinary debts of the business, such as money owed to banks, landlords, suppliers and other creditors. LLC owners, on the other hand, do receive protection from these liabilities as long as owners do not agree to be personally liable for the business's debts.

And keep in mind that, as your business grows and becomes more profitable, so too does your exposure to lawsuits. The reason is that increased profits are invariably tied to increased business activity—for example, more customer transactions—and this means more potential for getting sued. And, of course, the very fact that your business is making more money often means that you look like a better target for lawsuit-prone customers and their attorneys who, it's sad to say, often decide to sue the "deepest pockets" they can find when a dispute or accident happens.

Example: *Rita and Ron move to Kona, Hawaii, buy a six-seat outboard-motor zodiac boat, and start earning a little cash giving whale-watching tours with their new business, Kona Coast Roamer Tours. In the early days business is slow and very homespun, and the two partners alternate taking out clients for a couple of hours a few times each week. But as the mainland economy booms and tourists flock to Hawaii, so too does their business. In fact, it improves so much the duo buy two additional boats and hire two staff members to provide morning and afternoon tours, seven days a week. This increased activity makes Ron and Rita nervous—more tours means the potential* *for more accidents and personal liability exposure for the owners. This nervousness increases more than a little when Rita discovers she's pregnant and the couple decide to buy a house. To help restore calm, Ron and Rita decide to form an LLC to wrap themselves up in its personal limited liability protection, and to sleep a little better at night. This is, after all, why they moved to Hawaii in the first place.*

When it comes to tax costs, sole proprietorships and LLCs come out about even on the main tax issues:

- *Income taxes.* Sole proprietorships and LLCs are both automatically treated as pass-through tax entities. Therefore, sole proprietors and LLC owners can count on about the same amount of tax complexity, paperwork and costs. Of course, if a one-person LLC elects corporate tax treatment, the LLC's tax situation will change significantly (see Chapter 4, Section C), to mirror that of a corporation.

- *Self-employment taxes.* Both sole proprietors and the sole owners of one-person LLCs will likely have to pay the same level of self-employment taxes. (See Chapter 4, Section D, for a full discussion of self-employment taxes for LLC members.)

C. What Is a General Partnership?

A partnership is a business in which two or more owners agree to share profits (and losses). If you go into business with at least one other person, even if you never sign a formal partnership agreement, state law says you have automatically formed a general partnership. Or put another way, a general partnership really can be started with a handshake (although it makes far more sense to prepare and sign a written partnership agreement—see "All Partnerships Should Create a Written Partnership Agreement," below).

Example: Two employed Web designers set up a side business to design websites for nonprofit organizations. They are too busy working to bother to think about the best business structure for their new sideline business. Without taking any formal action or creating a partnership agreement, they have formed a partnership. If the partners were to have a dispute—over the division of profits perhaps—in the absence of an agreement, state partnership law would control the outcome. This is one good reason why taking the time to prepare a partnership agreement in this sort of co-owned business is so important. For now, working as partners suits these two Web designers, since there are no significant personal liability issues involved in operating their tiny business. If their business grows, and along with it their business debt, to become more than a sideline business, they might consider filing articles to form an LLC.

All partnerships should create a written partnership agreement. While not required by law, general partners should always create a written partnership agreement. Without an agreement, the one-size-fits-all rules of each state's general partnership laws will apply to the partnership. These provisions usually say that profits and losses of the business should be divided up equally among the partners (or according to the partner's capital contributions in some states), and they impose a long agenda of other cookie-cutter rules. Rather than relying on state law, general partners should prepare a written partnership agreement (much like an LLC operating agreement) that covers issues important to their business relationship, including division of profits and losses, partnership draws (payments in lieu of salary) and the procedure for selling a partnership interest back to the partnership or to an outsider, should a partner die or want to move on.

1. Number of Partners

General partnerships may be formed by two or more people; by definition, there is no such thing as a one-person partnership. Legally, there is no upper limit on the number of partners who may be admitted into a partnership, but, because of the lack of the organizational and management structure that is built into corporations and LLCs, general partnerships with many owners may have problems reaching a consensus on business decisions and may be subject to divisive disputes between contending management factions. In larger partnerships, one or more partners may be designated as managing partners to eliminate day-to-day bickering, but using a partnership agreement to delegate authority to a select group of managing partners is rare in small business partnerships. Why? Because doing so can be risky for the nonmanaging partners—who, by definition, wouldn't keep a close eye on the business. Remember, all general partners are personally liable for partnership debts, whether they show up for work every day or not. To minimize their risks and to keep all the partners honest, all general partners usually take an active hand in management.

2. Personal Liability for Business Debts

As I just mentioned, each owner of a general partnership is personally liable for all business debts and any claims (including court judgments) against the business that the business can't pay. For example, if the business fails to pay its suppliers, the partners are personally responsible for paying these business debts and may have to use their houses, cars and personal bank accounts to provide funds to repay them.

What's more, if the business owes money it can't pay, the creditor may go after any general partner for the entire debt, regardless of her partnership ownership percentage (although if this happens, the partner who is sued can in turn sue her other partners to force them to repay their shares of the debt).

Personal liability for business debts becomes even more worrisome when you realize that each general partner may bind the entire partnership (and all of its partners) to a contract or business deal. In legal jargon, this authority is expressed by saying that each partner is an *agent* of the partnership. (Fortunately, there are a few significant limitations to this agency rule—to be valid, a contract or deal must generally be within the scope of the partnership's business, and the outside person who makes the deal with a partner must reasonably think that the partner is authorized to act on behalf of the partnership.) And as mentioned above, if a partnership can't fulfill a valid contract or other business deal, each partner may be held personally liable for the amount owed. This personal liability for the debts of the entire partnership, coupled with the agency authority of each partner to bind the others, makes the general partnership riskier than a sole proprietorship (where only the proprietor can legally bind the business) and far riskier than LLCs, corporations, limited partnerships and RLLPs (all of which offer at least some of the owners limited personal liability for business debts).

3. General Partnership Income Taxation

Like a sole proprietorship, a general partnership is treated as a "pass-through tax entity." Again, this IRS jargon means profits (and losses) pass through the business entity to the partners, who pay taxes on any profits on their individual returns at their individual tax rates.

Partnership taxation, however, is a lot more complicated than sole proprietorship taxation, and most partnerships of any size will likely need an accountant. Although a partnership does not pay its own taxes, it must file an informational return each year, IRS Form 1065, U.S. Partnership Return of Income. In addition, the partnership must give each partner a filled-in IRS Schedule K-1 (Form 1065), *Partner's Share of Income, Credits and Deductions*, which shows the proportionate share of profits or losses each person carries over to his or her individual 1040 tax return at the end of the year. Note that, just like LLC members, each partner must pay taxes on her entire share of profits, even if the partnership chooses to reinvest the profits in the business rather than distributing all of them to the partners. The technical way of saying this is that the owners are taxed on their "allocated" profits, not their "distributed" profits. (I discuss this in the LLC context in Chapter 4, Section A3.)

What about self-employment (Social Security and Medicare) taxes? General partners, although not considered employees of the partnership, must pay self-employment taxes on their share of partnership income.

4. General Partnerships Compared to LLCs

General partnerships are less costly to start than LLCs because most states do not require startup paperwork to be filed with a state agency, meaning there are no filing fees for forming new general partnerships (although publication in a local newspaper is required in some states). By contrast, an LLC will have to file organizational papers (called "articles of organization" in most states) and pay state filing fees (see Chapter 1, Section C3, for a list of state filing fees). Also, operating a co-owned LLC often requires more ongoing recordkeeping than running a partnership—it's wise to record ongoing LLC management decisions to avoid disputes among LLC owners, and as a hedge against anyone outside the LLC trying to sue the LLC members personally. (As I discussed in Chapter 1, Section B4, outsiders can ask a court to disregard the existence of the LLC because it was operated as a personal extension of the owners and not as a separate business entity—an unlikely, but possible scenario.) Partnerships, too, should try to keep written records of key business and ownership decisions, but there are fewer potential legal consequences if they fail to do so.

Again, the downside to running a general partnership is each partner's exposure to personal liability. A general commercial insurance package, possibly supplemented by more specialized coverage for unusual risks, can significantly lessen the partners' exposure to personal liability for accidents. However, most affordable commercial insurance policies contain high deductibles and do not cover certain transactions, such as mismanagement or risky behavior by the business owners, and most smaller businesses can't afford to buy full coverage for all foreseeable risks. In addition, no insurance policy will cover the failure of the business to pay ordinary debts of the business, such as money owed to banks, landlords and other creditors. LLC owners, on the other hand, normally avoid the problem of personal liability as a matter of law.

General partnerships and LLCs come out about even on a couple of important issues:

- *Ownership Agreements.* Even a small general partnership should start off with a written general partnership agreement. Creating one, of course, takes time and, if a lawyer is hired to write it, is likely to cost between $1,000 and $5,000 in legal fees, depending on the complexity of your partnership and the thickness of your lawyer's rug. Of course, many partners do the work themselves saving a bundle of money using a self-help tool (such as those mentioned previously in this section). Creating a partnership agreement with one of these tools takes about as much time as it takes to create an LLC operating agreement on your own.

- *Income Taxes.* General partnerships and LLCs are both automatically treated as pass-through tax entities, and both prepare and file standard partnership tax returns. (There are no separate LLC tax returns at the federal level; LLCs are treated as partnerships for tax purposes and use the same informational tax returns and tax procedures as partnerships.) Therefore, partnership and LLC owners can count on about the same amount of tax complexity, paperwork and costs. Even though you'll probably turn over most year-end tax work to a tax advisor who'll prepare your business tax return, understanding and following basic business reporting tax procedures takes a fair amount of time and effort for either type of business. Of course, this can change since both LLCs and partnerships can elect corporate tax treatment (see Chapter 4, Section C).

As for self-employment taxes, as the IRS regulations now stand, partners can usually avoid self-employment taxes. LLC members who are active in their business, on the other hand, will probably have to pay self-employment taxes, which can be as much as 15% of their income. (See Chapter 4, Section D, for a full discussion of self-employment taxes for LLC members.) However, these rules are expected to change soon so that all owners of pass-through businesses will be treated the same.

Self-Employment Tax Rules May Change. The emergence of the LLC has thrown dealing with federal self-employment tax regulations into a state of turmoil, since partners, LLC members and S corporation shareholders are treated differently when it comes to self-employment taxes, even though they are all owners of "pass-through" businesses. The U.S. Treasury Department has been unsuccessfully trying to revamp the entire self-employment tax scheme to make it apply uniformly to all of these entities. So far, final regulations have not been adopted, but everyone in the tax field expects an eventual change in how the self-employment tax rules apply to all multi-owner pass-through tax entities—partnerships, LLCs and S corporations alike. Ask your tax advisor for the latest information.

Start-Up Information for Partnerships. If you're considering forming a partnership rather than an LLC, Nolo offers several helpful resources for learning about partnerships and creating a partnership agreement. Nolo's free Partnership Center at www.nolo.com/keyword/partnerships_home.html offers free Encyclopedia articles and FAQs about starting a partnership. In addition, Nolo's reasonably priced *The Partnership Book*, by Denis Clifford and Ralph Warner, explains how to form a partnership and create a partnership agreement. Nolo's website also offers a new WebForm for creating a partnership agreement. Simply go to www.nolo.com/product/webforms_home.html and choose "Partnership Agreement." You'll be asked a few questions in an online interview, after which you can download and print your customized partnership agreement.

D. What Is a Limited Partnership?

A limited partnership is similar to a general partnership, except it has two types of partners. A limited partnership must have at least one general partner that manages the business and is personally liable for its debts and claims. (General partners have the same broad rights and responsibilities as the partners discussed in the general partnership section above.) And by definition, a limited partnership must also have at least one limited partner, and usually has more. A limited partner is typically an investor who contributes capital to the business, but is not involved in day-to-day management. As long as limited partners do not participate in management, they do not have personal liability for business debts and claims. Instead, they function much like passive shareholders in a small corporation, investing with the expectation of receiving a share of both profits and the eventual increase in the value of the business.

To create a limited partnership, you must pay an initial fee and file papers with the state—usually a "certificate of limited partnership." This document is similar to the articles (or certificate) filed by a corporation or an LLC, and includes information about the general and limited partners. Filing fees are about the same for limited partnerships as they for a corporation or an LLC.

As for income taxes, limited partnerships generally are treated like general partnerships, with all partners individually reporting and paying taxes on their share of the profits each year. The limited partnership files an informational partnership tax return *(IRS Form 1065, U.S. Partnership Return of Income*, the same tax form that applies to a general partnership), and each partner receives *IRS Schedule K-1 (1065), Partner's Share of Income, Credits and Deductions,* from the partnership. Each partner then files this form with her individual IRS 1040 tax return. Limited partners, as a rule, are exempt from payment of self-employment taxes—that's because, since they are not active in the business, their share of partnership income is not considered "earned income" for purposes of the self-employment tax.

Limited partnerships and LLCs look alike in many ways. Both provide the limited liability owners with protection against business debts and claims, and both are treated as pass-through tax entities under the default tax rules. But there are two major differences. First, a limited partnership must have at least one general partner, who is personally liable for the debts and other liabilities of the business (unless the general partner goes to the trouble of setting up his own corporation or LLC, which I discuss below). This differs from LLCs, where all members are automatically covered by the cloak of limited liability protection.

Second, limited partners are generally prohibited from managing the business. If a limited partner becomes active in the business of the limited partnership, she typically loses her limited liability. (Some states have carved out some new exceptions to this ban, however, usually meaning that a limited partner can vote on issues that affect the basic structure of the partnership, including the removal of general partners, the termination of the partnership, the amendment of the partnership agreement or the sale of all or most of the assets of the partnership.) In contrast, all LLC members can freely manage and run any aspect of the business without running the risk of losing their limited liability.

This second restriction of the limited partnership normally makes it an unsuitable ownership form for small, actively run businesses, since all or most owners will want to participate in decision making, which would subject them to personal liability for business debts in a limited partnership. If an owner of a limited partnership wants the benefit of limited liability protection, she must step back from active management of the business, and invest in it as a passive investor only—something that is all but impossible for the millions of small business people who plan to be active in their own businesses. Owners who all want to be active in their company are better off forming an LLC or a corporation, where all owners/investors can run the business while enjoying the protection of limited liability for business debts.

Although you can readily see that a limited partnership is far less versatile than an LLC, some companies still operate as limited partnerships. This usually happens in certain types of investment firms, where the investors insist that the managers of the company (the general partners) be on the hook for bad business decisions—with the thinking that the managers will be less likely to make unsound investments if their personal assets are at stake. But in other, usually larger, limited partnerships, the general partner is actually a limited liability enterprise such as an LLC or a corporation. This way the general partner avoids personal liability altogether.

Example: In 1985, Situs Holdings, a limited partnership, was established as a real estate development company. Its general partner is The Situs Corporation, and it has 20 limited partners. The limited partners are individuals who invest capital to purchase and improve the company's real estate holdings, while the general partner, The Situs Corporation, manages Situs Holdings' properties in exchange for a management fee. The Situs Corporation is owned by Sid Block and his two daughters, Elizabeth and Jackie. All of the partners, The Situs Corporation and the limited partners, share in a percentage of the profits of Situs Holdings.

Note that the general partner is a corporation. This is a standard technique used to limit the personal liability of the general partner in larger limited partnerships, particularly where the liabilities of the company may be hefty. In this situation, the company's real estate debts are substantial, and the potential liabilities associated with the renovation and sale of properties also are considerable—general contractor liability claims, purchaser rescissions and other disputes that may end up in court can go into the millions of dollars range. Of course, the whole Situs ownership scheme was established before the LLC came into existence. If Sid and his daughters and the limited partners had to do it all over again, no doubt their legal and tax advisors would recommend a much simpler setup—namely, forming one manager-managed LLC to hold and develop the properties. All of the LLC managers and the nonmanaging members (the investors) would enjoy limited liability protection.

E. What is a C Corporation?

A "C" corporation is just another name for a regular for-profit corporation—a corporation taxed under normal corporate income tax rules. The letter C comes from Subchapter C of the Internal Revenue Code and is used to distinguish regular corporations from "S" corporations, a more specialized type of corporation that is regulated under Subchapter S of the Internal Revenue Code. In a nutshell, an S corporation gets the pass-through tax treatment of a partnership (with some important technical differences) and the limited liability of a corporation, much like an LLC. I discuss S corporations in more detail in Section F, below.

To form a corporation, you pay corporate filing fees and prepare and file formal organizational papers, usually called "articles of incorporation," with a state agency (in most states, the Secretary or Department of State). Once formed, the corporation assumes an independent legal life separate from its owners. This separate legal life leads to a number of familiar traditional corporate characteristics, which I discuss below.

1. Number of Shareholders (Owners) and Directors

A corporation can have as many or as few shareholders and directors as it wants. Even one-person corporations can be formed in all states. Since every corporation is required to have directors and officers to manage and run the day-to-day business, that one person would be sole shareholder, director, president and secretary of the corporation.

2. Limited Liability for Shareholders

A corporation provides all of its owners—that is, shareholders—with the benefits of limited personal liability protection. That means if a court judgment is entered against the corporation, or if the corporation can't pay its bills, the shareholders stand to lose only the money that they've invested. Creditors cannot go after the personal assets of the shareholders.

Traditionally, the main reason why business owners formed corporations was to wrap themselves in the legal mantle of limited liability, to avoid personal exposure to business debts and claims. Of course, now that LLCs have entered the picture, small business owners now can choose between the two if they are looking for limited liability protection. I compare the two entities in Section 4, below.

3. C Corporate Income Taxation

First, let's quickly review how unincorporated businesses are taxed. In an unincorporated business, the owners pay individual income taxes on all net profits of the business, regardless of how much they actually receive each year. For example, assume that a partnership or an LLC has two owners and earns $100,000 in net profits. If the owners split profits equally, each must report and pay individual income taxes on $50,000 of business profits. Now here is the rub. This is true even if all of the profits are kept in the business checking account to meet upcoming business expenses rather than paid out to the owners.

Now, let's compare how net profits are paid out and taxed in a corporation. A corporation is a legal entity separate from its shareholders and files its own tax return, paying taxes on any profits left in the business. Unlike most LLC members, shareholders who work for the corporation are treated as employees who receive salaries for their work in the business. The owners' salaries are deducted by the corporation as a business expense when it computes its net taxable income. But since the owners of a small corporation also manage the business as its directors, they have the luxury of deciding how much to pay themselves in salary. In short, the owners decide how much of the profits will be taxed at the corporate level or paid out to them and taxed on their individual returns.

Two results follow from this: 1) the owners only pay individual income taxes on salary amounts they actually receive, not on all the net profits of the business, and 2) the corporation—which, remember, is a separate tax entity—pays corporate taxes on the net profits actually retained in the business—that is, profits that remain after paying normal business expenses, including the salaries paid to the working owners. In effect, the corporate tax scheme actually does a better (or at least a more accurate) job of taxing the business for profits actually retained in the business, while taxing the owners only on profits they actually receive.

As I'll discuss shortly, this type of income splitting between the company and the owners can lead to tax savings, at least for small corporations.

Now let's look more closely at the fact that a corporation pays corporate taxes on the net profits actually retained in the business. How does this actually work? The corporation's owners file individual income tax returns and pay taxes, at their individual tax rates, on the salaries and any bonuses they receive. At the end of the year, the corporation files a corporate tax return, *IRS Form 1120, Corporate Income Tax Return*, and pays its own income taxes on the profits left in the company. Corporate tax rates are normally lower than shareholders' individual tax rates for the first $75,000 of income (15% for the first $50,000, 25% for the next $25,000). This means that if the owners decide to retain profits in the business for expansion or other business needs, profits of up to $75,000 will be taxed at rates that are almost surely lower than the owners' individual tax rates, resulting in overall tax savings.

TAX RATES ON TAXABLE CORPORATE INCOME

$0	to	$50,000	15%
$50,001	to	$75,000	25%
$75,001	to	$100,000	34%
$100,001	to	$335,000	39%
$335,001	to	$10,000,000	34%
$10,000,001	to	$15,000,000	35%
$15,000,001	to	$18,333,333	38%
Over $18,333,333			35%

Note: Personal service corporations are subject to a flat tax of 35% regardless of the amount of income.

Example: Justine and Janine are partners in Just Jams & Jellies, a specialty store selling gourmet canned preserves. Business has boomed and their net taxable income has reached a level where it is taxed at the highest individual tax rate of 39.6%. If the owners incorporate, they can leave $75,000 worth of profits in their business, which will be taxed at the lower corporate tax rates of 15% and 25%, saving overall tax dollars on business income. In fact, because corporate tax brackets on all net taxable income never reach the highest individual tax rate of 39.6% (the highest corporate tax rate is 39%), the owners can keep as much income in the corporation as they want and still reduce their overall income tax bill.

For some small businesses, however, this corporate tax strategy—called income-splitting—isn't useful, since their owners pay out all net profits to themselves at the end of each tax year.

Example 1: Remember our friend Winston, who set up his own computer graphics company as a sideline to his day job? (See the Introduction, Section A, Example 3.) Like many other small service-business owners, he does not reinvest profits of his self-employment business, but happily deposits every last cent into his own personal checking account. Would corporate tax treatment benefit Winston? No. He does not have any reason to accumulate money in his business, so he would not benefit from lower corporate tax rates.

Example 2: Linux and Colleen own and work part-time for their own LLC, a retail sales business that employs one full-time worker, Vince. Linux and Colleen share in the LLC's profits as owners, not employees (the normal set-up for LLC members). Gross sales revenue of the business this year is expected to be $200,000. Cost of inventory will be $50,000, so net sales revenue is $150,000. Linux and Colleen annually pay Vince $50,000 in salary and their landlord $25,000 to rent their storefront property. Other normal business expenses total about $20,000 per year, with the result that net profits will be about $55,000. The partners need to pay out all of this money to themselves for their hard work and to help meet their own living expenses (past savings *also help them pay their personal expenses as their business gets going). Again, as in the example above, income-splitting between this business entity and its owners is not a viable tax strategy.*

But for other small businesses, even ones that make modest net incomes, this is not the case. Many small business owners are forced to retain net profits in their business to handle upcoming costs of doing business such as the purchase of inventory or to pay employee salaries and other necessary and regular business expenses such as rent and insurance. In short, retaining net profits in the business can be necessary even if the owners are not paying out as much of the profits to themselves as they would like. In these situations, being able to apply the lower corporate tax rates on net income left in the business does result in tax savings.

Example: *Let's visit Linux and Colleen a few years from now and assume that their LLC has begun to make more money. For the past two years, their gross sales have averaged $500,000, and their cost of inventory has remained level at 25% of gross sales, or $125,000. Vince, the one full-time employee, and the owners have had to work harder to meet increased customer demand, giving up many of their weekends to the business. Vince's salary has increased to $75,000, but other expenses have stayed almost level at $60,000. Net partnership profits now average $240,000 per year, with each owner taking home a $120,000 share.*

Linux and Colleen agree to look for a slightly more upscale storefront, hoping to sell more expensive items (with higher margins) to a more affluent clientele. They know that they'll have to come up with a chunk of cash to move into a new space, and they also expect to have to come up with additional funds to start stocking the higher-priced inventory. In addition, they discuss the possibility of hiring another full-time worker—if only to allow themselves to have more weekend time away from the business. They each realize they'll have to take a temporary cut in their share of paid-out profits to fund the move and expansion. Realizing they will need to begin retaining a substantial amount of partnership profits in the business in order to accomplish these plans, they decide to elect corporate tax treatment so that the profits kept in the business will be taxed at lower corporate income tax rates.

Now for one last income tax item: when a corporation is sold or dissolved, the shareholders and their corporation must each pay taxes on any increased value (appreciation) of the assets owned by the corporation—this means that a double tax is paid. For businesses that regularly make investments, hold real estate or buy other types of property that are likely to increase in value, this can be a big disadvantage. The rules here are complex and tricky—just realize that one of the more technical issues of deciding to incorporate has to do with the tax consequences that will occur when you sell or dissolve your business. If your business will invest in assets that are likely to increase in value, this is definitely one of the areas where expert tax advice is needed.

4. Corporate Management

Because a corporation has a separate legal existence from its owners, you must pay more attention to its legal care and feeding than you would for a sole proprietorship, a partnership or an LLC.

As mentioned above, corporations are owned by shareholders and managed by a board of directors. This means the owners of a small corporation must periodically don different legal hats. As directors they must hold annual meetings required under state law. And they must keep minutes of meetings, prepare formal documentation (in the form of resolutions or written consents to corporate actions) of important decisions made during the life of the corporation, and keep a paper trail of all legal and financial dealings between the corporation and its shareholders.

To make corporate life even more complicated, the board of directors needs to appoint officers to supervise daily corporate business. State law usually requires that, at the least, a president (CEO) and a secretary be appointed and, in many states, a treasurer as well. In practice, however, since a small corporation's shareholders act as both its board of directors and its officers, this consists of little more than handing out a couple of titles (legal hats) to the same people.

Example: *Tornado Air Conditioning Service, Inc. is owned and operated by Ted and his spouse Valerie. They name themselves as the only two directors in the corporate articles they file with the state. At the first organizational meeting of the board, they appoint Valerie as both President and Treasurer, and Ted as both corporate VP and Secretary. They also approve the issuance of the corporation's initial shares to Ted and Hilda, its only two shareholders.*

5. Corporate Capital and Stock Structure

A corporation issues stock to its shareholders in exchange for capital invested in the business. The manner in which corporate stock allows corporations to structure ownership remains unique in the world of business entities and leads to a few special benefits. For example, a corporation alone can parcel out ownership interests in the form of shares, which can be divided into classes, each with different rights to vote, receive dividends, participate in management and receive cash if the business is liquidated.

The existence of corporate stock is also very useful to fund employee stock option or bonus plans. In addition, it can be used to fund a buyout of another business or can be exchanged or converted into the shares of another corporation to effect a merger or consolidation. And, of course, the corporate stock structure is almost essential if a business wants to raise money from the public in an initial public offering (IPO). The state corporation statutes flesh out the full potential of corporate stock ownership and provide a ready-to-use set of legal standards and procedures that are used throughout the banking, investment and legal community to funnel private and public capital into corporate coffers.

6. Employee Fringe Benefits

Even small corporations have the opportunity to offer fringe benefits such as fully deductible group life and disability insurance and enhanced retirement plans to their employees, as well as the stock purchase, option and incentive plans mentioned above. The owner/employees who receive these benefits are not taxed on their individual tax returns for the value of these benefits.

7. Corporations Compared to LLCs

A good way to compare the C corporation to the LLC is to revisit the traditional corporate characteristics just discussed to see if and how each of these features would survive if the business organized as an LLC instead. In overview, you'll find that many, but not all, of the advantages associated with incorporation can also be achieved by forming an LLC (which also provides owners with several unique benefits).

- *Limited liability for all owners.* Like corporate shareholders, all LLC owners are protected from personal liability for business debts and claims under the state LLC statutes. The limited liability provided by LLCs is just as strong as that provided by corporations.

- *Corporate formalities.* Corporations are similar to LLCs in the type of paperwork and fees necessary to get them started. Both must prepare and file organizational papers with the state and pay a filing fee. And it is essential that both adopt a set of operating rules that set out the basic legal requirements for operating the business: corporations adopt bylaws and LLCs adopt operating agreements. But when it comes to ongoing paperwork hassles, LLCs come out ahead. That's because by statute small LLCs are usually authorized to be more relaxed when it comes to a lot of the ongoing formalities required of corporations, such as holding and documenting formal meetings. Sure, LLC members still should take the time to document important legal, tax and business decisions, and even hold and document the occasional important member meeting if for no other reason than to make sure everyone's on the same page and to record everyone's mutual understanding. But for the most part this is a practical, not a legal, requirement, unlike in corporations, which must hold shareholders' and directors' meetings at least annually, whether they are really needed or not. Or put another way, unlike a corporation, LLCs needn't worry that a court or the IRS will ignore their owners' limited liability status just because their LLC records binder is a little thin.

- *Corporate management.* As an added bonus, LLCs are not required to have the three-tiered organizational structure of corporations: shareholders, directors and officers. In an LLC, all you need are owners, who by now you should know are called members. Some LLCs choose to select some of the members to be managers (discussed in Chapter 1, Section A6), but most members of smaller LLCs usually choose to operate their LLC themselves, without a separate management team. Even if an LLC does appoint managers to handle the day-to-day business, living with the manager/member dichotomy can be a lot simpler than trying to juggle management roles in the corporate shareholder, director and officer context.

- *Corporate stock structure.* As mentioned above, the corporation's special stock structure remains a unique part of the corporate way of life. While LLCs can issue informal "membership units," these units don't have the same legal or financial standing that corporate shares do—most importantly, there is no system in place for public offerings of membership units. And, of course, since LLCs don't issue stock, there can be no stock options. For these reasons, the small minority of small businesses that want to issue options to employees or sell shares to venture capitalists will find that organizing as a corporation makes the most sense.

• *Tax treatment of profits and losses.* For the great majority of companies that will never need the stock structure of corporations, LLCs can be the best choice if for no other reason than that an LLC can split profits and losses among owners as the owners choose. For example, even in an LLC owned equally by four people, profits and losses can be apportioned in unequal percentages as long as special IRS rules are followed (see Chapter 3, Section E). By comparison, corporate capitalization is more straight-laced. Because of the stock ownership model set out in corporate statutes, corporate profits and losses must normally be allocated in proportion to stock ownership. (While special classes of shares can be created to deviate somewhat from the standard corporate model, this involves creating a complex stock structure.)

Example: Manny and Linda present a business idea to Nate, who agrees to give them financial backing. Nate puts up the cash to get the business started, while Manny and Linda contribute full-time work and personal know-how. The three each own one-third of the LLC (each owns one of three membership units), but Nate reasonably insists on getting 50% of any LLC profits until he is paid back his cash investment plus 10% annual interest. The LLC structure easily accommodates this arrangement—they simply set out these terms in their operating agreement.

If the three had instead formed a corporation, a more complicated ownership arrangement would be required to effect the uneven profit distribution. One approach would be to issue Nate a separate class of shares that alone participated in dividends. But this setup would not be optimal, since dividends can't *be deducted from corporate income, but must be paid with after-tax profits of the company (and would be taxed a second time on Nate's individual tax return). Instead, they'd probably decide to exclude Nate totally from stock ownership in the business and have Nate lend money to the corporation, issuing him an interest-bearing note. But this approach, too, would be problematical—since it would deny Nate a capital stake in the enterprise money, he wouldn't profit if the business was later sold for a great price. Again, the point here is that disproportionate profit-sharing arrangements are the bread-and-butter of the LLC, but they are not so easily implemented in the corporate context.*

- *Corporate income tax treatment and income splitting.* Traditionally, what set the corporate form apart from other limited liability structures like the LLC was corporate tax treatment, and specifically, the ability to split income between the business and its owners, as discussed in Section 3, above. In years past, owners of an unincorporated business such as an LLC or a partnership had to actually convert their business into a corporation in order to be treated as a corporation for income tax purposes. That's no longer true. Today, if you find that your LLC or partnership regularly retains profits to meet its future needs instead of distributing these profits, you have the option of keeping your present ownership structure, while at the same time electing to be taxed as if you were incorporated. By doing this, you'll pay individual income taxes on only the amount of profits actually paid to you for working in your business and let the business itself pay taxes on retained profits, at reduced corporate income tax rates (at least for the first $75,000 of profits). The net result may be a substantial income tax savings to you and the other business owners (for example, if your individual tax bracket is 31%, you'll save approximately $10,000 in taxes on $75,000 of retained profits).

As a practical matter, of course, most new LLCs don't elect corporate tax treatment until their owners are able to take home plenty of profits to cover their living expenses. And then they do so only if their tax advisor agrees that the income tax savings that can be achieved by splitting income between owners and the business entity itself are worth the trouble and the collateral tax costs of electing corporate tax treatment. To find out more about corporate tax splitting for LLCs, see Chapter 4, Section C.

But for our purpose here—comparing corporations to LLCs—the point is: now that the IRS allows LLCs to elect corporate tax treatment, the benefit of corporate income splitting is no longer unique to the corporation. So whenever you read about the advantages of lower corporate tax rates, or the ability to split income, feel free to substitute "LLC" in place of "corporation" as long as you realize that to receive corporate tax treatment, an LLC must make a special tax election (discussed in Chapter 4, Section C3).

- *Taxation on appreciation.* Unlike shareholders and their corporations, LLC members and their LLC are not subject to double taxation on the increased value of company assets when the LLC is dissolved. That's because the LLC's tax liabilities are all passed through the business to the LLC members; the LLC itself does not pay a tax on any of its income, including any appreciation on its assets.

- *Taxation of benefits.* As I mentioned above, corporations can offer employees fringe benefits like group insurance and retirement plans and deduct them as a business expense. While some of these fringe benefits are available under federal and state tax rules to sole proprietors and owners of partnerships and LLCs, unincorporated business owners who receive these benefits will ordinarily be taxed on their value (unless they have elected corporate tax treatment). However, before you decide this is a big corporate advantage, remember that many new businesses can't afford the cost of these expensive benefits for all of their employees. And some types of employee benefits must be provided on a nondiscriminatory basis to all employees or none—not just to the owners of the corporation. In short, the cost of setting up and maintaining elaborate benefit programs for all of a corporation's employees may offset the tax advantages for the owners.

That's the short list of key corporation and LLC similarities and differences. To cut to the point, with the arrival of the LLC, many business owners will realize that incorporation normally only makes sense if the business needs to take advantage of the corporate stock structure to attract key employees and investment capital (including the possibility of raising public capital by making a public offering of shares). No question, a corporation will probably have an easier time attracting capital investment by issuing stock privately or publicly. And businesses in Internet and other hot technology industries may find it easier to attract and retain key employees by issuing employee stock options. But for businesses that never go public, or for businesses that will go public, many years from now, choosing to operate as an LLC rather than a corporation normally makes the most sense because of its simplicity and flexibility.

Start-Up Information for Corporations. If you decide your circumstances may make forming a corporation a better route for you than forming an LLC, Nolo offers several helpful resources for learning about and forming corporations. Nolo's free Corporations Center at www.nolo.com/keyword/corporations_home.html offers free Encyclopedia articles and FAQs about starting a corporation. In addition, I have written books on how to form a corporation in California, Florida and Texas (all published by Nolo), and am currently writing a national book good for forming a corporation in any state (all books include articles of incorporation forms on disk).

F. What Is an S Corporation?

As I mentioned at the beginning of Section E, above, an S corporation is a corporation that qualifies for special tax treatment under the Internal Revenue Code (and state corporate tax statutes as well). Forming one requires jumping through the same state incorporation hoops as does forming a regular C corporation. This means filing articles of incorporation with the state and paying a state filing fee. Then, to convert the new corporation into an S corporation, the shareholders must sign and file an S corporation tax election, IRS Form 2253. But as you'll see below, choosing S corporation status is a tax, not a legal, election—the same legal corporation rules applicable to C corporations also apply to S corporations.

LLCs have largely replaced S corporations. The S corporation used to be the only way that all owners of a business could obtain personal liability protection while retaining pass-through taxation of business income. Since the advent of the LLC, S corporations have largely fallen out of favor. That's because the LLC provides substantially the same benefits as an S corporation without several of the significant restrictions that are part and parcel of S corporations. (I discuss these below.)

1. Number of Shareholders (Owners) and Directors

Generally, an S corporation may have no more than 75 shareholders, all of whom must be individuals who are U.S. citizens or residents, or certain types of trusts or estates. While the 75-shareholder limit may not be much of an inconvenience—after all, most small businesses have fewer than 5 owners—the other shareholder restrictions can be significant.

2. Limited Liability for Shareholders

Because S corporations are the same legally as C corporations under state law, all S corporation shareholders have limited personal liability protection from the debts and other liabilities of the corporation. See the discussion of corporate limited liability in Section E2, above.

3. S Corporation Income Taxation

Once a corporation makes an S corporation tax election, its profits and losses pass through the corporation and are reported on the individual tax returns of the S corporation's shareholders. This means that any profits an S corporation retains at the end of the year are not taxed at the business entity level at corporate tax rates (as is the case for a regular C corporation), but are passed through to the S corporation's owners. In other words, S corporation profits are allocated and taxed to each shareholder each year at the shareholder's individual income tax rates (again, this is the same basic pass-through tax treatment afforded partnership and LLC owners).

4. S Corporations Compared to LLCs

As I mentioned above, before the LLC business form came along, forming an S corporation was the preferred way for business owners to obtain personal liability protection while retaining pass-through taxation of business income. However, now that the LLC is on the scene, S corporations no longer hold much allure for most business owners. Here's why:

S Corporation Formation. To form an S corporation, you must first form a regular C corporation, then convert it to an S corporation by filing an S corporation tax election with the IRS. This involves more paperwork than simply forming an LLC.

- *S Corporation Limited Liability.* S corporation shareholders, like LLC members, are protected from personal liability for the debts of the business. But to keep this limited liability protection, you have to follow the corporate rules when running your business to preserve your limited liability status. This means issuing stock, electing officers, holding regular board of directors' and shareholders' meetings, keeping corporate minutes of all meetings, and following the mandatory rules found in your state's corporation code. By contrast, if you form an LLC, most of these legal hoops needn't be jumped through—you just make sure your management team is in agreement on major decisions and you go about your business. Yes, it makes sense to hold formal LLC meetings from time to time to record important management decisions, but *you* get to decide when you really need to do this.

- *S Corporation Ownership Restrictions.* Because S corporation stock ownership is limited to individuals who are U.S. citizens or residents, it doesn't have the same organizational flexibility of the LLC. (Special types of trusts and other special entities can own shares too, but these exceptions don't help the average business person.) Even if an S corporation initially meets the U.S. citizen (or resident) requirement, its shareholders can't sell shares to a foreign citizen or a company (like a corporation or an LLC), on pain of losing S corporation tax status. (This also means that some of the C corporation's main benefits—namely the ability to set up stock option and bonus plans and to bring in public capital with an IPO—are pretty much out of the question.) In an LLC, any type of person or entity can become a member—a U.S. citizen, a citizen of a foreign country, another LLC, a corporation or a limited partnership.

- *S Corporation Allocation of Profits and Losses.* Because an S corporation is a corporation, profits and losses of the entity are distributed to the shareholders in proportion to their stockholdings. LLCs have more flexibility in this regard, since they can tailor the allocations of profits and losses to meet the needs of investors—for example, an LLC can bring in an investor for a share of LLC profits or losses that's disproportionately larger than his capital interest (see Chapter 3, Section E, for details).

Example: *Ely and Natalie want to go into business designing solar-powered hot tubs. Ely is the "money" person and agrees to pitch in 80% of the first-year funds necessary to get the business going. Natalie is the hot tub and solar specialist and will operate the business. One half of Natalie's first-year salary, plus a cash payment of $20,000, will fund her initial 20% share in the enterprise. In exchange for his investment, the two agree that Ely will receive two-thirds of the profits of the business for five years, at which point they will be divided equally. While doling out profits in a way that is disproportionate to business ownership makes practical sense for Ely and Natalie, it is not permitted under S corporation rules. Far better for Ely and Natalie to form an LLC, which does allow them this flexibility.*

- *Limitations of S Corporation Tax Treatment.* A full discussion of S corporation taxes is beyond the scope of this overview book on LLCs. Nevertheless, I want mention one aspect of S corporations that can make a huge difference to some business investors. An S corporation's business debts cannot be passed along to its shareholders unless they have personally co-signed and guaranteed the debt. This means that the tax basis of an S corporation shareholder does not increase when the company takes on debt. Conversely, LLCs normally can give their owners the tax benefits of any business debt, co-signed or not, meaning that their tax basis will increase when the company takes on debt. This increase in basis means that, in the long run, each of the LLC owners is less likely to be taxed on all of the profits they receive from the LLC. In short, if a company will incur substantial debt, as would often be the case if it borrows money to open its business or buy real estate, the investors who form an S corporation will be at a disadvantage as compared to those who form an LLC.

Example: *An LLC borrows $400,000. This debt is allocated equally to four LLC owners. This means it increases the basis each owner holds in his capital (ownership) interest. This basis increase, in turn, means that each owner can receive $100,000 in distributions of profits from the LLC without being taxed (distributions are only taxed when they exceed an owner's basis). By contrast, S corporation shareholders do not increase their basis in their shares when the corporation borrows money, so an entity-level loan of this sort would not provide a tax benefit to them.*

Benefits of Entity-Level Debt. This a highly technical area that a tax advisor can fill you in on if you want more information.

S Corporations have an advantage when it comes to self-employment taxes. S corporation owners do enjoy one advantage over standard LLCs with respect to self-employment taxes (Social Security and Medicare taxes). S corporation shareholders normally do not have to pay self-employment taxes on any portion of S corporation profits that pass to them at the end of each year, over and above any actual salary they receive. As of this writing, the self-employment tax situation for LLC owners is in a state of flux. Currently, the general rule for LLCs is that LLC members who are active in their business must pay self-employment taxes on all profits that pass through to them at the end of the year, which means that they must pay more self-employment taxes than if they had formed an S corporation. In other words, not only do LLC members have to pay self-employment taxes on any salary they receive, they must also pay these taxes on all of the company's profits that are allocated to them.

Example: Sam owns a one-person S corporation that nets $250,000 in profits (before payment of Sam's salary). Sam pays himself $100,000 by way of salary, with the remaining $150,000 being allocated to him at the end of the year as a profit on his investment (since an S corporation is a pass-through tax entity, all money ends up being credited to Sam for tax purposes). Sam pays income taxes and self-employment taxes only on the first $100,000; for the next $150,000, he pays only income taxes, not self-employment taxes. By contrast, if Sam had organized his business as a one-person LLC, he would normally be subject to payment of self-employment taxes on the entire amount.

5. Disadvantages of the S Corporation Compared to the C Corporation

Just in case you're wondering, the S corporation's ownership restrictions and its inability to issue special classes of stock also makes the S corporation a lot less flexible than a regular C corporation when it comes to attracting key employees and investment capital—two of the advantages a regular C corporation enjoys as compared to an LLC. First, because an S corporation cannot have more than 75 shareholders, it can't adopt an employee stock option, stock bonus or stock purchase plan, nor can it make a public offering of its shares. Second, because an S corporation must have one class of shares, it can't easily accommodate the needs of outside venture capital firms and other investors who require special dividend or conversion rights in return for a capital investment in a company.

G. What Is an RLLP?

In all 50 states, professionals may set up a special type of partnership, called a registered limited liability partnership (RLLP), as an alternative to forming an LLC. In some states (like California), this new type of ownership structure was invented because state law didn't allow professionals to form LLCs. In others, this business structure was established to help professionals in a multi-member practice be certain that they could avoid personal liability for the malpractice of the other professionals in their firm. If you are not forming a professional practice along with professional co-owners, the RLLP is probably not of interest to you.

What an RLLP really amounts to is a partnership in which all of the owners remain personally liable for their own acts (malpractice), but receive limited liability for any malpractice of other partners in the firm. Most state RLLP statutes also give the professionals personal liability protection from other tort liabilities (slip-and-fall lawsuits) of the RLLP as well as from business debts.

1. Number of Partners

At least two partners are needed to form an RLLP. Typically, under state statutes, the partners must be licensed in the same or related professions. Usually professionals that are eligible to form an RLLP include people who work in the legal, medical and accounting fields, as well as in a short list of other professions in which a special "professional-client" relationship is assumed to exist. In some states engineers, veterinarians and acupuncturists are also allowed to form RLLPs. It's important to realize that in some states, not all categories of licensed professionals can form an RLLP.

Professionals eligible to form professional corporations can usually form RLLPS. The list of professionals who may form an RLLP in a particular state is normally the same as the one used to determine which professionals are eligible to form a professional corporation. For example, physicians can incorporate only as a professional corporation in most states, and are also eligible to form an RLLP in those states. Call your state LLC filing office to find out what professionals are eligible to form RLLPs in your state.

2. Limited Liability

RLLP owners enjoy a benefit not available to the owners of other partnerships: While the owners remain liable for the financial consequences of their own malpractice, RLLP statutes specifically say that they are not liable for the malpractice of the other professionals in their partnership. In addition, in more than one-half of the 50 states, the RLLP act says that a partner in an RLLP is not personally liable for any type of liability, whether arising from contracts, torts or the professional malpractice of another professional in the firm. This sort of sweeping protection is known as "full shield" limited liability protection.

Look Up Your State RLLP Act. You can look up your state's RLLP act by using the Internet. One way is to go to Nolo's Legal Research Center at www.nolo.com/research/index.html. Click on your state and then either do a search or browse your state's code to find the RLLP act.

Again, before forming an RLLP or converting an existing professional partnership to one, it's important to find out how much personal limited liability protection your state RLLP statute provides. In addition to reading your state's law yourself, one good way to do this is to consult your professional trade or licensing organization, since they almost surely keep up with the law in this area. Also, the wording of these state RLLP statutes varies widely, and, if you are thinking of forming a multi-member professional practice, a knowledgeable business lawyer in your state can help you sort out just how much protection your state RLLP statute provides.

3. RLLP Income Taxation

Like partnerships and LLCs, RLLPs are taxed as pass-through tax entities. This means that the owners are taxed on all profits on their individual income tax returns at their individual tax rates; the RLLP itself is not taxed on profits (see Section C3, above, for a review of partnership taxation). In most professional firms that provide services and not goods, this is appropriate since all profits are usually available to be paid out to the professionals each year—there is normally little need to accumulate funds in professional service firms (as there often is in a nonservice business that needs to accumulate earnings for inventory, equipment or future expansion).

4. RLLPs Compared to LLCs

For practical purposes, RLLPs are very similar to LLCs. They both have pass-through taxation; they both provide limited personal liability. The big difference is that RLLP statutes specifically provide protection for professionals from the malpractice of their partners, while LLC statutes do not. This is not normally a problem for the typical LLC owner—legal liability in most businesses comes about as a result of contract disputes, accidents on the premises (for example, slip-and-fall injuries), customer or product complaints, and the like—not as a result of an owner's direct, negligent conduct toward a client. But, of course, in a professional practice, things are very different; here professionals are routinely sued for alleged direct or indirect harm caused by the professional's own actions.

One other difference between the LLC and the RLLP is their ability to distribute profits freely. Many professional firms want to have the ability to distribute all net profits of the business to its owners. After all, most professional firms offer services, not goods, and do not need to keep profits in the company to accumulate inventory, buy expensive equipment or expand the enterprise. But technically, under most state LLC (and corporate) laws, LLCs cannot make distributions to owners if doing so would make the business insolvent—that is, unable to pay its debts as they become due—or would make the business's liabilities exceed its assets by a certain percent (see Chapter 1, Section A4). An RLLP has no such limitations. However, many LLCs will not want to distribute every last penny of profits to owners each year, so these technical limitations will have little significance for them.

H. Deciding Between an LLC and Another Business Type

This is a good place to recap the previous points in this chapter and reach some preliminary conclusions as to which type of legal entity may be best for your business. Here I'll take a practical approach and discuss the types of business that may benefit from the LLC business structure. For some real-life examples that lend an additional perspective of whether or not the LLC makes sense for your business, read the Introduction, if you haven't already.

1. Businesses the LLC Structure Usually Benefits

LLCs generally work best for:

- *Businesses with a limited number of active owners.* With an LLC, all of the owners of the business are able to enjoy limited liability and have a full hand in LLC management. This said, it's also true that member-managed LLCs work best when there are relatively few owners. (See Chapter 1, Section A1, for a larger discussion of how many members are practical in an LLC.) True, a larger LLC can limit the number of cooks in the kitchen by adopting a manager-management structure, where a select group of members manage the LLC on behalf of a larger, inactive membership, but establishing a more complex manager-managed LLC does require additional thought and paperwork, and could bring up securities issues (see Chapter 5, Section A2, for a discussion of the manager-management option). As an alternative, companies with more than 15 or 20 owners and investors may be better off forming a corporation.

- *Businesses that want to split profits and losses flexibly without an extra level of income taxation.* LLC members can split up profits and losses pretty much the way they want, plus they have only one level of income taxation to deal with since profits and losses automatically pass through to their individual tax returns each year. If LLC owners start making more money each year than they need or want to take out of the company, and they want to shelter it in the business at lower corporate income tax rates, they can elect corporate income tax treatment for their LLC.

- *Startup companies that may lose money.* New businesses often lose money the first year or two. That explains why startups want the ability to pass early-year losses along to owners to deduct against their other income (usually salary earned working for another company or income earned from investments). Fortunately, LLC members can deduct their LLC losses against other income.

- *Companies that aren't 100% insured.* Especially if your enterprise is at risk of being sued by customers, employees, suppliers, members of the public or competitors, and you can't afford to fully insure yourself against all of these risks, you'll want to protect your personal assets against the threat posed by lawsuits. Unless your business needs to raise money from a number of investors or plans to go public (see Section H2, below), the best way to do this is to form an LLC.

- *Existing sole proprietorships or general partnerships.* If you are self-employed—full- or part-time—or if you own or operate an unincorporated business with others, you may worry that even though things are going well, a business reverse or just an unlucky accident could result in a huge business-breaking debt. Even though the chances of this occurring may be small, you still worry. One of the best ways to restore your peace of mind is to take a few minutes to fill out LLC articles and file them with your state. Once you do, your personal assets are legally off limits to be used to pay off business debts. And to get this benefit, you don't have to change your current income tax filing status. As explained in Chapter 1, if you convert a sole proprietorship to an LLC, you continue reporting taxes on your 1040 Schedule C. If you convert an existing partnership, you keep reporting profits on your 1065 partnership return. (And the changeover is not a taxable event under IRS rules, just a change in your way of doing business.) Simply put, converting your existing one- or multi-owner business to an LLC is a quick and legal way to give yourself an extra measure of needed personal insurance in your business.

- *Anyone thinking of forming an S corporation.* To a large extent, the LLC was invented to streamline and fix things that were clunky or broken in the S corporation. The upshot is that LLC members more easily get the same limited liability protection as S corporation shareholders, and perhaps a more advantageous form of pass-through tax treatment.

2. Businesses the LLC Structure Usually Does Not Benefit

LLCs generally work less well for:

- *Businesses without debt or liability risks.* If you are thinking of starting a very small business that is unlikely to experience a problem that will be solved by forming an LLC, then don't form one. For instance, if your home-based consulting business won't take on any debt and is highly unlikely to be sued, you may not need the protection that the LLC offers against personal liability for business debts, and it follows that it makes sense for you to begin your business life as a sole proprietor. For example, a freelance proofreader who works at home and doesn't ever anticipate needing a loan to run her business probably doesn't need the limited liability that an LLC offers. After all, making a profit is hard enough—there is no sense in complicating your life if you don't need to.

- *Professional firms.* If you are a professional in a multi-member firm, an RLLP may do better at protecting you from personal liability for the malpractice of other professionals in your firm. I discussed how an RLLP can do this in Section G, above. Also, in some states, such as California, professionals are not allowed to form LLCs. In those states, their only choices are to form an RLLP or a professional corporation.

- *Capital-intensive and fast-track startups.* If your company expects to seek outside investment capital, offer stock options to employees, or undertake a public offering of its stock, the corporate form is your only good choice. I discussed how a corporation provides these benefits in Section E6, above.

I. Business Structures Comparison Table

In the tables below, we highlight and compare general and specific legal and tax traits of each type of business ownership structure. We include a few extra technical issues to tweak your interest. Should any of the additional points of comparison seem relevant to your particular business operation, talk them over with a legal or tax professional.

BUSINESS ENTITY COMPARISON CHART—LEGAL CHARACTERISTICS

	Sole Proprietorship	General Partnership	Limited Partnership	C Corporation	S Corporation	LLC
Who owns business?	sole proprietor	general partners	general and limited partners	shareholders	same as C corporation	members
Personal liability for business debts	sole proprietor personally liable	general partners personally liable	only general partner(s) personally liable	no personal liability of shareholders	same as C corporation	no personal liability of members
Restrictions on kind of business	may engage in any lawful business	may engage in any lawful business	same as general partnership	some states prohibit formation of banking, insurance and other special businesses	same as C corporation —but excessive passive income (such as from rents, royalties, interest) can jeopardize tax status	same as C corporation
Restrictions on number of owners	only one sole proprietor	minimum two general partners	minimum one general partner and one limited partner	most states allow one-person corporations; some require two or more shareholders	same as C corporation, but no more than 75 shareholders permitted	some states still require two members but are expected to allow one-person LLCs soon
Who makes management decisions?	sole proprietor	general partners	general partner(s) only (not limited partners)	board of directors	same as C corporaton	ordinarily members; or managers if manager-managed LLC
Who may legally obligate business?	sole proprietor	any general partner	any general partner (not limited partners)	directors and officers	same as C corporation	ordinarily any member; or any manager if manager-managed LLC

	Sole Proprietorship	General Partnership	Limited Partnership	C Corporation	S Corporation	LLC
Effect on business if an owner dies or departs	dissolves automatically	dissolves automatically unless otherwise stated in partnership agreement	same as general partnership	no effect	same as C corporation	In some states, dissolves unless remaining members vote to continue business
Limits on transfer of ownership interests	free transferability	consent of all partners usually required under partnership agreement	same as general partnership	transfer of stock may be limited under securities laws or restrictions in Articles of Incorporation or Bylaws	same as C corporations—but transfers limited to persons and entities that quality as S corporation shareholders	unanimous consent of nontransferring members may be required under state law or operating agreement
Amount of organizational paperwork and ongoing legal formalities	minimal	minimal; partnership agreement recommended	startup filing required; partnership agreement recommended	startup filing required; Bylaws recommended; annual meetings of shareholders required	same as C corporation	startup filing required; operating agreement recommended; meetings not normally required
Source of startup funds	sole proprietor	general partners	general and limited partners	initial shareholders (in some states, cannot invest with promise to perform services or contribute cash in the future)	same as C corporation—but cannot issue different classes of stock with different financial provisions	members (may usually invest with promise to perform services or contribute cash in the future)

	Sole Proprietorship	General Partnership	Limited Partnership	C Corporation	S Corporation	LLC
How business usually obtains capital, if needed	sole proprietor's contributions; working capital loans backed by personal assets of sole proprietor	capital contributions from general partners; business loans from banks backed by partnership and personal assets	investment capital from limited partners; bank loans backed by general partners' personal assets	flexible; outside investors (may offer various classes of shares); bank loans backed by shareholders' personal assets (if corporation has insufficient credit history); may go public if need substantial infusion of cash	generally same as C corporation—but can't have foreign, or partnership corporate share holders; must limit number shareholders of to 75; can't offer different classes of stock to investors except for shares without voting rights	capital contributions from members; bank loans backed by members' personal assets (if LLC has insufficient credit history)
Ease of conversion to another business form	may change form at will; legal paperwork involved	may change to limited partnership, corporation or LLC; legal paperwork involved	may change to corporation or LLC; legal paperwork involved	may change to S corporation by filing simple tax election; change to LLC can involve tax cost and legal complexity	generally same as C corporation—may terminate S tax status to become C corporation but cannot reelect S status for five years after	may change to general or limited partnership or corporation; legal paperwork involved
Is establishment or sale of ownership interests subject to federal and state securities laws?	generally not	generally not	issuance or sale of limited partnership interests must qualify for securities laws exemptions, otherwise must register with federal and state securities laws offices	issuance or transfer of stock subject to state and federal securities laws or must qualify for securities laws exemptions	same as C corporation	probably not, if all members are active in business

	Sole Proprietorship	General Partnership	Limited Partnership	C Corporation	S Corporation	LLC
Who generally finds this the best way to do business?	owner who wants legal and managerial autonomy	joint owners who are not concerned with personal liability for business debts	joint owners who want partnership tax treatment and some nonmanaging investors; general partners must be willing to assume personal liability for business debts	owners who want limited liability and ability to split income between themselves and a separately taxed business	owners who want limited liability and individual tax rates to apply to business income; must be willing to meet initial and ongoing S corporation requirements	owners who want limited liability and either pass-through or corporate taxation (see below); particularly beneficial for smaller, privately held businesses
How business profits are taxed	individual tax rates of sole proprietor	individual tax rates of general partners	individual tax rates of general and limited partners	split up and taxed at corporate rates and individual tax rates of shareholders	individual tax rates of shareholders	individual tax rates of members, unless LLC files IRS Form 8832 and elects corporate taxation
Tax-deductible fringe benefits available to owners who work in business	sole proprietor may set up IRA or Keogh retirement plan; may deduct a portion of medical insurance premiums	general partners and other employees may set up IRA or Keogh plans; may deduct a portion of medical insurance premiums	same as general partnership	full tax-deductible fringe benefits for employee-shareholders; may fully deduct medical insurance premiums and reimburse employees' medical expenses	same as general partnership, but employee-shareholders owning 2% or more of stock are restricted from corporate fringe benefits under partnership rules	can get benefits associated with sole proprietorship, partnership or corporation, depending on tax treatment of LLC
Automatic tax status	yes	yes	yes, upon filing certificate of limited partnership with state corporate filing office	yes, upon filing Articles of Incorporation with state corporate filing office	no; must meet requirements and file tax election form with IRS (and sometimes state); revoked or terminated tax status cannot be re-elected for five years	yes, with IRS; unless LLC wishes to elect corporate tax treatment (by filing IRS Form 8832); most states treat LLC same as IRS for state income tax purposes

	Sole Proprietorship	General Partnership	Limited Partnership	C Corporation	S Corporation	LLC
Are taxes due when business is formed?	generally tax-free to set up	generally tax-free to set up; individual income taxes may be due if a general partner contributes services as capital contribution	usually same as general partnership	generally not taxable unless existing business is incorporated and new owners are brought into the business	same as C corporation	generally tax-free to set up; individual income taxes may be due if a member contributes services as capital contribution
Deductibility of business losses	owner may use losses to deduct other income on individual tax returns (subject to active-passive investment loss rules that apply to all businesses)	partners may use losses to deduct other income on individual tax returns if "at risk" for loss or debt	same as general partnership, but limited partners may only deduct "nonrecourse debts" (for which general partners are not specifically liable)	corporation may deduct business losses (shareholders may not deduct losses)	shareholders may deduct share of corporate losses on individual tax returns, but must comply with special limitations	follows sole proprietorship, partnership or corporate loss rules depending on tax status of LLC
Tax level when business is sold	personal tax level of owner	personal tax level of individual general partners	personal tax level of individual general and limited partners	two levels: shareholders and corporation may be taxed on liquidation if it includes sale or transfer of appreciated property	normally taxed at personal tax levels of individual share-holders, but corporate level tax sometimes due if S corporation was formerly a C corporation	follows sole proprietorship, partnership or corporate tax rules depending on tax status of LLC

Members' Capital and Profits Interests

In this chapter, I look at the financial arrangements typically used to set up an LLC and to divide LLC profits and losses among the LLC owners (members). I also discuss some of the basic tax ramifications associated with these arrangements.

Let's start with some background on how most start-up LLCs are funded—that is, how the organizers of a new LLC pay capital into their LLC. Of course, these start-up considerations don't loom as large for existing businesses, such as sole proprietorships and partnerships, that are converting their organizations to LLCs. In that case, the assets of the existing business simply carry over to the LLC, usually with no change in the owners' capital interests and profits and loss interests, or the tax positions of the business owners (more on converting existing businesses to LLCs in Section C, below).

A. The Creation of LLC Capital Interests

The initial members of a new LLC ordinarily make financial contributions (called "capital contributions" in business lingo) to the business to get it started. These contributions can consist of:

- cash

- property

- services, or

- a promise to contribute cash, property or services in the future.

In return, each LLC member normally gets a percentage of ownership in the assets of the LLC (this is called a member's "capital interest"). This interest reflects the portion of the assets of the LLC that each member is entitled to when an LLC member sells his membership interest or when the LLC itself is sold. For example, if a member has a 50% capital interest in an LLC whose assets, including goodwill, are valued at $500,000, he can expect to be paid approximately $250,000 if he asks the other LLC members to buy out his interest. Of course, a good LLC operating agreement (or buy-sell agreement) will clearly say how members' interests will be valued so that a member can anticipate how much he'll get when he sells his interest and when he'll get it (in a lump sum, in installment payments or in a combination of the two).

Example 1: *Tim, Dan and Ellory are about to form Home Page Designs, a website development company. The capital necessary to start the LLC is minimal, and all three expect to contribute an equal amount of work in operating the enterprise. Tim plans to contribute his sophisticated, power-user computer equipment, worth $12,000, and Dan plans to contribute $12,000 in cash, enough to buy two scaled-down work stations for himself and Ellory. Ellory, who doesn't have any ready cash or property, agrees to contribute $12,000 by simply leaving the first $12,000 of his share of allocated profits in the business. The three become equal one-third owners of the LLC, each with a one-third capital and profits interest in it (I discuss profits interests in Section D, below).*

Example 2: *After reading Section B3 of this chapter, below, Ellory realizes that he may have to pay income tax on the value of his capital interest if he contributes services to the LLC. Instead, he asks the other owners if they will extend a personal loan to him of $12,000 cash, which he will use to buy a one-third interest in the LLC. He agrees to pay back the personal loan, with interest, from his share of LLC profits earned during the first year of LLC operations.*

B. Tax Considerations of Start-Up Capital

As you can see from the above example, members may make capital contributions to their LLC in the form of cash, property and/or services, or the promise to provide any of these in the future. However, any member who contributes property or services rather than cash should be aware of several important tax considerations, which I discuss below.

1. Paying for an LLC Interest With Cash

If your LLC members simply contribute cash to start up your LLC, the tax considerations are straightforward. The members are not taxed on the transaction. Instead, their membership interest is given an "income tax basis" equal to the amount of cash each member invests. This tax basis will go up and down during the life of the LLC as profits and losses are allocated and paid to members and as the LLC's liabilities fluctuate. When a member finally sells his membership interest or when the LLC itself is sold, the tax basis at that time will be used to compute the amount of taxable gain that the member owes taxes on.

Example: Jethro pays $1,000 to start his gold-mining LLC in the Sierra mountain foothills. He buys an inexpensive silt strainer, then sets up camp by a small stream, spending his days slowly sifting for gold and daydreaming of future wealth and luxury. A year later, when he sells his LLC to his cousin Ned for $2,000, his income tax basis still sits at $1,000. This means Jethro's taxable gain on the sale is $1,000, which is the amount he must pay capital gains taxes on.

2. Paying for an LLC Interest With Property

Another popular way to fund an LLC is through the contribution of property. For example, a member may transfer her title (ownership document) to a piece of real estate to her LLC in return for a membership interest. Vehicles, business equipment and machinery, as well as patents and trademarks, are also commonly exchanged for membership interests. As long as other LLC members (if there are any) accept the property at an agreed value, there is no legal impediment to doing this. But in some circumstances, contributions of property (especially property that has appreciated in value) can lead to special tax consequences.

a. Transfer of Appreciated Property

Tax issues arise when a member contributes property that has increased in value (appreciated) since the time it was purchased, inherited or received by gift. Appreciation is most likely to have occurred on real estate (a building or land) prior to its transfer to the LLC. First, the good news. Contributions of appreciated property to an LLC are generally tax-free at the time they are made (there are some technical exceptions, of course—see just below). The not-so-good news is that a member who transfers appreciated property to the LLC must eventually pay taxes on the past appreciation (the increase in value that occurred prior to transferring the property to the LLC). Typically, the member who originally transferred the property to the LLC pays taxes on the past appreciation when his interest in the LLC, or the entire LLC itself, is sold.

Example: Jim owns a building he bought outright for $20,000 in 1996. It is worth $120,000 when he transfers it to his newly formed LLC in 2001 (it has appreciated $100,000). In exchange for transferring this real estate to the LLC, Jim receives a capital stake in his LLC worth $120,000 (based on the property's current fair market value). Jim's tax basis in his membership interest is $20,000—his "cost basis" in the transferred property. (This simplified example assumes there have been no adjustments to his basis in the *property for capital improvements or depreciation.) Jim pays no taxes when he transfers the property to the LLC.*

Jim sells his membership interest in 2003 for $120,000. (For simplicity's sake, let's assume his interest is worth the same amount when he sells it as when he transferred it to the LLC—another unlikely assumption.) His amount of gain—the amount he'll have to pay capital gains taxes on—equals the amount he receives for the sale of his LLC interest ($120,000) minus the amount of his basis in the membership interest ($20,000). In other words, Jim has to report a gain of $100,000 and pay taxes on that amount at the time of the sale. As you can see, Jim doesn't avoid paying taxes on appreciation by transferring his building to the LLC; he simply defers paying the taxes on the appreciation.

There are, however, a couple of big exceptions to this general rule of no immediate tax consequences when appreciated property is transferred to an LLC. For one, if the LLC distributes profits to a member within two years after he contributes property to the LLC, he'll owe taxes on the appreciation at this time. And if the LLC sells the property contributed by the member, or distributes it to another member, taxes will also be due. Ask your tax advisor for the details.

b. Property Subject to Debt

This section does not apply to one-person LLCs. If you are the only member of your LLC, you can skip this next section. It only applies when you transfer some debt to your LLC, and the other LLC members are allocated a portion of it. In a single member LLC, if you contribute property that's subject to debt, you'll be allocated all of the debt, so there'll be no change in your tax position.

If a member of a multi-member LLC contributes property subject to debt—for example, a building encumbered with a mortgage—there are immediate tax consequences for that member. To understand why, remember that LLC members share profits and losses (debts) with each other. So when a member transfers mortgaged property to the LLC, the debt is allocated among all LLC members, including the member who transfers the property. (Each member theoretically takes on a share of the debt that's in proportion to their profits and loss interest, or distributive share, discussed in Section D, below. This allocation of debt increases each member's tax basis in her interest, which, in turn, reduces the taxable gain that will occur later, when a member sells her interest.)

In the sense that the debt is now shared, the transferring owner is benefited since she now only owes a portion of the debt. The IRS treats this decrease in debt obligation as a payout of cash to that member. For example, if you transfer property worth $100,000 to your LLC to become one of five equal members in the LLC, and the LLC assumes the $50,000 mortgage attached to the property, the IRS treats the transaction as though you were paid income of $40,000 (the amount of the mortgage assumed by the four other LLC members—4/5 times $50,000). You are obligated to pay tax on this assumed payout (based on the amount your debt has decreased) if it exceeds your current income tax basis in your membership interest. Detailed rules in this area are too complicated to explain more fully here. Just be sure to ask your accountant for details if you're considering transferring debt-burdened property to an LLC.

Helpful LLC Tax Resources. Most books and articles that cover the tax consequences of LLC and partnership taxation assume a substantial amount of prior knowledge, and do a poor job of explaining the basic terms and concepts necessary to fully appreciate the material they cover. One exception is Prentice-Hall's *Comprehensive Federal Taxation* book, updated annually (the current edition is *Federal Taxation 2000, Comprehensive*). It is used primarily as a text for students entering the tax field, and may be available at a local business or law library. It doesn't contain many fully developed examples of how the tax rules apply to smaller businesses, but you can use the material to get a basic understanding of the fundamental tax concepts that apply to an LLC, partnership or corporation.

3. Paying for an LLC Interest With Services

Sometimes an LLC member receives a capital interest in an LLC in return for the past performance of personal services or for a promise to perform services in the future (often in addition to a cash payment). For example, in exchange for a capital interest a member might pay $10,000 plus a promise to perform 500 hours of work (without pay) to set up the LLC's website. The IRS views this type of transaction as "payment for services." This means the member must pay income taxes on the value of the membership interest she receives in exchange for the hours she puts in, just as she would if she were to instead receive a paycheck for those hours of work. In other words, whenever LLC members sign an operating agreement that issues a capital interest to a member in exchange for services, that member obligates herself to pay income tax for the value of those services as recorded on the LLC's books.

Example: Five Austin computer programmers start Computer Tex, LLC. Four put up $20,000 each as their 20% capital contributions. In return, they each get a 20% capital interest in the LLC (their membership interest). Cash-strapped Sharon, the fifth member, receives her 20% membership interest in exchange for a promise to do programming work for the company for six months without pay. The IRS considers this payment to be personal service income to Sharon. She'll owe individual income taxes on the $20,000, and she'll have to estimate and pay it during the year even though she never pockets a nickel.

Contact a tax expert if a member will pay for a membership interest with services or property instead of cash. The payment for an LLC membership interest with services or property can get complicated, and the above examples are simply meant to introduce you to these areas. Please consult your tax advisor if you or another member is thinking of paying for an interest with services or property.

4. Paying for an LLC Interest With Borrowed Money

Fortunately, there are several ways that a member who doesn't have cash or property to contribute can get around the immediate income tax bite that results if she obligates herself to contribute services.

One approach is for the impecunious member to borrow the needed cash, then buy her capital interest outright. The loan can be from an outside source, such as a bank, from another LLC member or even from the LLC itself. The member who receives the loan signs a promissory note specifying repayment terms, including a competitive, commercially reasonable interest rate. The member can pay back the loan with payments of profits from the LLC or from some other source of funds. Of course, depending on the lender's requirements, the member may also be required to pledge property as security for repayment.

Example: Bella and Xavier kick around the idea of forming Happy Hoofs Equestrian Academy LLC—a proposed horse-riding and boarding facility in the rolling foothills of Mesa de Oro, California. Bella can contribute the cash and property to finance a down payment on a pleasantly weather-worn barn with surrounding acreage, and otherwise get the business off happily running. But Xavier, who is champing at the bit with energy that he'll use to convert the farm to a riding academy, is low on funds. Realizing that their venture is far more likely to succeed if Xavier is a co-owner—not just a hired hand—Bella agrees to lend Xavier the money to become a member of the LLC. This means Xavier will receive a capital interest in the LLC without having to immediately pay taxes on the value of the services he promises to perform. This way Xavier can take part in the LLC's profits while repaying Bella over several years.

It can be a bad idea to wait to buy a membership interest until some point in the future. An obvious way to avoid paying income taxes on a capital interest that's received in exchange for services is simply for a member-wanna-be to wait until he has earned sufficient cash to buy a membership interest. But if the LLC increases in value right off the bat, the member-wanna-be may not be able to afford the increased capital required to buy an interest in the business.

Example: Let's return to the Happy Hoofs Equestrian Academy LLC. Now assume Bella and her husband, Clyde, form the LLC as the two initial members. Xavier, who can't afford to become a member right away, works for the ranch as an employee and saves his money. Xavier plans to buy out Clyde's capital interest in the LLC when he has sufficient cash. Unfortunately for Xavier, the ranch becomes profitable quickly, and Xavier can't afford to pay Clyde the fair value of his capital interest, which has shot up in value since Bella and Clyde opened the Academy. Not only is Xavier not able to buy into a chunk of the LLC assets, he hasn't been able to share in its hefty profits for the time he's been working there.

5. Receiving a Profits-Only Interest

An LLC member can also avoid an obligation to pay taxes resulting from the performance of services if the LLC gives him what is called a profits-only interest in the LLC (not an ownership interest in LLC assets) in return for a promise to render future services. Income taxes won't be due immediately, since a capital (ownership) interest won't be issued. Of course, like any member, the member with the profits-only interest must pay taxes on LLC profits as they are allocated to him.

Example: Hubert Allis Overalls, Ltd. Co., which supplies denim fabric to clothing manufacturers, brings in Hank Allis (son of founding member Hubert) to help run the LLC. Business is busting at the rivets, with the LLC supplying fabric to several brand-name jeans manufacturers. In return for signing a ten-year employment contract, Hank is given a 25% stake in LLC profits for that period, plus a guaranteed annual salary. Because Hank does not receive a capital interest in the LLC, he will not be taxed up front on his promise to perform services for the LLC.

Although a profits-only interest is a true economic interest in an LLC, it is not the same as a capital (ownership) interest, since it doesn't give the holder a right to a portion of LLC assets when the LLC is sold. (Although, if the business does well, of course, the holder of a profits-only interest will benefit by sharing in the profits *until* the company is sold.) Typically, the holder of a profits-only interest will buy a capital interest in the LLC as soon as he is financially able to do so—using the profits distributed to him (true, as discussed above, the value of the interest may go up during the period that the owner draws profits only, but this is the risk he takes for not buying into the LLC from the beginning). Alternatively, the holder of a profits-only interest can sell that interest as long as the sale is not prohibited by the LLC's operating agreement, although the holder may not be able to find a buyer for it unless the LLC has a proven profitmaking track record.

C. Converting a Pre-Existing Business to an LLC

Many sole proprietors and partners decide to convert their existing business into an LLC. As discussed throughout this book, it's a quick and legal way for business owners to limit their personal liability for business debts and claims. Since these businesses already exist under a different legal structure, it's no surprise that owners of pre-existing businesses fund their LLCs differently from the new LLCs discussed above. In most cases, the assets and liabilities of the pre-existing business are simply transferred to the LLC, and the old owners take over as owners of the new business, with the same percentages of ownership they had in the old business.

Example: *Imogene and Bethany convert their 50-50 partnership, Rugby Sales Group, into an LLC. They prepare an LLC operating agreement that gives each new LLC owner a 50% capital interest, plus a 50% distributive share of LLC profits and losses.*

One nice part of converting an unincorporated business to an LLC is that it is not treated as a taxable sale, meaning the old business owners don't pay taxes as a result of the conversion. That's true because the IRS recognizes that converting a sole proprietorship or a partnership into an LLC is simply a change in the legal structure of an existing business, not a sale of assets from one business to another.

After converting an unincorporated business to an LLC, the business and the owners continue to file the same tax returns they filed prior to the conversion (for a sole proprietorship that converts to an LLC, a 1040 Schedule C; for a partnership that converts to an LLC, the 1065 partnership tax return). Of course, if the LLC then elects corporate tax treatment (as discussed in Chapter 4, Section C), the owners must change their tax filing procedures and begin filing a corporate tax return for their LLC.

When converting a pre-existing business to an LLC, the owners should make sure to change the business's name on business licenses, permits, insurance policies and titles to personal property and real estate. They also need to change their federal employer ID number, their state employer registration number and all other formal business numbers, licenses and permits to the name of the new LLC. An LLC operating agreement should also be prepared, even if the owners don't change their percentages of capital interests, profits and losses and management power. (For more on operating agreements, see Chapter 6, Section A2.)

The conversion of a corporation to an LLC is far more difficult. And it can be costly, since there's often a substantial tax bite. In fact, after considering the difficulties and legal expenses involved, most corporation owners who want to get rid of their corporate tax status and be treated as pass-through tax entities opt instead for S corporation tax status (see Chapter 2, Section F, for more on S corporations). Indeed, allowing owners of existing C corporations to obtain pass-through tax status is one of the few remaining practical uses of the S corporation.

D. The Creation of LLC Distributive Shares (Profit and Loss Interests)

When LLC members receive a capital interest in an LLC in exchange for cash, property or services, they are also given a share of its profits and losses, called their "distributive share." (This only applies to LLCs with pass-through taxation. Owners of LLCs that elect corporate tax treatment instead receive their share of profits as salaries or dividends.) You'll see the term "distributive share" a lot in IRS publications and tax forms. It refers to how much of the LLC's profits and losses will be allocated to each LLC owner at the end of the year. It is a bit of a misnomer, because under the pass-through tax rules an LLC's owners are taxed on all the of profits allocated to them at the end of each LLC tax year, even if these profits are not distributed. (I'll discuss the taxation of profit allocations and distributions in Chapter 4.) An owner's distributive share is sometimes also referred to as his "profits interest" in the LLC. (Remember, I discussed the difference between a capital and a profits interest in Section C5 of this chapter.)

Each member's distributive share of profits and losses must be specified in the LLC operating agreement. Most often, an operating agreement will provide that each member's distributive share corresponds to his capital interest in the LLC.

Example: *Tony and Lisa set up Antler Artifacts, LLC, a retail outpost in Jackson Hole, Wyoming, that sells antler-shaped back scratchers, wapiti-musk potpourri and other animal kingdom miscellany conscientiously made only* *with synthetic materials and resins. The two members contribute equal amounts of cash as start-up capital. The LLC operating agreement specifies that Tony's and Lisa's capital interests correspond to the amount of capital each contributed, and that their distributive shares of profits and losses are proportionate to their capital interests. Since Tony and Lisa contributed equal amounts of cash, they each have a 50% capital interest and a 50% distributive share of LLC profits and losses.*

One flexibility of doing business as an LLC is that the operating agreement can provide that profits and/or losses can be distributed in a manner that is not proportionate to capital interests. For example, an LLC member with a 30% capital interest could receive 40% of the yearly profits. The ability to mete out allocations of profits and losses in different ways is one of the special advantages of setting up an LLC (or a partnership). By contrast, the founders of a corporation are unable to do this sort of disproportionate profit-splitting without a lot of tinkering with the standard corporate model. Splittings of profits and losses that are disproportionate to members' relative capital interests are called "special allocations" under the tax law and are subject to IRS tax rules, which I fully discuss in Section E, below.

Example 2: *Assume Tony and Lisa set up the same LLC, but this time Tony puts up all the cash, while Lisa signs a promissory note to contribute her share in installments over the first two years of the life of the LLC. Their operating agreement still says that Tony and Lisa each have a 50% capital interest, but it also says that Tony will be allocated 75% of the LLC's profits (and losses) for the first two years, and Lisa will be allocated 25% of the LLC's profits (and losses) during this initial period. After the first two years, the agreement says that both members will split LLC allocations of profits and losses 50-50 (that is, according to the value of their capital interests). Since this set up constitutes a "special allocation of profits and losses" for the first two years, their tax accountant included language in their operating agreement to make sure the IRS would respect the special allocation (again, see Section E, below).*

E. Special Allocations of LLC Profits and Losses

I promised you more information on special allocations of LLC profits and losses, and since this is a technical area of the LLC rules, I saved it for last. Start by understanding that making special allocations of profits and losses will require you to get more detailed information than you'll find here, probably including professional tax advice.

As discussed throughout this book, LLC members can decide not to follow the usual practice of splitting up profits and losses proportionately to each member's capital interest when they form an LLC. Instead, they can agree to split profits and losses *disproportionately* to members' capital contributions by making what is called a "special allocation." For example, a special allocation would be necessary if an LLC allocates a 20% share of profits and losses to a member who contributes 10% of the initial LLC cash or assets.

1. "Substantial Economic Effect"

Unfortunately, the IRS regulations covering special allocations go on for pages (Sections 1.704.1 through 1.704.3 of the Income Tax Regulations, to be exact). Basically, these regulations state that for special allocations of profits and losses to be valid for tax purposes, they must have what it calls "substantial economic effect." This jargon means that special allocations must be based on real economic factors of the business and the owners' circumstances to be valid—they can't simply be used to shift income around to reduce an owner's income taxes. For instance, the IRS would probably balk if an LLC allocated all its losses to the one member with significant income from non-LLC sources, to allow that member to fully deduct the LLC losses and pay fewer income taxes.

Example: Up Up and Away Ventures, LLC, is a passive investment company that puts investors' money into business operations run by others. Its prime moneymakers are its investments in multi-tiered car parking garages and businesses that operate vending machines. Joe and Kenneth have invested equally in the LLC, and each holds a 50% capital interest in the business. Joe wants the parking lot income each year and Kenneth wants the vending machine profits (let's just say their accountants see this as the best way for each to maximize personal income and minimize taxes on their individual tax returns). Will the IRS object? Probably, unless neither Joe nor Kenneth can come up with a real economic justification for the division. Absent this, the IRS would probably say that this special allocation does not have a "substantial economic effect."

2. Safe Harbor Rules for Special Allocations

If your LLC can follow the "safe harbor" rules that I discuss below, you can ensure that any special allocations you make will have "substantial economic effect" for IRS purposes by incorporating special language to this effect in your LLC operating agreement. "Safe harbor" simply means that, by using these rules, a business can be assured that it complies with a tax or legal provision.

Nolo's Legal Research Center. You can find the special allocations rules in Nolo's free Legal Research Center at www.nolo.com/federal/codes/findlaw.html. Find them by searching the Code of Federal Regulations for Income Tax Regulations Sections 1.704.1 through 1.704.3, but be warned, they are contained in 93 pages of hopelessly complicated legalese.

The reason the IRS lets you make special allocations after you adopt the special safe harbor language in your operating agreement is that there are some real financial and tax consequences associated with adopting this language. The language contains three basic requirements as follows:

- *Maintenance of capital accounts.* The LLC's capital accounts must be carried and handled on the financial books under special rules that do not mimic generally accepted accounting practices (known as GAAP in the accounting trade) and may not be immediately obvious even to tax practitioners unfamiliar with pass-through tax treatment. This is not a particular problem, just a quirk that must be taken into consideration by your tax advisor.

- *Liquidation of the LLC according to capital account balances.* The tax implications of an LLC liquidation (when you dissolve your LLC) can be very complicated. At the risk of oversimplifying, when an LLC is liquidated, distributions of assets to the members must normally be made in accordance with their capital account balance. For example, if, at the termination of an LLC, Joe's capital account balance is $25,000 and Sam's $50,000, Joe should receive one-half of the assets distributed to Sam.

- *Payback of negative capital account balances.* When an owner sells his interest, or the LLC is sold or liquidated, any members with a negative capital account balance must restore their account to a zero balance. (Capital accounts typically go negative in any number of ways; here's two: 1) a member can be allocated losses in excess of his capital account balance, or 2) distributions to a member can exceed the member's initial capital contribution plus profits that have been allocated but not paid out.) A member can restore a negative capital account balance to zero by contributing cash or property to the LLC before his membership interest or the LLC itself is sold or liquidated.

  There are a few ways to get around the last requirement to restore negative capital accounts, but they are beyond the scope of this overview book. If you're interested in making special allocations, talk to your tax advisor.

Example: *Cuneiform Widgets Works Ltd. Liability Co. is founded by Sol Shimmaker. The business makes wedge-shaped objects of all descriptions, including a unique form-fitting door stopper named the Toe-Hold 2000. Expanding orders spur Sol on to seek additional capital to retool and expand the LLC's fabrication facilities. Arnie and Lillian Roeder, friends of Sol's, have the bucks and agree to contribute an amount of cash equal to one-half of the existing capital of the enterprise. They insist, however, on receiving a five-year 65% profits interest in the Toe-Hold 2000, plus a 50% share of net profits derived from other LLC product sales. The LLC protects itself from IRS challenge to these special allocations by asking its tax advisor to prepare and add to its operating agreement special language taken directly from the IRS regulations.*

Tax Resources. Again, you may find Prentice-Hall's *Federal Taxation 2000, Comprehensive,* useful for delving a bit deeper into tax laws. It discusses the safe harbor rules for special allocations in more detail than I do here, but still in an understandable—if limited—fashion.

Get help with special allocations. This special allocations area is a difficult one. Unless you want to get a degree in tax accounting, it's not something that most nonspecialists will want to tackle. The best way to adopt and implement these special allocation regulations is with the help of a very knowledgeable accountant—one who provides advice on this area of pass-through tax law as a regular part of her practice and who can sort through the special allocation language to pick out the parts that you should include in your LLC operating agreement.

CHAPTER 4

Taxation of LLC Profits

In this chapter I'll help you understand the tax treatment that applies to LLCs under the current federal tax scheme. Fortunately, the basics of LLC taxation are straightforward and easy to grasp. There are, however, several areas of LLC taxation, such as electing corporate tax treatment, that can get complex in a hurry. I'll alert you to these more complicated areas and suggest that you check any preliminary conclusions you arrive at with a savvy small business tax advisor before reaching any firm decisions about tax strategies for your LLC.

Believe it or not, one of the most exciting areas of recent LLC development is its tax treatment. LLC legislators, lawyers and accountants were not content to simply shake up small business law by successfully getting all states to legalize the LLC. They forged ahead and got the IRS to change the entire federal business classification system to enable an LLC (or a partnership) to elect to be taxed either as a pass-through entity (with income tax paid by LLC owners) or as a corporation, if the LLC owners concluded this would be beneficial. In this chapter, after covering the standard tax rules that apply to all new LLCs, I also discuss whether and when it might make sense for your LLC to choose corporate tax status.

A. Standard LLC Pass-Through Tax Treatment

Unless you choose otherwise, "pass-through" income tax status is automatic for all new LLCs. This means that all of the LLC's profits and losses "pass through" the business and are reflected and taxed on the owners' individual tax returns. But before I go further into income tax issues, let's get real for a moment and discuss how typical LLC members normally pay themselves for actively working in or managing their business.

1. Distribution of Profits to LLC Members

In an unincorporated business like a partnership or an LLC, the owners share in the net profits of the business. They usually don't pay themselves a salary up-front—instead, each year (or often, each quarter), they see how much net profit remains after deducting all regular business expenses. Then they decide how much of this profit to distribute to themselves and how much to retain in the business. The next step is to actually divide the profits among the owners according to their "distributive share," or "profits interest," as set out in the LLC operating agreement. (See Chapter 3 if you are hazy on how this works.)

Even if some owners operate the business full-time and others (passive investors) don't work in the business at all, the working/managing owners usually do not get a guaranteed salary. Instead, the working owners split the net profits with the passive owners according to their LLC operating agreement. In recognition of the larger contribution made by the active owners, typically the operating agreement states that they get a larger share of profits than the passive owners do. In addition, the working owners sometimes get all business profits up to a certain level, with any additional profits divided with the passive owners according to the operating agreement.

Of course, it's also possible for an LLC owner who works in the business to receive a salary. This is particularly likely in a small business that produces profits year after year, or in a business where one managing owner does all the work for a bunch of passive investors. In this scenario the working/managing owners may receive a guaranteed salary that is paid regardless of yearly fluctuations in the profit-level of the business. Since the salary is guaranteed to be paid regardless of profits, it is a business expense and can be deducted by the business in computing its net profit. This, in turn, reduces the amount of profits the other owners are allocated and taxed on (of course, the other owners also receive less profits under this scenario). The working/managing owners who are paid guaranteed salaries pay individual income taxes on the salary payouts plus, of course, their allocated share of any additional money (profits) they divide with the other business owners. But again, arrangements of this sort are the exception, not the rule, for most smaller unincorporated businesses. Before setting up a guaranteed salary for you or one of your co-owners, talk to your tax advisor.

2. Pass-Through Taxation in a Nutshell

Now let's look at how LLC business profits are taxed. For a co-owned LLC, pass-through tax treatment means the LLC will be taxed in the same way as if it were a partnership. For a one-person LLC, it means the sole owner will be taxed as if he were a sole proprietor. In both instances, this means LLC profits will "pass through" the LLC and be allocated and taxed to the LLC owner or owners at the end of each LLC tax year. Or put another way, the LLC owners, not the LLC itself, will be responsible for paying income taxes on business profits on their individual returns.

In a co-owned LLC, the amount of income allocated to each LLC member (owner) at the end of the year is as specified in the LLC's operating agreement (in a one-member LLC, of course, all income will pass through to the sole owner). Typically, each member is allocated a percentage of LLC profits and losses that corresponds with each member's capital interest in the LLC, which, in turn, is usually based on the member's investment (capital contribution) in the LLC.

Example: Kirk contributes $10,000, and Scotty $20,000, to set up their LLC enterprise. The capital interests of these two members are stated in the form of membership units in the LLC operating agreement. Because both men will work full time in the business, but one has contributed twice as much as the other, the agreement states that Kirk owns 10,000 membership units and Scotty 20,000. The operating agreement further states that each member is allocated a percentage of LLC profits and losses (and management votes) that corresponds to his capital units. Therefore, Kirk gets one-third of the profits and losses and management voting power while Scotty receives two-thirds.

Each LLC member pays individual income taxes on the amount of LLC profits allocated him each year.

Example: *Continuing with Kirk and Scotty's LLC, let's say their first year net taxable LLC profit is $300,000. Since, according to the LLC operating agreement, Kirk is due one-third of the profits and losses and Scotty two-thirds, Kirk must report and pay taxes on $100,000 of net profits, while Scotty must report and pay taxes on $200,000.*

3. Members Pay Income Taxes Even If They Aren't Paid Any Profits

This is a good time to step back and consider the implications of pass-through tax treatment. A big one is that, while LLC members must pay individual taxes on all LLC net profits "allocated" to them each year under their operating agreement, their LLC is not required under the tax laws to distribute all—or, for that matter, any—of the LLC's profits at the end of the year. (If it helps you grasp this concept, think of an owner's allocated profits as profits that are "earmarked" as belonging to that owner, but that may or may not actually be distributed to that owner.) It follows that even if a member's allocated profits are retained by the LLC, the member must pay income taxes on those profits as if she received them. At bottom, this is the big idea behind pass-through tax treatment—the IRS wants its income tax money each year; it doesn't want to wait until the LLC decides to put the money in the owners' pockets. If the owners were allowed to avoid taxes on profits by waiting until they felt like paying them out, you can be sure that in very good income years, when profits would cause LLC owners to be taxed in higher marginal tax brackets, owners would retain the profits in the business. Then in leaner years, when LLC owners would otherwise receive little or no income, they would pay them out so as to be taxed in lower individual tax brackets.

To deal with the potential problem of owing taxes if you don't receive a payout of profits one year (say the majority of LLC members vote to keep the money in the business), many LLC operating agreements contain a provision that says the owners must receive at least a minimum percentage (typically 25% to 30% or more) of their share of allocated profits each year. This minimum payout assures each owner will have at least enough cash on hand to pay individual income taxes on his share of allocated profits. (State and federal individual income taxes, after taking into account individual deductions, exemptions and credits, often reach the 25% or 30% figure.)

When it comes to actually paying out profits to the members, LLCs do have to pay attention to a few legal rules. In many states, there are financial tests that an LLC must meet before profits can be paid out. In general, a distribution of profits is valid if, after the distribution:

- the LLC remains solvent—that is, the LLC will be able to pay its bills as they become due in the normal course of business, and

- LLC assets remain equal to or exceed LLC liabilities (or, in some states, a statute sets out a higher asset-to-liability ratio that the LLC must be able to satisfy after distributing profits).

Courts may ignore limited liability if these standards are ignored and the company is later sued. Members or managers who approve a distribution in violation of statutory standards can be held liable for the amount of the invalid distribution. The moral here is, don't let your LLC pay out more profits to its owners than the business can afford.

4. Pass-Through Taxation Compared to Corporate Taxation

To truly understand the practical implications of choosing pass-through treatment, you should also understand the basics of corporate tax treatment. Only then can you fully grasp the differences between the two. Start by understanding that the IRS taxes corporations, as well as unincorporated businesses that choose corporate tax treatment, in a fundamentally different way. Instead of passing all profits and tax liabilities through to its owners, the corporate business is taxed on the profit it retains in the business, while the owners are personally taxed only on profits they actually receive. Payouts of profits in a corporation can be made in the form of salaries and bonuses to owners who work as employees of the business, or as dividends to owners who invest in the business. Since payouts of profits as salaries and bonuses are tax-deductible business expenses, the corporation doesn't pay taxes on them. They get taxed once—to the owner-employees at their individual income tax rates. By contrast, payouts of profits in the form of dividends end up getting taxed twice—once to the corporation at the corporate tax rate (since they're not deductible expenses) and another time to the owner to whom the dividends are paid, at his individual income tax rate (which, of course, explains exactly why most small corporations rarely pay dividends).

This two-tiered level of taxation—where the business pays taxes on retained profits while the owners pay taxes only on the profits they receive—results in a corporate tax benefit I call "income-splitting." Any profits left in the business (up to $75,000) will be taxed at the lowest corporate income tax rates of only 15% and 25%. These rates, of course, are often substantially lower than the individual tax rates that unincorporated business owners pay on the profits that are passed through to them. I'll have more to say about corporate income tax rates and income-splitting in Section C1, below.

Perhaps LLC pass-through tax treatment may appear inflexible as compared to corporate tax treatment. In some ways (being taxed on all allocated profits, for instance), it is. But for most small businesses this is no bad thing. Here's why:

- Many LLC owners, especially if they're just starting out, pay out (distribute) all or most of the net business profits that are allocated to them each year. As a result, they end up paying taxes only on money actually paid to them, just like the owners of a corporation. In other words, since most LLC owners leave little or no earnings in the business at the end of the year, they're not paying taxes on money that they don't take home.

- Sole proprietors, partnerships and S corporations, tax cousins to the LLC, are subject to the same set of pass-through tax rules: For owners who have experience operating one of these businesses, pass through tax status is familiar and easy to work with.

- If an LLC becomes so profitable that there are profits left over after the owners take out enough for their own personal needs, or if an LLC needs to regularly keep substantial profits in the business to pay upcoming expenses, the LLC can at that time elect to be taxed like a corporation (without having to convert the business into a corporation). After this election is made, the owners are taxed only on profits actually paid to them, and the business pays corporate income taxes on any net profits left in the business. (And as I mentioned above, because the initial corporate tax rates of 15% and 25% are lower than most individual tax rates, this ability to split income can result in substantial tax savings.) A corporate tax election has no effect on the LLC's legal status—the LLC remains an LLC for all purposes except taxes and can continue to operate under the rules set up in its operating agreement. (I discuss this corporate tax treatment election in detail in Section C, below.)

B. How LLCs Report and Pay Federal Income Taxes

If your LLC has only one member (and you haven't elected corporate tax treatment), the tax reporting process is simple. The LLC itself does not have to prepare and file any tax returns. The owner simply files his regular 1040 form and attaches *Schedule C, Profit or Loss From a Business*, on which he reports his share of allocated LLC profits or losses, and *Schedule SE, Self-Employment Tax Return*, on which he figures the self-employment (Social Security and Medicare) tax he owes.

Tax tip: use a double-entry bookkeeping system. For multi-member LLCs, the IRS requires a double-entry bookkeeping system. Since this requirement doesn't apply to one-member LLCs, some use a single-entry bookkeeping system such as a simple business check register to keep track of their expenses and income. But even if not required, double-entry procedures help owners to organize and track the financial progress of the business. So if yours is a one-person LLC, consider setting up a double-entry system for your business. You can do this by consulting a self-help resource, such as *Small-Time Operator*, by Bernard Kamoroff (Bell Springs Publishing), by using a software system such as QuickBooks (Intuit), or by having a short visit with an accountant.

For LLCs with two or more owners, the LLC itself must prepare and file *IRS Form 1065*, the same tax forms used by a partnership, unless it elects corporate tax treatment as explained in Section C, below. Since LLCs themselves don't pay income taxes on profits (their owners do), this annual partnership income return is informational only. Unfortunately, *Form 1065* is a bit complicated for the uninitiated. It requires that the business use a standard double-entry bookkeeping system, with a journal of accounts that are periodically posted to a general ledger. These general ledger accounts, in turn, are used to generate an income statement and balance sheet, both of which are necessary to complete *Form 1065*. The form must also show a reconciliation of each owner's capital (ownership) account that shows his capital contributions and distributions as well as the allocations and distributions of profits to each owner.

Form 1065 also includes *Schedule K*, where the income, losses, credits and deductions allocated to all owners must be reported. And finally, the LLC must give a *Schedule K-1* form to each owner, on which it reports the profits, losses, credits and deductions allocated to that owner—called the owner's "distributive share." Each owner uses the *Schedule K-1* to prepare her individual income tax return for the year and then attaches a copy of it to her 1040.

Use an Accountant and/or Bookkeeper. By now, if you are inexperienced in bookkeeping and accounting concepts, you may be a little daunted by the idea of setting up a tax reporting system for multi-member LLCs (and partnerships). No question, it's a surprise to some when they first learn how complex the pass-through tax rules and procedures can be. So unless you have a good handle on basic accounting, use a software program such as QuickBooks or strongly consider hiring an accountant to help you set up a good system and a part-time bookkeeper to help maintain it.

A Resource for Operating Your LLC. For more information on how taxes and tax basis play out in ongoing LLC business transactions, like when an owner's interest transferred or when the business itself is sold, see my book, *Your Limited Liability Company: An Operating Manual* (Nolo). This book also can give you a deeper understanding of how to legally care for and feed your LLC on an ongoing basis, and contains minutes forms as well as over 80 different resolution forms for recording tax, legal and management decisions.

C. Election of Corporate Tax Treatment

In 1997, the IRS issued new business tax classification rules. Because of these rules, an unincorporated business such as an LLC or a partnership no longer needs to convert itself into a corporation to enjoy corporate tax treatment. At first it may seem strange that an unincorporated business can choose to be taxed as an incorporated entity, but it's nevertheless true. An LLC can file a simple form with the IRS to receive corporate, rather than "pass-through," tax treatment. And make no mistake, this new ability for an unincorporated business to change its tax classification is a ground-breaking event—never before have small businesses been given this kind of tax flexibility by the IRS.

You can read IRS regulations for yourself. If you're interested, the new business entity tax rules discussed here are set out in Internal Revenue Code Regulations §§ 301.7701-1 to 301.7703T. (The Code of Federal Regulations citation for the first of these rules is 26 CFR 301.7701-1.) You can browse these regulations online by going to the federal area of Nolo's Legal Research Center at http://nolo.com/federal/codes/findlaw.html. Scroll down to the Code of Federal Regulations, and where it says Title, Part and Section, enter 26, 301 and 7701-1, respectively.

1. Corporate Taxation and Income Splitting

First, I want to review how corporations can benefit from corporate tax treatment. Then in Section 2 I will discuss why some LLC owners might want to elect it. Finally, in Section 3 I'll show you how to make the election.

As I mentioned above, unlike a sole proprietorship, a partnership or an LLC, a corporation starts out as a separate taxable entity. Corporate shareholders who are employees of the corporation pay income taxes on their salary (and any bonuses) on their individual income tax returns. (Since salaries and bonuses are business expenses like any other, they are tax-deductible to the corporation.) The corporation itself pays corporate income taxes on any net profits left in the business—that is, on profits that are not paid out to the owners in the form of salary (or bonuses). If all corporate net income is paid out in the form of salaries and bonuses, there is no corporate tax due. As you now know, this type of income tax treatment is different from the pass-through tax treatment that LLCs and partnerships start out with. Of course, that's because these unincorporated business owners pay individual income taxes on all net business profits each year, whether or not any profits are distributed to them.

The basic reason why corporate tax treatment can sometimes save a business owner in overall income taxes compared to pass-through tax treatment is that, for corporate income up to $75,000, the tax rates are only 15% and 25%. These are far lower than most individual owners pay on the profits that are passed through to them. (Individual income tax rates jump to 31% and higher fairly quickly, particularly if a business owner has other income or files a joint income tax return with a working spouse.)

**TAX RATES
ON TAXABLE CORPORATE INCOME**

$0	to	$50,000	15%
$50,001	to	$75,000	25%
$75,001	to	$100,000	34%
$100,001	to	$335,000	39%
$335,001	to	$10,000,000	34%
$10,000,001	to	$15,000,000	35%
$15,000,001	to	$18,333,333	38%
Over $18,333,333			35%

Note: Personal service corporations are subject to a flat tax of 35% regardless of the amount of income.

Note that, because corporate tax rates on net taxable income never reach the highest individual tax rate of 39.6% (the highest corporate tax rate is 39%), owners in high tax brackets can keep as much income in the corporation as they want and still reduce their overall income tax bill.

What this means is that owners of a business that will retain some profits in the business from one year to the next can usually save taxes by choosing to be taxed as a corporation. I call this technique of retaining some profits in the business to be taxed at corporate tax rates while also paying owners salaries and bonuses "income-splitting." But fortunately, because of changes in the federal tax rules, LLC owners who retain profits in the business can also get the benefit of corporate tax treatment too. I explain how all of this can work for LLCs immediately below.

Businesses with corporate tax treatment have a slight advantage when it comes to medical expenses. Until 2003, owners of an LLC with pass-through treatment can deduct only part of their medical expenses on their individual tax returns, unless they qualify to itemize their medical expenses, in which case they can deduct 100% of the medical expenses. But for an LLC with corporate tax treatment, the LLC can pay 100% of the owners' health insurance premiums and deduct them as business expenses. But this won't remain exclusively an advantage of corporate tax treatment for long—in the year 2002, owners of pass-through LLCs will be able to deduct 70% of their health insurance premiums, and by the year 2003, they'll be able to deduct the full cost of their premiums.

2. Income Splitting in an LLC

As a practical matter, most new LLCs don't elect corporate tax treatment until their LLC is able to pay its owners very livable salaries. And then they do so only if their tax advisor agrees that the income tax savings that can be achieved by splitting income between owners and the business entity itself are worth the trouble and the collateral tax costs of electing corporate tax treatment.

But for those businesses profitable enough to retain profits in the business from one year to the next—and especially for those with inventory or other liquid assets on their books that can't be distributed to owners—income splitting can result in significant tax savings.

Example: *Jed and Beth own a retail sales LLC. Since they haven't elected corporate tax treatment, the LLC's profits are automatically subject to pass-through tax treatment. Net taxable profits of the LLC allocated to Jed and Beth at the end of the year are $200,000, or $100,000 apiece. But Jed and Beth decide that they need to keep $100,000 in the business bank account for upcoming business expenses, so the LLC doesn't distribute all of the income that was allocated to them. Thus they each take home $50,000, yet they still pay taxes on the whole $100,000 that was allocated to them.*

Let's look at how this affects Jed's tax situation. Because Jed is single, under current federal individual tax rates his individual income tax is about $25,779 on the $100,000 of allocated profits. (For simplicity, I'm not including the personal exemption or any deductions and credits Jed can undoubtedly take to reduce his individual income taxes; nor am I considering any other income Jed might have to report on his individual income tax return that could bump him into a higher individual income tax bracket.) If Jed and Beth elect corporate tax treatment for their LLC, Jed could "split" his LLC profits by paying himself a salary of $50,000, still retaining the other $50,000 in the business. Jed would pay $10,652 in individual taxes on his salary of $50,000, and the LLC would pay $7,500 in corporate income taxes on the $50,000 kept in the business, for an overall tax bill of $18,152. This would be a total tax savings of $7,627 ($25,779 − $18,152)! And, of course, if Beth is in roughly the same tax bracket, she would qualify for the same savings.

JED'S INDIVIDUAL INCOME TAX—NO INCOME SPLITTING

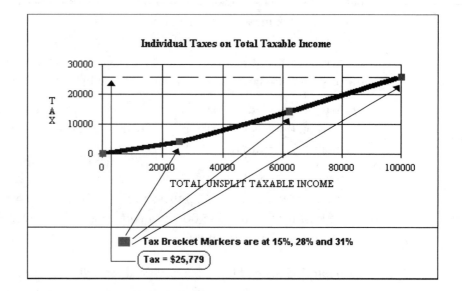

INDIVIDUAL AND BUSINESS INCOME TAX COMBINED—WITH INCOME SPLITTING

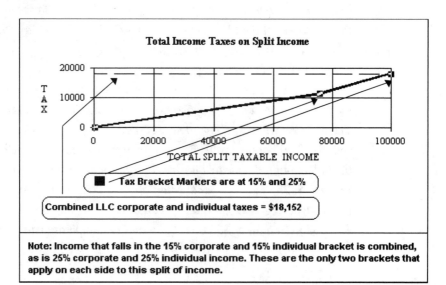

Note: Income that falls in the 15% corporate and 15% individual bracket is combined, as is 25% corporate and 25% individual income. These are the only two brackets that apply on each side to this split of income.

In case the concept of income-splitting is still not completely transparent to you, let's quickly review how income splitting can work for an LLC. If an LLC makes a tax election to be taxed as a corporation (I explain how in the next section), it has the ability to split its income between the business, which will pay taxes at the corporate rate, and its owners, who are taxed as individuals. This allows the LLC to:

- pay out tax-deductible salaries and bonuses to owners, just like a corporation. The owners pay individual taxes on these payouts on their own returns.

- retain some profits in the business, like a corporation. The corporation pays income taxes on these profits at corporate tax rates, which at least for the first $75,000 of income are almost always lower than the owners' individual rates.

Example 1: Sally and Randolph are friends as well as co-owners of their own lumber supply LLC. They are both married (but their spouses don't work outside of the home) and they each file a joint income tax return with their spouses. Sales for the year are $2.2 million. After deducting the cost of goods sold and the payment of business expenses, including salaries and bonuses to the employees of the LLC, the LLC shows a $250,000 net taxable profit. In addition to their capital interests, Sally and Randy each have a 50% profits interest in the LLC (meaning they are each entitled to half the profits of the company). At the end of the year, the owners decide to retain some earnings in the LLC to make a down payment on a much needed piece of new equipment. The machine will cost them about $100,000, meaning they can only afford to split $150,000 of the profits between themselves. However, each must report the full amount of allocated business profits on their individual income tax returns ($125,000 each—that's half of $250,000, the net taxable business profit). Ignoring deductions and credits, each pays an individual income tax of $30,032 for a total of $60,064. Sally and Randolph are frustrated and *annoyed that they have to pay personal taxes on money they never got to spend personally.*

If Sally and Randolph elect corporate tax treatment for their LLC, they would only have to pay taxes on the profits actually distributed to them in the form of salaries ($150,000). They would each pay $15,404 in taxes on their individual tax returns (on income of $75,000 each). The LLC would pay corporate taxes on the retained amount—$100,000—for a corporate tax of $22,250. The total of the LLC and individual taxes would be $53,058 ($22,250 + $15,404 + $15,404). This would be an overall tax savings of $7,006 ($60,064 − $53,058).

Example 2: Now let's assume Sally and Randy divorce their spouses and marry each other. You might guess that income splitting now saves them more in taxes than it did when they were married to nonworking spouses. That's because they're in a higher income bracket now that they're a dual-income family. Since they have more taxable income now, having some of that income taxed at the lower corporate rates will benefit them even more—their income-splitting tax savings should be greater. Let's see if this is true.

They now have to report all $250,000 of the profits on their one joint return. Absent any other income, their tax obligation would be $73,354. If they make a corporate income tax election, only the $150,000 that they are paid in salary by their LLC would be reported on their joint income tax return. The personal income tax on this amount would be $37,782. The LLC would pay corporate taxes of $22,250 on the remaining $100,000 of profits. Total taxes would be $60,032 ($37,782 + $22,250), and the resulting tax savings would be $13,322 ($73,354 − $60,032). Just as we thought—the tax savings now is greater than in the previous example (where it was $7,006).

SALLY AND RANDY'S TAX BRACKETS—FOR UNSPLIT AND SPLIT INCOME

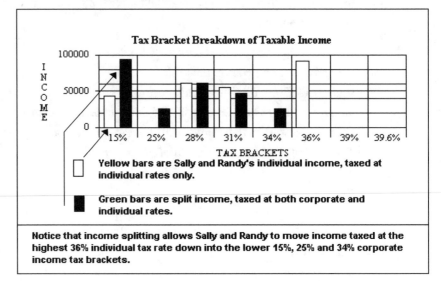

Tax Bracket Breakdown of Taxable Income

☐ Yellow bars are Sally and Randy's individual income, taxed at individual rates only.

■ Green bars are split income, taxed at both corporate and individual rates.

Notice that income splitting allows Sally and Randy to move income taxed at the highest 36% individual tax rate down into the lower 15%, 25% and 34% corporate income tax brackets.

3. How to Elect Corporate Tax Treatment

If you form an LLC and you (and any co-members) decide that you want your LLC to be taxed like a corporation, you can obtain this result by filing *IRS Form 8832, Entity Classification Election*, with the IRS. You simply check the correct box on the form to elect corporate tax treatment—this is the box on the line that reads, "A domestic eligible entity electing to be classified as an association taxable as a corporation." All owners of the business must sign the form, or they must authorize one person to sign it (for example, by signing a simple statement, which is later placed in the LLC records binder, that says one particular LLC member is authorized to sign the form).

Online Tax Forms. You can get the tax form mentioned above from the IRS website. Go to http://www.irs.treas.gov/forms_pubs/index.html. There you can print blank forms to be filled in by hand or typewriter, or even better, you can view a "Fill-in Form," insert your information and print it out.

The tax election takes effect on the date you specify on Form 8832, which must be no more than 75 days before, or 12 months after, you file the forms. If you don't specify a date, the tax election will take effect on the date the form is filed with the IRS. The LLC must attach a copy of Form 8832 to its corporate tax return filed during the first tax year that the election takes place.

Example: On January 15, 2002, Dorothy and Jim, owners of a two-person LLC, file IRS Form 8832 to elect to have their LLC taxed as a corporation. They request that the corporate tax election be retroactive to January 1, 2002. Their LLC files its first corporate tax return March 15th of 2003, for its 2002 corporate tax year (most LLCs follow the calendar tax year). They attach a copy of Form 8832 to the corporate tax return.

If your LLC makes the corporate tax election, it will have to use a double-entry accounting system, start filing corporate income tax returns and pay estimated corporate income taxes.

Choosing corporate tax status is a tax, not a legal, election. Even if you elect corporate income tax treatment, your LLC will not be treated like a corporation for any purpose besides taxation. This means your state's LLC statutes will still govern its operations, meaning you won't have to suddenly appoint a board of directors or issue corporate stock. Plus, you still must file annual LLC statements (if required by your LLC filing office) and possibly pay an annual fee.

4. Changing Your Corporate Tax Election

A corporate tax election made with *IRS Form 8832* stays in effect until you file another election asking to return to pass-through treatment. However, once a business makes a corporate tax election, it normally cannot change its tax status back to pass-through treatment until at least five years after the initial election. This rule points out an important aspect of making a corporate tax election: before making the election, a business not only should make a profits projection for the current year, but also for future years. Typically, it only makes sense to elect corporate tax status if it looks like your business is likely to remain solidly profitable for at least several years.

There is, however, one exception to the five-year rule. If more than 50% of the ownership interests in the business change after the effective date of the tax election, you can ask the IRS to change your tax status in the form of a private letter ruling request. You'll have to pay the IRS for the privilege, plus pay a tax advisor to help you prepare the request, but it may be worth it if your profits picture changes substantially with a change in ownership.

5. Other Issues to Consider

If you and you tax advisor figure out that electing corporate tax treatment will save you enough income tax dollars to be worth considering, you will want to review other issues before filing *IRS Form 8832*. Included among these issues are the following:

- LLC owners who work for the LLC will become corporate employees, and be subject to the withholding, reporting and payment of payroll taxes, self-employment taxes, unemployment taxes and the like. If your LLC already employs workers, this should be no big deal.

- A conversion to corporate tax treatment should be tax-free under Internal Revenue Code Section 351 as long as the LLC owners are still "in control" of the company after the conversion. Most actively managed LLCs should have no problem with this requirement. If for any reason you are unsure if you'll meet the Section 351 requirements, talk to your tax advisor.

- Corporate capital gains tax treatment, corporate loss carryover treatment and other technical corporate tax provisions are different from the rules that apply to pass-through LLCs. For example, corporations often must pay double taxes on appreciated assets when they are liquidated. Also, corporations are less flexible in passing operating losses through to owners—these losses normally stay with the corporation. You will want to thoroughly review these issues with a knowledgeable tax advisor before electing corporate income tax status.

D. LLC Owners and Self-Employment Taxes

I mentioned in Chapter 2 that, if you are an active owner in your LLC (you manage it or work for it), you'll have to pay self-employment (Social Security and Medicare) taxes on any profits paid to you by your LLC. Inactive owners—nonmanaging members in a manager-managed LLC—do not have to pay self-employment taxes.

This isn't a big deal—it's the same way sole proprietors and general partners are treated under the current federal tax system, and unless your LLC will bring in huge profits, this extra tax isn't likely to impact your income much. For the 1999 tax year, for example, the self-employment tax was set at 15.3% on earnings up to $72,600 and 2.9% on earnings over $72,600, and you get to deduct half of that self-employment tax from your income before you pay taxes.

But it's also true that limited partners and S corporation shareholders don't have to pay self-employment taxes on their allocated profits (money they receive over and above any salary they receive). You may wonder why active LLC owners are treated differently. This question has been asked by scores of commentators since the creation of the LLC. And many proposals have been made which would have the effect of placing all owners of limited liability enterprises—S corporations, LLCs and limited partnerships—on an equal footing. But as of this writing this hasn't been done, meaning that for now, active LLC owners will have to pay self-employment taxes on all money they receive, but owners of highly profitable S corporations don't. There will likely be movement in this area soon, but, for now, if you think you'll make big bucks, you may want to look to the old regulations (under IRC § 402) to plan your self-employment tax strategy. Chances are you'll decide to form an LLC anyway, but this is one area where an S corporation does have a small advantage over an LLC.

For More Information. There are also ways to change your LLC operating agreement to make an argument that the nonmanaging members of an LLC should be treated like limited partners and let off the hook for some self-employment taxes. Going into this uncertain and complex area of tax law is beyond the scope of this book. If you are concerned about limiting the self-employment tax bite on some of your LLC allocated profits, talk to your tax advisor.

■

LLC Management

In every business, at least one person needs to be responsible for the overall management of the business, and the LLC is no exception. As discussed throughout this book, under most states' legal rules, all LLC members are automatically equally responsible for managing the LLC. For example, in an LLC which has four members, all four are its business managers. In LLC legal jargon this arrangement is called member-management. But as you should now know, there is another possible LLC management approach—manager-management—by which LLC members can specifically choose one or more members and/or nonmembers to manage their LLC. In most states, you must specify whether your LLC is member- or manager-managed in the organizational document (your LLC articles or certificate) that you file with the LLC filing office.

A. Member vs. Manager Management

Here's an overview of each type of LLC management, and examples of which type of management works best for which types of businesses.

1. LLC Member-Management

The owners of most smaller LLCs choose the standard member-management approach. Again, this means that all LLC members are responsible for managing the LLC. (A few states, such as Minnesota and North Dakota, have copied terminology found in their unincorporated association statutes, and call the managers "governors.") The reason this approach makes sense is that, in most smaller LLCs, all members plan to be active in the business, and all want to be able to vote to decide how the LLC will be run.

Example: James and Amy form Tree Trimmers, LLC, a landscaping business. Amy transfers title to her Ford Ranchero pickup to the LLC to help with hauling, and James contributes an equivalent amount of cash. Both want to manage the LLC, so they select member-management in their articles of organization.

Again, it's likely that you and your co-members will all want to run your LLC, so you'll choose member-management in your articles of organization. In the sections that follow, I talk more about the day-to-day responsibilities of members, including how members hold meetings, vote, and make decisions in general.

2. LLC Manager-Management

Member-management, however, isn't the best choice for all LLCs. Under the other management option—manager-management—an LLC is managed by a single manager or a small group of managers consisting of:

- one or more selected LLC members

- one or more nonmembers (usually either officers or outside investors), or

- a mixture of the two.

The main reason to opt for manager-management instead of member-management is that you're planning to bring in outside investors who do not want to take a management role in your business.

Example 1: Let's continue with Tree Trimmers, LLC. Even before James and Amy open the doors to their new landscaping business, they immediately sign up more customers than they can handle. Amy and James realize that they'll need extra cash up-front to buy a second pickup truck so that each can go out on separate landscape jobs. A friend of theirs, Antonio, agrees to put up the necessary cash to buy the second truck, in exchange for a proportionate interest in the new LLC. A busy programmer with no interest in landscape gardening, Antonio does not want to work for or run the LLC. As a result, James and Amy form a manager-managed LLC, with themselves as the two managers. Antonio is simply a nonmanaging member.

Example 2: *Jason is an electronics engineer who works for a design company. A co-worker, Jamal, is a highly skilled engineer who wants to quit his day job and strike out on his own, doing custom electronics design for client companies. Jason has some extra cash on hand and agrees to invest in Jamal's new LLC. Jamal will work full-time managing and working for the new business, and Jason will merely invest in it and do occasional design jobs for a fee. The new LLC is managed by Jamal only, and Jason becomes a nonmanaging member.*

Manager-management also may make sense for an LLC if:

- The LLC owners decide to hire a chief exec more qualified or suitable than the current LLC members to manage the LLC.

- The LLC wishes to give an outsider (a nonmember) a vote in management (for instance, an outsider wishes to lend money to the LLC, but only on the condition that he be given a say in management decisions). To give the nonmember management authority, the LLC must select manager-management and create a management group made up of the members of the LLC and the outsider.

- The sole member of an LLC wants to manage the business but gifts membership interests to nonmanaging family members, who will step into a management role only when the current owner-manager steps down.

As these bullet points indicate, the people you select as managers do not need to be owners of the LLC. You can select LLC officers and executives or anyone else you wish as a manager.

Fortunately, an LLC can easily choose manager-management to handle any of these situations. You just select manager-management in your articles (required in most states) or in your operating agreement (required in the other states). In all states, just one manager is required to manage a manager-managed LLC, but there is no limit to the number of managers you can have.

In most small LLCs, managers serve for an indefinite term—that is, until the members of the LLC vote to replace or remove them. Typically, LLC operating agreements allow an LLC manager to be removed or replaced for any or no particular reason upon the vote of the full membership (nonmanaging members as well as managing members). Another way of saying this is that state law lets LLC members decide for themselves when managers can be removed. Some larger LLCs, however, prefer to have managers serve for a definite term, such as one year, at the end of which the members re-elect or replace the managers. This procedure is usually only used in more formal LLCs with at least several outside investors (who are nonmanaging members). That's because, unlike corporations, where shareholders re-elect or replace the board of directors each year, most LLCs choose not to deal with the formality of a periodic review and election of managers, unless they have outside investors who demand it. In fact, most LLCs pick an initial management team and stick with it for the long-term, unless there is a problem and one or more managers need to be replaced.

Manager-management will not affect limited liability. In a manager-managed LLC, all members, managing as well as nonmanaging, get to keep their personal liability protection. Note that this is a fundamentally different approach than the liability protection that applies to limited partnerships, where at least one general partner must be personally liable for partnership debts and liabilities.

If you do choose to go the manager-management route, it's important to realize that state law still leaves certain voting rights in the hands of the nonmanaging members. As just mentioned, LLC members have the right to remove and replace managers. Also, nonmanaging members have the right to approve fundamental changes to the LLC and its membership, including the power to amend the articles or operating agreement of the LLC, to merge or dissolve the LLC, to approve or deny the admission of new members and to approve or deny the transfer of an LLC membership from an existing member to an outsider.

Members who don't work in or manage the LLC do not pay self-employment taxes. Under current IRS regulations, LLC members who are not active in the business should be able to avoid paying self-employment taxes on their share of allocated LLC profits. This is because the IRS does not consider nonmanaging members' profits to come from their own efforts, but from the work of others. For more on self-employment taxes, see Chapter 4, Section D.

Securities law consequence of manager-management. If you choose manager-management for your LLC, ownership interests in your LLC may be classified as securities because some owners will be investing their money in a business that they're not actively participating in—again, they'll expect to make money from the efforts of others. See Chapter 6, Section C, for more on securities issues.

B. Legal Authority of LLC Members and Managers

Any member of a member-managed LLC, or any manager of a manager-managed LLC can legally bind the LLC to a contract or business transaction. In other words, each member in a member-managed LLC and each manager in a manager-managed LLC acts as an agent of the LLC, and can single-handedly commit the entire LLC to a contract or business deal. This is the same legal authority given each partner in a general partnership. However, there are some exceptions to the legal authority of LLC members and managers. An LLC usually can't be held to a contract or deal if it was clearly outside the normal course of business of the LLC, or if the outsider contracting with the member or manager knew that the LLC member or manager did not have specific authority to conduct that transaction. For example, if a member of an LLC that operates a small local fish store tries to commit the LLC to purchasing a TV station, the sellers would be well advised to be sure that member really had authority to do the deal. If they didn't check up and a court fight followed, a judge would probably find that because TV stations and fish stores are completely unrelated, the ambitious LLC member had no legal authority to bind the LLC. In that case, the member might be held personally to the contract, but the LLC would not be bound carry it out. Unfortunately, when it comes to trying to disavow the actions of rogue LLC members or managers in more moderate situations, this lack of authority can be hard to prove.

Example: Gary is a member and VP of Fish and Fritters Fast Foods LLC, a member-managed LLC. He orders $5,000 of goods from Joe's Office Supply Company, a local merchant, consisting of $4,000 of LLC stationery and routine office supplies plus $1,000 of personal letterhead and an expensive pen with his name embossed on it. When he places the order, he does so on behalf of his LLC, and charges the bill to his LLC's account. Joe, the owner of the office supply company, gets a check from the LLC for $4,000, with a note from the LLC accounts payable officer advising Joe to collect the $1,000 balance from Gary, saying that the order for personal letterhead and the pen had nothing to do with the LLC. Would a small claims court let Joe recover the $1,000 balance from the LLC itself? Yes. Joe would normally be justified in believing that a member of the LLC had authority to place the full order on behalf of the LLC.

The moral should be clear. Local fish markets trying to buy TV stations aside, it's always safest to assume that your LLC will be legally bound by any contract or transaction signed or entered into on behalf of your LLC by any member or manager, no matter how unreasonable the deal is. This broad legal authority should not present a problem if you make sure you choose the right people to be members or managers of your LLC in the first place. But it can be poison if you work with the wrong people. If you're uncomfortable with the idea that a particular co-owner could obligate your entire business, you shouldn't go into business with that person. And it follows that, if you don't like the fact that any co-owner can bind your business to any deal, a multi-owner LLC is probably not the right type of business for you. Instead, you may want to form a one-owner LLC, where you have the only say.

C. Members and Manager Meetings

Before looking at the basic rules for holding LLC meetings, I want to make one point clear: routine business decisions made in any type of LLC—whether member- or manager-managed—are decided without holding formal LLC meetings, recording votes in written minutes or signing written consent forms. (See Chapter 6, Section B2, for more on minutes and consent forms.)

Example: Xenon X-Ray Systems, a medical electronics firm, decides to increase inventory in anticipation of a surge of upcoming orders. The decision is made by the VP of Manufacturing, after getting a nod of approval from the LLC's CEO. A formal LLC meeting, documented by written minutes, is not held, nor do the LLC's managers or members sign written consent forms.

Major items of LLC business, however, are often discussed and voted on in formal member or manager meetings. "Major" items are usually those that affect the basic structure of the company, including the removal of managers, the termination of the LLC, the amendment of the operating agreement, and the sale of all or most of the assets of the LLC. In addition, meetings can be held anytime an LLC member or officer feels a decision should be formally approved by a full vote, such as the approval of a large LLC bank loan, the purchase of LLC real estate, the expansion of the LLC product line, or the acquisition of a new business venture by the LLC.

Most states do not have rules in their LLC act on when and how formal LLC meetings should take place. Several states do, but, as is usual in most areas of LLC law, these rules only apply if you don't set out your own rules in your operating agreement. Either way, you should obviously spell out in your LLC operating agreement who can call LLC meetings, how notice of a meeting should be given and how many participants must be present for a valid meeting to take place, as well as the basic rules to be used to conduct an LLC meeting. Or put another way, if you don't create sensible procedural rules for governance of your LLC, you may have to follow the rules set out in your state's LLC statutes.

That said, your LLC operating agreement does not have to require that particular meetings be held at particular times during the year (required meetings of this sort are called "regular" or "annual" meetings). Instead, it can simply set up procedures to allow any LLC member or manager to call a "special meeting" when the need arises—which typically occurs when an important legal, business or tax decisions needs to be voted on. Does this mean that LLCs never hold annual meetings? No. It just means that LLC operating agreements rarely require that such meetings be held. In fact, LLCs with investors who are not involved in the business often do call a meeting at the end of each year, to keep the nonmanaging investors aware of how well LLC management is meeting the LLC's financial goals and what management's financial objectives and goals are for the upcoming year.

Example: *Castoff Clothing, LLC, started as a clothing wholesaler that supplied used designer clothes to antique clothing boutiques. Business boomed, and an investment company with 12 individual owners (called Pinnacle Investments) bought a one-third interest in Castoff. After the investment, Castoff changed from member-management to manager-management and added a seat on its management team for the Pinnacle CEO. Since the changeover, Castoff has held biannual management meetings to which all Pinnacle investors are invited. This annual meeting keeps the investment group fully informed on how Castoff is doing, keeping the lines of communication open between the partnered companies.*

Again, in smaller LLCs without a broad investor base, annual meetings of this sort are less common. Instead, special meetings are called when an important item of business needs to be formally approved or where the issue at hand is controversial, making it sensible to hold face-to-face discussions that will be recorded with written minutes. Here are a few examples of scenarios that may give rise to the calling of a special meeting in a smaller LLC:

- An important legal or tax formality needs to be approved and recorded. For example, your LLC is admitting a new member or approving the buy-back of a departing member's interest in the LLC.

- You need to meet face-to-face with your full membership—including any less active investors—and formally approve an out-of-the-ordinary or important business decision. For example, if the LLC will sell important LLC assets or purchase real estate, the decision should be recorded.

- A controversial business decision needs to be discussed or a dispute resolved; for example, some members of your LLC want to dissolve or sell the business and others don't, or one member wants to acquire a new product line that another thinks is nuts. Holding a formal meeting means no one can later claim that a decision was made secretly or without disclosure of all key facts.

- A member has a conflict of interest in an upcoming deal that the LLC is considering. For example, if one of your co-members is proposing a business deal for the LLC that will personally benefit him more than you and your other co-members, a frank discussion where the member discloses how he will profit from the deal, complete with minutes, is clearly in order.

- In a manager-managed LLC, you need to re-elect managers to another term (assuming managers serve for a fixed term). For example, if you adopt a two-year term for your managers in your operating agreement, you will want to hold membership meetings every second year to re-elect your managers.

Self-Help Resource for Holding Meetings. For practical information on calling and holding LLC meetings, see my book, *Your Limited Liability Company: An Operating Manual* (Nolo). This practical manual also contains ready-to-use minute forms and consent forms necessary to formally approve ongoing LLC decisions and document them for your LLC records binder, as well as over 80 resolutions for the various decisions LLC members can make.

D. Member and Manager Voting Rights

Your operating agreement should specify how much voting power each member or manager gets to exercise at a member or manager meeting. If it doesn't, your state's statutory rules will determine how your members and manager vote. In most states, the law requires that LLC members' voting rights be allocated according to their capital (ownership) interests (unless you provide otherwise in your articles or operating agreement). For example, a member contributing 50% of the capital to the LLC gets

50% of the voting power of the LLC unless there is an agreement providing otherwise. However, in some states, the default voting rule is that, absent an agreement, members are given voting rights on a per capita basis (one vote per member).

Most LLCs want to mete out votes in proportion to the members' contributions of capital. After all, the level of each member's risk for poor management decisions is really the amount each invests in the LLC—that's what each member has to lose. But in special circumstances, you may decide instead that a per capita (one vote per member) management voting pool makes the best sense. Here's an example that makes the point:

Example: Dorothy and Frances start Bungee Jump Adventures LLC. Dorothy contributes most of the startup capital for a 90% capital interest, while Frances adds a bit of cash for a 10% share. Frances will be the jump operator, who often will strap herself in for dual drops with novice jumpers. Aside from purchasing reliable bungee gear and paying for a telephone answering service to take calls from clients, initial expenses are minimal. In their LLC operating agreement, Dorothy insists on equal voting power, reasoning that although she has only a 10% capital stake in the enterprise, her personal risk of life and limb should qualify her for a 50% share in important management decisions.

No matter how voting power is allocated among members, under state statutory rules, most LLC matters brought to a vote of the members must be approved by at least a majority of the LLC's voting power—that is, by more than 50% of the full voting interests of the members whether the members have various percentages of voting power or they have one vote each.

Example: Sit-u-ational Awareness, LLC, a California ergonomics consulting firm, has parceled out its voting interests in its operating agreement according to the capital interests of its three members as follows: Kathlyn – 30%, Evan – 25% and Alyson – 45%. The operating agreement (and California's LLC act) further says that the vote of a majority of LLC voting power is required to decide an issue brought to the membership for resolution. This means that, because of the capital and voting interests of the members, at least two of the three members must agree to approve a membership resolution brought to a vote at a members' meeting.

Of course, your operating agreement can state that a decision can only be approved by the vote of a larger majority of the membership. For instance, you can require that any matter brought before the members be approved by two-thirds of the voting interests of the members.

If an LLC is manager-managed, state statutory rules typically give managers one vote each in situations where there is more than one manager. And most states' LLC laws also require a majority of the manager votes to approve management decisions. Although LLCs can adopt different manager voting rules (state law only applies when LLCs fail to state a different rule in their operating agreement), most simply copy the "one manager, one vote" procedure from their state LLC act, believing that it works well.

Example: Dollars to Donuts, LLC, which uses the trade name D2D, an emerging franchiser and promoter of the one-buck-per-dozen-donut discount offer on every tenth donut purchase, is owned by four entrepreneurs. But D2D is managed by a team of five managers consisting of the four members and a nonmember pastry chef, Pierre (who brings to the business the secret recipe for the "twissant," a delectable French pastry, plus his formidable baking skills). Their LLC operating agreement says that, for management votes, each manager gets one vote, and the vote of at least three of the five managers is required to resolve a disputed issue. In short, far from functioning as a fifth wheel on the management team, Pierre has become the all-important dead-lock-breaking vote should the four owners split their votes.

CHAPTER 6

Starting and Running Your LLC:
The Paperwork

In this chapter I focus on the basic legal documents you'll use to set up your LLC. Then I'll review the legal formalities you'll need to follow to organize and operate your LLC, including ongoing recordkeeping requirements and necessary government filings. Finally, I'll alert you to an issue that all multi-member LLCs should be aware of: in some circumstances, there's a small chance that federal and state securities agencies could treat membership interests in your LLC as securities (like shares in a publicly traded corporation)—in Section C I'll explain the issues involved and your options if it appears likely that you'll have to comply with any of these securities laws.

A. Paperwork for Forming an LLC

Except in Massachusetts and the District of Columbia, where at least two people are required, one person can own an LLC any place in the United States. As a result, it is now routine for a sole proprietor to convert his existing businesses to a one-person LLC, and equally as common for a one-person start-up to organize as an LLC. But, of course, there are also many small businesses with two or more members that form LLCs. Businesses with more than a few members often follow the LLC manager-managed approach (which I discussed in Chapter 5).

Setting up your own LLC is easy—it should take you relatively little time to turn your idea for an LLC into a legal reality. In most states, one person—called the "LLC organizer"—can prepare and file all of the necessary paperwork on behalf of the other initial members of the LLC.

⚠ **Not all professionals can form LLCs.** As I discussed in Chapter 1, Section C1, California and Rhode Island don't allow professionals to form LLCs at all (but they can form RLLPs—see Chapter 2, Section G). A few other states require professionals to follow special rules when forming an LLC, including putting profession-specific language in their articles of organization. And in some states, professionals who want to form an LLC must obtain a statement from their state licensing board that certifies they have a current state license, which they must file with the LLC articles. If you have a vocational or professional license, call your state LLC filing office to check if you can form an LLC in your state, and if so, whether there are special rules or restrictions.

Self-Help Resources to Form Your LLC. If yours will be a small business, you can very likely organize your LLC safely on your own, instead of paying a lawyer to do it for you. While this book does not contain forms for creating an LLC, Nolo has several products that can help you accomplish this:

- *LLC Maker*™. A software application (for Windows 95 and later) that assembles filable LLC organizational documents (articles or a certificate) according to all 50 states' legal requirements. The comprehensive program also allows the user to quickly and easily prepare other LLC documentation, such an LLC operating agreement, an application for reservation of an LLC name (to make sure your proposed name is available for your use when you file your articles), manager and membership lists and more. The program includes extensive state-by-state legal help. In addition, it allows you to quickly launch your Web browser to access your state's LLC filing office website and LLC act so you can easily check to see if there are any last-minute updates, plus get tax and business license information for your state. You can purchase LLC Maker from Nolo's website at http://www.nolo.com/product/sb.html.

- *Nolo WebForms.* You can now create your own articles of organization on Nolo's website. After answering a few basic questions in an online interview guided by online help, you'll be able to print out your LLC articles, which you can file with your state LLC filing office to create your LLC. These forms are simple and easy to use, but contain less background legal help than does LLC Maker. Available at http://www.nolo.com/product/webforms_home.html.

- *Form Your Own Limited Liability Company* (Nolo) is a workbook (with forms on disk) that provides a full treatment of state LLC laws and legalities. It contains step-by-step instructions for preparing articles for all 50 states, plus an LLC operating agreement.

1. LLC Articles of Organization

In most states, the only formal legal step normally required to create an LLC is to prepare and file LLC articles of organization with your state's LLC filing office. (In some states, this organizational document is called a "certificate of organization" or a "certificate of formation"—see Appendix A for the terminology your state uses.) A few states require an additional step, however: prior to filing your articles, you must publish your intention to form an LLC in a local newspaper.

The LLC filing office is usually the same one that handles your state's corporate filings, typically the Secretary or Department of State's office, located in the state's capital city. More populous states also often have branch offices in other major cities. The name, address and website address of your state's LLC filing office is in Appendix A.

Your LLC articles of organization needn't be lengthy or complex. In fact, you may be able to prepare your own by filling in the blanks and checking the boxes on a form provided by your state's LLC filing office. Or, if you want more handholding and step-by-step instructions, you can use either Nolo's comprehensive software program, LLC Maker, or Nolo's WebForms (online interactive LLC articles forms for your state), as mentioned above. Typically, you need only specify a few basic details about your LLC, such as its name, the address of its main office, the agent and office you're designating to receive legal papers, and the names of its initial members. Here's an example of LLC articles of organization for a member-run LLC that is typical in most states.

ARTICLES OF ORGANIZATION
OF
LUXOR LIGHTING LLC

The undersigned natural persons, of the age of eighteen years or more, acting as organizers of a limited liability company under the Anystate Limited Liability Company Act, adopt the following Articles of Organization for such limited liability company.

Article 1. Name of Limited Liability Company. The name of this limited liability company is

Luxor Light LLC.

Article 2. Registered Office and Registered Agent. The initial registered office of this limited liability company and the name of its initial registered agent at this address are:

Robert Johnston, 1515 San Estudillo, Anycity, Anystate, 00000.

Article 3. Statement of Purposes. The purposes for which this limited liability company is organized are:

to operate a custom home and commercial lighting and fixture

store, and to engage in any other lawful business for which

limited liability companies may be organized in this state.

Article 4. Management and Names and Addresses of Initial Members. The management of this limited liability company is reserved to the members. The names and addresses of its initial members are:

Robert Johnston, 1515 San Estudillo, Anycity, Anystate, 00000

Rebecca Johnston, 1515 San Estudillo, Anycity, Anystate, 00000

Gregory Luxor, 3021 Los Avenidos, Anycity, Anystate, 00000.

Article 5. Principal Place of Business of the Limited Liability Company. The principal place of business of the limited liability company shall be:

56 Rue de Campanille, Anycity, Anystate, 00000.

Article 6. Period of Duration of the Limited Liability Company. The period of duration of the limited liability company shall be: **perpetual** .

In Witness Whereof, the undersigned organizer of this Limited Liability Company has signed these Articles of Organization on the date indicated.

Date: **date**

Signature(s): *Gregory Luxor*

Gregory Luxor , Organizer

If you're designating a special management team to run the LLC, you'll usually have to add the names of your managers to your articles form.

Converting a partnership to an LLC may require a different form. Some states require pre-existing partnerships that are converting to an LLC to file a special articles form for their new LLC. This form is often called a certificate of conversion. Call your state's LLC filing office and ask if they have a special conversion form (again, the contact information is in Appendix A).

Note that your LLC articles will be rejected by the LLC filing office if the proposed name of your LLC is already in use by another LLC, corporation or other type of business in your state. The best way to make sure you don't run into this problem is to check with your state LLC filing office, before you settle on a name and prepare your paperwork, to see if your proposed name is available for your use. If it is, in most states you can reserve it for 60 days or more for a small fee. Once you reserve your name, it is guaranteed to be available for your use when you file your LLC articles (assuming you file the articles within the reservation period). Many states allow you to check name availability online, and they often provide a downloadable reservation form you can use to reserve a name that's available.

Here are some issues to address when picking a name for your LLC:

- Your proposed business name shouldn't be similar to another business's name or trademark. While the LLC filing office will tell you if another LLC in your state is already using your proposed name, you're on your own as to the names and trademarks of other businesses in your state and in the rest of the country. To be sure another business in your field isn't already using the name or trademark you want to use, you should learn the basics of trademark law and conduct a trademark search.

- The name should do a good job of marketing your goods and services.

- The name must end with an LLC designator, such as "Limited Liability Company" or "Limited Company," or an abbreviation of these words, such as "LLC" or "Ltd. Liability Co."

- The name usually can't include special words such as banking, trust, insurance or similar words that refer to financial services businesses.

Choosing a Business Name. My primary goal in this section is to alert you to the steps you'll need to take to form an LLC in your state, so I don't explore a number of potentially complicated and important legal issues that can come into play when you choose and use a business name. To learn more about trademark law, get a copy of *Trademark, Legal Care for Your Business & Product Name*, by Kate McGrath and Stephen Elias (Nolo). In addition to educating you about trademark law, this book will help you choose a strong marketing name and search for possibly conflicting trademarks.

Protecting Your Business Name. Once you have chosen a business name and your articles of organization have been accepted, you may wish to take extra steps to protect it. If you will be using the name to sell goods or services, you may wish to register it as a trademark with your state and the U.S. Patent and Trademark Office. The application procedures are relatively simple and reasonably inexpensive, and are fully explained in *The Trademark Registration Kit*, by Patricia Gima and Stephen Elias (Nolo).

2. The LLC Operating Agreement

Even though operating agreements need not be filed with the LLC filing office and are not explicitly required by state law, it is a practical necessity that LLC members should create a written operating agreement to define the basic rights and responsibilities of all LLC members and managers. Specifically, an LLC operating agreement sets out member-ship rights such as the members' capital (ownership) interests and distributive shares (the profits that will be allocated to the members). An operating agreement should also specify whether any actual distributions of profits must be made to the members (or whether the LLC can retain all of the profits in the business)—see Chapter 3, Section D, for a review of the difference between distributive shares and actual distributions. How the LLC will be managed and the voting power of all the members (and any managers) is also covered in the operating agreement, as well as housekeeping details like rules for holding meetings and taking votes. Lastly, an operating agreement should contain "buy-sell" provisions (unless the LLC will have a separate buy-sell agreement), which lay down a framework for what happens when a member wants to sell his interest, dies or becomes disabled.

What happens if you don't prepare an operating agreement and you later run into a serious conflict with other members? Your LLC's legal life will be controlled by your state's LLC statutes. This means that state law, not the choices you and your business associates make, will dictate how the dispute is resolved. For example, many states have a default rule that says LLC profits and losses must be divided up among the members equally, regardless of each member's capital contribution. Is this really how you would split up profits in your LLC, even if one of your members invests twice as much as the others? If not, you've got to state a different rule in your operating agreement.

Example: *Yvonne and Joe form an LLC with Yvonne contributing 30% of the capital and Joe contributing 70%. Under their state's default rule, Yvonne and Joe would each be entitled to one-half the profits of the LLC each year, even though they paid unequal amounts to get the LLC started. But if Yvonne and Joe prepare their own operating agreement, they can agree to divide profits according to their capital contribution percentages, or any other way they wish. (See Chapter 3, Section E, for more on special allocations.)*

For reasons like this, I believe it's a big mistake to run an LLC without an operating agreement. Without an agreement defining the rights and responsibilities of members, you won't have control over the answers to basic questions like these:

- When your members are faced with an important management decision, does each get one vote, or do they vote according to their LLC capital interests or profits interests (distributive shares)? How many members make up a quorum (the minimum number of members who must be present before a vote is taken)? Also, if your LLC has managers, does each manager get one vote? And how many managers make up a quorum?

- What if a member wants to increase her capital interest percentage? Can other members stop her or will their relative capital percentages decrease if they decide not to match her investment?

- How much—if any—of the allocated profits of the LLC must be distributed to LLC members each year? Can members at least expect their LLC to pay them enough to cover the income taxes they'll owe on each year's allocations of LLC profits? (Remember—members are allocated and taxed on profits each year whether or not any profits are actually paid to them—see Chapter 4, Section A3.)

- Does your LLC have to hold an annual membership meeting? Who can call special meetings of the membership during the year? What are the procedures for giving notice of special a meeting to the LLC members?

- If your LLC needs additional operating capital after it gets started, are the owners expected to make additional capital contributions (invest more money in the business)?

- Can a member leave the LLC any time she wishes? If so, is the LLC, or the LLC members, required to buy back the member's interest? What if they can't agree on a fair price?

- Is a departing member allowed to sell an interest to an outsider? If so, can the remaining members stop the sale, or not admit the purchaser as a new, voting member?

These kinds of unanswered questions can, and frequently do, come back to haunt small business owners, particularly if they have a falling out and haven't written down the details of their agreement. You can almost guarantee that in times of tension these details will be remembered differently. The best tack is to discuss these and other key issues at the beginning of your venture and record these points in a written operating agreement. That way, you can get on with LLC business without having to worry too much about future changes or disputes.

Sample Operating Agreement. Appendix B contains an example of an operating agreement for a member-run LLC that is typical in many states. However, the laws do vary from state to state, so don't model your operating agreement on our sample alone. As mentioned above, Nolo's software program LLC Maker™ can prepare an LLC operating agreement for you, helping you to answer the above questions according to your state's particular legal requirements.

3. Filing a Fictitious or Assumed Business Name

There are a few additional steps associated with setting up an LLC—the remaining items in this section cover the legal formalities necessary to perfect the organization of your LLC. The first one I'll turn to is selecting an assumed or fictitious business name for your LLC.

Many LLCs will operate under their formal LLC name—the name they put in their articles of organization. For example, a computer repair shop files its articles under the name Fix Me LLC and also does business under that name. In that case, the LLC doesn't have to file its business name anywhere. But some LLC owners like to operate their LLC under a name that's different from the formal name of their LLC listed in their articles of organization.

Example: The owners of Solar Plexus Flex and Fitness Center Ltd. Liability Co. decide to operate their fitness centers under the fictitious name "Flextime Fitness Center." The LLC owners don't want to change their formal LLC name as stated in the state-filed LLC articles of organization, but they want to operate the centers under the second version, Flextime Fitness Center.

Fortunately you'll usually have no problem operating your business under a different name than the one you used to organize your LLC. To do this, most states simply require your LLC to file a "fictitious" or "assumed" business name statement and pay a small fee (in legal slang this name is often called a "DBA"—short for "doing business as"). The purpose of this filing is to allow vendors, creditors and customers who encounter your fictitious name to track down the real owners of your business. You normally file this paperwork with the Secretary of State's office or the local county clerk's office. In some states, both a state and county filing are required. Find out your state's rules by calling your LLC filing office or going to its website—you'll find phone numbers and Web addresses (urls) in Appendix A.

Some states also require you to publish your intention to use a fictitious name in a local newspaper one or more times. Newspapers with legal notice classified sections will perform the required publications for you for a modest fee and will file an affidavit of publication with the state or local county clerk. Calling a local newspaper is generally the easiest way to discover whether your state requires the publication of a fictitious or assumed name statement and how to satisfy any related state requirements.

Small Business Legal Resources. Nolo's Online Legal Encyclopedia (www.nolo.com/encyclopedia/index.html) contains lots of free, helpful information on other start-up steps that apply to all businesses, not just the particular steps that apply to forming an LLC. For instance, in the small business section of the encyclopedia, you'll find tips on writing a business plan, choosing a business name, selecting a business location, arranging for financing, and setting up bookkeeping and accounting systems.

For more in-depth information, you might want to read Nolo's most comprehensive small business legal reference book, the *Legal Guide to Starting and Running a Small Business*, by Fred Steingold. It offers a comprehensive, two-volume treatment for entrepreneurs on how to start and operate a business. And for step-by-step advice on how to get your business off the ground quickly, *Nolo's Small Business Start-Up Kit: A Step-by-Step Legal Guide*, by Peri Pakroo (Nolo), explains all the hurdles you'll have to clear before opening the doors of your new business, from getting a business license and complying with local zoning laws, to getting necessary tax and employer numbers and licenses.

4. Additional Steps for Pre-Existing Businesses

These extra steps only apply to owners of pre-existing businesses. If your business is a start-up—that is, you are not converting a sole proprietorship or a partnership into an LLC—you can safely skip this section. Go to Section B, Ongoing LLC Paperwork.

If you're converting a pre-existing business to an LLC, you'll need to notify the IRS, your state taxing authority and other governmental agencies that you've changed your business's legal status to an LLC, and you'll need to give them your new LLC name. As part of this process, you will need to transfer I.D. numbers, licenses and permits to your new LLC name, including:

- your federal Employer Identification Number (FEIN)

- your state employer identification number

- your sales tax permit

- your business license

- your professional licenses or permits, if applicable, and

- your fictitious or assumed business name statement (this applies if you'll operate your LLC under a name other than its formal name, as explained just above).

Of course, you'll also want to change your stationery, business cards, brochures, advertisements, signs and other marketing and business miscellany to reflect your new LLC status and name. In addition, you'll want to let your suppliers, your customers, your business associates and your bank know your new business name and LLC status. You can do this simply by sending a letter to each company on your new LLC letterhead stationery, telling them that you converted your business to an LLC.

Review your files and other papers for more contacts. If you go through your lists of customers, suppliers, professional directories and the like, you'll surely discover the names and addresses of other agencies and businesses that you'll want notify that you are now operating your business as an LLC.

a. Termination of a Prior Partnership

If you're converting an existing partnership to an LLC, you may need to do a little extra paperwork to end the partnership's legal existence.

General partnerships normally don't file organizational papers with the state to get started, so if you are converting a general partnership to an LLC, you won't need to file a document with the state to terminate your partnership. But in some states you are required to publish a "notice of dissolution of partnership" in a local newspaper. (Failing to do this means that a creditor of the partnership could sue the owners of the new LLC personally for his unpaid debts, since the creditor wasn't aware that the partnership ended.) Any newspaper that handles legal filings should be able to explain your state's rules. Once you publish your notice, the newspaper should send you a copy of the published notice and an affidavit of publication to place in your files.

Limited partnerships—which, after all, have to make an initial filing with the state to create their partnership entity—must file a document letting the state know that the partnership no longer exists. But if your state provides a special form to convert a partnership to an LLC (often called a certificate of conversion), your partnership will be automatically terminated when you file this form—there's no need to file anything else. On the other hand, if your state does not provide a special articles form to convert your partnership to an LLC, you may need to terminate the partnership yourself. To do this, you'll probably file a "certificate of termination," or similarly titled document, with the state agency where you filed your original limited partnership papers. To find out exactly what's required, call your state LLC filing office or browse their website online to get instructions on how to terminate a prior partnership.

b. If Your Prior Business Owed Money

If you are converting a sole proprietorship or a partnership to an LLC, and the prior business has outstanding claims or debts, you and your co-owners will remain personally liable for these debts. Of course, this should never be a legal issue if your new LLC plans to assume and pay these bills as they come due. But as a courtesy, and to make sure all creditors of the prior business have notice of your new business form, you should send a letter to notify each creditor that you're converting your prior business to an LLC, and ask them to put future bills in the name of your LLC. If your prior business has significant disputed debts or claims that your LLC will not automatically pay when it begins doing business, I strongly urge you to check with a business lawyer as to your legal responsibilities and rights as to these disputed amounts, and whether you'll have to take any extra steps when converting your business to an LLC.

Some types of businesses that change their legal form to an LLC are required to comply with what is known as the "bulk sales law." In many states, this law applies when retail, wholesale, manufacturing and restaurant businesses are converted to a new legal form. This law requires the publication of various notices in a local newspaper, plus a waiting period before the conversion takes place, to allow creditors of the prior business to submit claims for the payment of unpaid bills. These requirements are meant to make it more difficult for the owners of a business that owes money to change its business form—usually to one with limited liability protection—without arranging to pay its past debts. However, even if you are converting a business that is subject to the bulk sales law, you may be able to exempt yourself from most of the law's notice requirements and waiting periods by agreeing to assume the debts and liabilities of the prior business.

Get help with your state's bulk sales rules. A local newspaper that publishes legal notices can help you understand and meet your state's bulk sales requirements. Normally the publication requirements are not onerous and the fees small. If you have lots of debts—especially if some are disputed—ask a local small business lawyer how to proceed. Trying to figure out every nuance of these laws yourself simply won't be worth your time.

B. Ongoing LLC Paperwork

Let's now take a look at the ongoing legal formalities an LLC should follow. Fortunately, LLCs can be run informally, and a lot of ongoing paperwork is not required.

1. Maintaining an LLC Records Binder

You will want to keep your important LLC documents, such as your articles (or certificate) of organization, LLC operating agreement, minutes of members' meetings (and managers' meetings, if your LLC is manager-managed), leases, major contracts, and the like in a safe, convenient place. I recommend setting up an organized system for arranging these LLC records, whether in 50-cent manila envelopes or file folders, or a slightly more expensive LLC records binder. There is no legal requirement to use a separate records binder, but many LLCs find it makes sense to go this more formal route if for no other reason than to emphasize the importance of maintaining an established recordkeeping system.

To help you organize your records, Nolo offers the *Nolo Advantage LLC Records Kit*, an LLC records binder that includes the following materials:

- a three-ring binder with a slipcase cover imprinted with the words "LLC Records"

- index dividers labeled for LLC articles of organization, operating agreement, membership register, membership certificates and minutes of LLC meetings, and

- 20 printed membership certificates to issue to each member, with your LLC's name printed on the face of each and with stubs to keep in the records binder. (The issuance of LLC membership certificates is not legally required in any state, but some LLCs like to distribute them.)

To order a *Nolo LLC Records Kit*, see the order page at the back of this book or call the Nolo Customer Service desk at 800-992-NOLO.

2. Written Records of Important Decisions

It's a good idea to document all important business decisions that require member or manager approval. Although LLCs are specifically empowered by many state statutes to conduct their affairs with less formality than corporations, it is nevertheless wise to document and record your major business decisions. In a worst case scenario, if an LLC keeps few or no records, a court might disregard the LLC's legal existence and hold its members personally liable for business debts (see Chapter 1, Section B4). (This is more likely to occur if the LLC is used as a device to defraud others or treat them very unfairly.) But an even more important reason to document key LLC decisions is to plan ahead to reduce the possibility of controversy and dissension among LLC members. Believe me, even in the ranks of a small, LLC where all of the members are friends, this is likely to occur if key decisions are not recorded. The 13th century legal scholar, Beaumanoir made this point beautifully in his *Coutumes de Beaumanoir*: "For the memory of men slips and flows away, and the life of man is short, and that which is not written is soon forgotten." Lastly, formally documenting key LLC action is a good way to keep any members who are not involved in the day-to-day management of your LLC fully informed of major LLC decisions.

The following are some examples of LLC decisions that should be recorded:

- a vote to change (amend) the LLC articles or operating agreement

- a vote on matters that require a member or manager vote, as set out in the LLC's operating agreement. Typically these matters include admitting a new member to the LLC, buying back a member's interest in the LLC and dissolving the LLC.

- a vote to make significant capital outlays, such as to purchase real property. (Also, banks and escrow and title companies often ask LLCs to submit a copy of written minutes or a written consent approving the transaction.)

- a vote to sell real estate or other major LLC assets. (Again, escrow and title companies, as well as buyers, will ask for paperwork approving the transaction.)

- the decision to fund a major or significant recurring LLC expense, such as contributions to an employee pension or profit-sharing plan, or the authorization of a significant loan or line of credit

- a vote to make significant state or federal tax elections (such as electing corporate tax treatment)

- a decision to expand or discontinue a line of products or services

- a decision to pursue or settle a lawsuit

- approvals of other important legal, business, financial or tax decisions.

State law may require unanimous or majority consent for some decisions. Your state's LLC act may require the consent of all or a majority of the LLC's members when a few types of fundamental decisions are made (regardless of what your operating agreement says), such as an amendment to the LLC articles or operating agreement, the departure of a member, the transfer of a membership to an outsider, or the approval of the admission of a new member. See Chapter 7, Section A5, for how to access your state's LLC statutes on the Internet.

Many of these decisions are made at LLC meetings—either an annual meeting (if you provide for one) or a special meeting called by the members during the year. (I discuss holding meetings in Chapter 5.) After each meeting, minutes that state the business discussed and approved at the meeting should be prepared in plain English, not legalese. Then a copy of the minutes should be placed, together with any notices of the meeting and documents or reports presented at the meeting, in the LLC records binder.

Many one- and two-person LLCs will not want to hold a meeting every time they have to make a major LLC decision. No question, holding a meeting with yourself is a bit silly. But even when meetings aren't helpful, it makes sense to keep good records of important decisions. That's why most states specifically allow LLC members to record important decisions on what are called consent forms—the member or members simply write down the important decision and sign at the bottom to show their consent.

A resource for ongoing paperwork. The legal formalities involved in operating an LLC are not difficult. I provide step-by-step instructions on how to legally care for and feed your LLC in *Your Limited Liability Company: An Operating Manual* (Nolo). You may want to take a look at this practical manual, which contains ready-to-use minutes and consent forms necessary to formally approve ongoing LLC decisions, as well as over 80 resolutions for the various decisions LLC members can make.

The good news is that you don't need to document *routine* business decisions—only those that require manager or member approval. In other words, it's not required by law that you clutter up your LLC record binder with unimportant documentation about the purchase of supplies or products, the hiring or firing of employees, decisions to launch new services or products or other standard business decisions.

3. Annual Report Filings

Most states require an LLC to file a short annual report form with the same state filing office where your articles of organization were filed—typically the Secretary or Department of State's office, in the state capital. Annual report forms are printed and supplied by the LLC filing office and are mailed out to LLCs annually. These forms typically require basic biographical information, such as the names and addresses of current

LLC members and/or managers and the name and address of the LLC's registered agent and office for service of legal process. In some states, you can leave items blank if there is no change in the information from the previous annual report filing. In most states, a small fee, usually in the $10 to $50 range, must be mailed with this form, but annual fees in a few states may be higher.

4. Real World Proof of LLC Status

Before deciding to do business with your LLC (enter into a contract, sign a lease, agree to sell or buy property or the like), financial institutions, trade creditors or other businesses you wish to deal with may want to see formal legal paperwork that establishes the existence of your LLC. This is particularly likely if you apply to borrow money, purchase securities or buy or sell real estate. You can normally show these status-seekers a copy of your articles of organization to help satisfy them that your LLC has handled all the necessary organizational formalities. But occasionally, you may be required to purchase a certified copy of your LLC articles of organization to show others. This should be available for a small fee from your state LLC filing office, and should be officially file-stamped by that office, and may also contain formal language stating that your LLC has met all necessary state formalities to begin doing business in your state. (A few even come with an embossed gold seal and ribbon!)

Once in a while, you'll find some outsiders who are such sticklers for detail that they may insist you prove your legal status is still valid on the date they are dealing with you. After all, they may point out your articles of organization only show that you met the state's legal require-ments when you originally formed your LLC—not that your legal status is currently valid. Most states will help you satisfy these sticklers for current information by allowing you to obtain, for a small fee, a certifi-cate of good standing that shows your LLC meets all state legal and tax requirements on the date of your status request. This should be plenty to satisfy even the most persnickety business that your LLC is a bona fide legal entity.

5. Income Tax Filings

Now let's look at the most common tax forms and formalities that crop up during the life of an LLC. I'll start with the income tax filings you'll have to make, which will vary depending on whether you stick with pass-through tax treatment or you make a special election to receive corporate tax treatment.

Make estimated tax payments. Your LLC's members will all have to make quarterly estimated income tax payments during the year. (Of course, if it looks like your LLC will not earn a profit and won't be allocating profits to members at the end of the year, the members probably won't have to estimate and pay income taxes to the IRS and state tax board during the year.) If you miss making required estimated tax payments, you will be charged penalties and interest. To make quarterly tax payments, each member sends in a payment four times a year along with *IRS Form1040ES*. For details, see *Publication 505, Tax Withholding and Estimated Payments* (available at the IRS's website at www.irs.treas.gov). In some cases, the LLC itself must make quarterly estimated income tax payments. This will be true if your state charges the LLC a separate entity-level fee or tax or if your LLC has elected corporate tax treatment.

a. For LLCs With Pass-Through Tax Treatment

For a quick review of pass-through tax treatment and what it entails, please re-read Chapter 3, Section A.

If you will be the only owner of your LLC, your tax returns will be relatively simple. Your LLC itself will not have to file any forms. You'll report all of your LLC income (or losses) on your yearly IRS 1040 form. You'll also have to fill out *Schedule C, Profit or Loss from a Business*, on which you'll report your LLC profits or losses, and attach it to your 1040 form.

If yours is a multi-owner LLC, you and your co-owners will also report their income from the LLC on their individual income tax returns, Form 1040. But in this situation, even though the LLC itself doesn't pay any income taxes, it does have to file an informational return, *IRS Form 1065*, each year (the same tax form used by partnerships). The LLC attaches a *Schedule K*, which reports the total profits, losses, credits and deductions allocated to the owners. In addition, the LLC must prepare a *Schedule K-1* for each owner, which reports that owner's share of profits, losses and other items shown on the *Schedule K* form. Each owner in turn attaches a copy of the *Schedule K-1* to her 1040, and uses the information on the K-1 to report LLC profits on their individual 1040 form.

b. For LLCs With Corporate Tax Treatment

For a review of corporate tax treatment, please re-read Chapter 4, Section C.

If your LLC elects corporate tax treatment (by filing *IRS Form 8832*), the IRS will treat it as a separate taxable entity. The LLC will have to file a corporate tax return, *IRS Form 1120, Corporate Income Tax Return*, and estimate and pay its own income taxes, at the appropriate corporate tax rate.

Online Tax Forms. You can get the tax forms mentioned above from the IRS website. Go to http://www.irs.treas.gov/forms_pubs/index.html. There you can print blank forms to be filled in by hand or typewriter, or even better, go to "Fill-in Forms," insert your information into a form and print it out. Some companies can now file their forms electronically—browse the IRS website if you're interested.

c. State Taxes

Most states follow the federal lead and classify your LLC the same way the IRS does. This normally means that, unless you file *IRS Form 8832* to elect LLC corporate tax treatment, your LLC will be treated as a pass-through entity at the state level, thereby avoiding the payment of entity-level (LLC) income taxes. Just as with the IRS, the members themselves will pay state income taxes on LLC profits and salaries (assuming your state has a personal income tax). However, even if your LLC itself won't be subject to state entity-level income taxes, it may have to file a state informational return or submit a copy of its federal tax return to the state business tax office.

Some states charge an annual LLC fee or tax. California, Florida and Michigan are among a handful of states that charge an annual entity-level fee (often confusingly called a tax), regardless of the LLC's income tax status. In some of these states, the fee is a flat yearly amount; in others it is graduated, depending on the gross income or net profits of the LLC. Contact your state's Department of Taxation or Franchise Tax Board for details.

If your LLC will have to pay a state franchise tax or state income taxes, you'll have to make estimated tax payments. Like federal income taxes, state franchise or income taxes usually must be prepaid in four installments during the tax year, with the first payment consisting of any minimum amount charged. If you miss making estimated tax payments, you will be charged penalties and interest. In some states, your LLC status can be suspended if you fail to pay these state taxes for a few years.

6. Employment Tax Filings

Your LLC will need to obtain a federal employer identification number (FEIN) using *IRS Form SS-4* and to register as an employer in your state. For salaried workers, your LLC must withhold, report and pay:

- federal and, if applicable, state income taxes

- federal employment taxes (unemployment, Social Security and Medicare taxes), and

- state payroll taxes (state unemployment, disability and workers' compensation insurance).

LLC members who receive a share of LLC profits are not legally treated as employees unless they also receive a guaranteed salary or other guaranteed compensation, such as interest payments. If LLC owners simply share in LLC profits without receiving any guaranteed payments, the LLC will still have to file for a federal employer identification number, but it won't have to pay employment and payroll taxes. Ask your tax advisor if you have questions.

An LLC member can be an employee who receives a salary and still receive additional distributions of profits. For example, an owner can be guaranteed $10,000 per year, regardless of profits, plus her share of any profits earned by the LLC. If the LLC makes no profits in a particular year, the owner only gets $10,000. Only the guaranteed $10,000 is treated as an employee salary, subject to withholding and other employment taxes.

7. Other State and Local Tax Filings

State sales tax, use tax and county property tax payments apply to LLCs. Counties and cities also may impose local and regional taxes. Check with your county and city tax offices for current information on reporting and payment requirements.

8. Signing LLC Paperwork Properly

I'm sure the separate legal existence of your LLC is important to you since it allows you to avoid personal liability for business debts and claims. Once you form your LLC, to help make sure you and other LLC members keep your limited liability legal protection, members should always sign LLC papers, documents, contracts and other commitments clearly in the name of the LLC, not in their own names.

The best way to do this is to first state the name of the LLC, then sign your name on its behalf.

Example: *Tom is one of two members of Park Place Plasterers, LLC. He enters into a long-term contract for the refurbishing of apartments in a high-rise condominium. Tom signs the contract as follows:*

Date: November 3, 2003
Park Place Plasterers, LLC.
By: _____[Tom's signature]_____ ,
Tom Park, Member

If you sign contracts in your own name without making it clear that you're acting for your LLC, as illustrated above, there's a chance you could be held personally liable to carry out the contract you've signed if the LLC can't (for example, pay money if the LLC goes broke). To be on the safe side, make this simple signing procedure a regular part of your standard day-to-day LLC business routine.

C. LLCs and Securities Filings

➡️ **One-member LLCs don't have to worry about securities law issues.** If you will be the lone member of your LLC and don't plan to take investments from outsiders, your membership interest will not be considered a security and you can skip ahead to Chapter 7. Securities laws are meant to protect investors from unscrupulous business operators; they are not meant to protect active business owners from the results of their own business decisions.

As I discussed in Chapter 3, Section A, the initial members of an LLC ordinarily make financial contributions to the business to get it started. Commonly, all initial members will be active in working for and managing the business. But sometimes, the LLC will solicit capital (funding) from outside investors, meaning there may be some LLC members who do not manage or work in the business. Either way, when someone buys into an LLC (whether as a working member or an outside investor) for a share of its profits, that person purchases a membership interest in the business. The question we need to focus on here is: Is a membership interest in an LLC, and more specifically, in your LLC, considered a "security" within the meaning of state and federal law? If the answer is "yes," your membership interests must either be:

- registered at the federal level (with the Securities and Exchange Commission—SEC) *and* with your state securities office, or

- eligible for an exemption from federal and state securities registration requirements.

If the answer is "no"—membership interests in your LLC do not fit within the definition of "securities"—you won't have to do anything. That is, you won't have to worry about seeking an exemption from securities registration rules or registering them.

1. Are LLC Membership Interests Securities?

Start by understanding that, like LLCs themselves, the question of whether and under what circumstances LLC membership interests may be treated as securities is relatively new, meaning that federal and state laws are in a state of developmental flux on this point. But a helpful generalization is that when the LLC owners rely on their own efforts to make a profit, their membership interests are normally not considered securities under federal and state law. On the other hand, if a person invests in a business with the expectation of making money from *others'* efforts, federal and state statutes, as well as the courts, usually treat that owner's membership interest as a security. How does this apply to real-life LLCs?

a. Member-Managed LLCs

If you and your co-owners plan to set up a member-managed LLC—where, by definition, all members should be actively managing the LLC—your membership interests should not be treated as securities. Why? Because by actively managing your LLC, you and your co-owners are expecting to profit from your own efforts and not from the efforts of others (don't worry, if you have employees, the fact that you may profit from their work doesn't matter in this context). Even if you or your co-owners don't plan to work in the business on a daily basis, if you plan to be active in business management, you should be considered active owners under the securities laws. For example, if you are setting up a small LLC with your spouse (say a car repair service), and one of you plans to manage the business end of it while the other will work in the service department from 9 to 5, you're probably safe deciding that your LLC is safely exempt from securities laws.

Some states have enacted legislation that codifies this rule—adopting a statute that says that if all LLC members actively participate in LLC management, their membership interests are not securities under state law. But in a few states with such statutes, "actively participating in management" is construed strictly. For example, California statutes say that for an LLC to be free of securities laws, it is not enough that its members have the right to vote or participate in management—an LLC must be able to prove that all of its members truly participate in the company on a regular basis.

My suggestion is that, even if you don't live in California or another state with similarly strict rules, it's best to insist that your members measure up to this strict participation standard—that is, if you want to be sure your membership interests will never be treated as securities, you should insist that all members, new and old, actively participate in LLC management. If this won't be the case, your safest tack is to assume all membership interests in your LLC are securities—see Section 2, below, for the next step. (Likewise, if any of your members for some reason don't even have the right to vote, you'd better assume your membership interests will be treated as securities.)

See a lawyer if one or more of your LLC members wants to be inactive. It's no joke to be out of compliance with securities laws (and could give rise to a lawsuit down the road by a disgruntled member). So if your members will include inactive investors, even if you haven't formally set up a manager-managed LLC, see a small business lawyer for advice about whether your membership interests must be registered with the government or if they'll qualify for an exemption (and the interests of most small LLCs will—see Section 2, below).

What if some members will truly be active participants in the LLC's management, but one or more will not? In that case, it's possible the feds and the state will treat *all* of the membership interests in the LLC as securities. Securities agencies have been known to take an all-or-none position: either all LLC memberships are exempt from securities laws or none are. Again, the bottom line here is, if any one of your members won't be active in your LLC, assume your membership interests will be treated as securities and pay to see a lawyer for an hour to discuss these issues.

b. Manager-Managed LLCs

If you set up a manager-managed LLC, it's likely that the ownership interests of at least the nonmanaging members (any members who have not been selected as managers) will be treated as securities under state and federal law. That's because these nonmanaging members won't actively participate in management, so by definition they'll expect to make a profit from the efforts of others. Nonmanaging members are usually outside investors who choose not to take a management role in your business, but wish to share in the profits of the LLC.

Example: Bert and Arnie, two chemical engineers, want to set up an LLC to market their invention, a flexible scuba-diving glove—called the "Claw"— that's made of waterproof polymers. Bert and Arnie plan to manufacture and distribute the glove themselves in their free time, with the help of a small group of employees. They invite a few co-workers at their chemical plant to invest in their new part-time business, but they make it clear to their co-workers that anyone who invests money won't be taking part in the day-to-day management decisions of the company (the co-workers will be nonmanaging members). Bert and Arnie are about to set up their LLC and issue membership interests to themselves and the initial investment group. Should they talk with a securities lawyer first before taking any money from their co-workers? Yes. The membership interests that Bert and Arnie will sell to their co-workers meet the definition of securities, since the co-workers will not actively participate in the business and will expect to make profits from Bert and Arnie's work. Before Bert and Arnie sell the membership interests to their co-workers, they'll have to make sure the issuance of these membership interests will be exempt under state and federal securities laws (which they probably will be— see Section 2, below) or they'll have to register them.

Of course, the interests of the managing members of a manager-managed LLC will probably not, on their own, be considered securities—they'll be considered active owners under the securities laws. But remember, securities agencies usually take an all-or-none position in this context. So, again, anytime you plan to bring in a new LLC member who won't take an active role, you should make sure your LLC fits into one of the exemptions discussed just below or you may have to register them as securities.

2. Exemptions to Securities Registration Requirements

So far I've talked about the definition of securities and why it's important to understand the issues, but I haven't told you why the securities laws exist in the first place. They do serve a purpose—namely, to ensure that people who are considering investing in a business (without managing it) are aware of any foreseeable risks associated with the business. They do this by making sure that the company discloses all relevant information on the company's risks to potential investors and that the investors are in a position to make an educated decision. (Some states, like California, even require that all sales of securities be generally fair to all of the investors!)

Make full disclosure your motto when taking money from investors. There is one basic provision of both federal and state law that applies to all securities transactions: provide full and fair disclosure of all relevant information, financial and otherwise. You should follow this rule regardless of whether your membership interests will be treated as securities or not. But particularly if you solicit investments from outsiders, disclose in writing all of the known and foreseeable risks of investing in your enterprise, and make all of your financial records fully available. If you go out of your way to disclose everything you know about your company, you'll stand a much better chance of fending off securities law problems later if your business does poorly and a member-investor becomes dissatisfied about the LLC's lower-than-expected profits.

But in some instances where potential investors are in a position to protect themselves (usually because of the their past investment history or acquaintance with the business owners), even though the interests in an LLC may be securities, the law says that their sale need not be regulated. This is where exemptions to the securities law come in. The exemptions define the situations where federal and state securities agencies either do not regulate the sale of the securities, or do so minimally. In short, if you think your membership interests may be considered securities, your next step is to see if they'll fall into an exemption from the registration requirements.

Below is a summary of the most commonly relied-upon exemptions from the federal securities law. (Many states either defer to or adopt these federal exemptions in their securities laws, meaning that if the sale of your membership interests will fit under a federal exemption, it's likely, though not certain, that the sale will also fit under a state exemption.) Note that the first exemption below does not require you to file any paperwork—you informally rely on it without having to notify any securities agency.

a. Private Offering Exemption

Under federal case law (law developed in the courts), as well as the securities laws of many states, the selling of securities privately (without advertising or promotion) to a limited number of people (usually no more than 35) is often eligible for a "private offering" exemption. Typically, you stand a better chance of being eligible for this exemption if you only sell membership interests in your LLC to a limited number of people, who have a close family or business relationship with you or one of your co-owners or have enough investment savvy to be able to protect themselves. Also, your investors should be buying the membership interests for themselves (that is, not for resale to other investors), and they shouldn't be able to transfer their membership interests freely. For example, you can place language restricting the further transfer of a membership interest right on the membership certificate, and you can make a conspicuous notation in the LLC records binder that your membership interests are nontransferable.

A typical statement that limits the transfer of membership interests, to be typed on the face of membership certificates, reads like this:

THE SECURITIES REPRESENTED BY THIS CERTIFICATE HAVE NOT BEEN QUALIFIED OR REGISTERED UNDER ANY STATE OR FEDERAL SECURITIES LAW, AND THEY MAY NOT BE TRANS-FERRED OR OTHERWISE DISPOSED OF WITHOUT SUCH QUALIFICATION OR REGISTRATION PURSUANT TO SUCH LAWS OR AN OPINION OF LEGAL COUNSEL SATISFACTORY TO THE ISSUER THAT SUCH QUALIFICATION OR REGISTRA-TION IS NOT REQUIRED.

This informal private offering exemption works for many small LLCs. Passive investors in many smaller LLCs will neatly fit within this traditional securities law exemption. Why? Because in a typical small LLC, memberships are issued to a limited number of people, memberships are a personal investment of the members, and the transfer of membership interests to outsiders is restricted under the LLC operating agreement.

Example: Value Added Ventures, LLC, is started by three active members, who work full-time in the business. In need of cash after their first year in business, they obtain $100,000 in investment capital from Joe, a mutual friend and business acquaintance, who will be a nonmanaging member. The LLC has now sold a total of four membership interests: one each to the founders, and one to the nonmanaging investor, Joe.

When the three initial, active members started their LLC, they felt comfortable that their LLC membership interests were not securities—after all, all three founders planned to work in the business. But when they considered taking an investment from Joe, they weren't so sure. If Joe planned to work in the business, or help manage it, that would be one thing—Joe's interest wouldn't be considered a security. But since Joe had no interest in doing either, they worried that they might be about to sell a security. So before Joe was brought in, the initial members retained a small business lawyer to make sure the sale qualified under an exemption from federal and state securities laws. They did this even though they planned to disclose all financial information and risks of the business to Joe, and even though they were on close terms with him. (And it made sense: in case their business didn't do well and Joe became disgruntled, as long as they had complied with the securities laws, Joe wouldn't be able to sue them for the return of his money by claiming a technical securities violation.) Fortunately, their lawyer assured them that they could safely rely on the private placement exemption—for both federal law and their state's securities law. That's because they didn't publicly advertise that they were seeking investors—Joe was a business aquaintance of theirs; they only sold a membership interest to one outsider; and Joe's ability to transfer his membership interests to others was restricted.

b. Regulation D Exemption

If you want an extra level of certainty when issuing memberships in your LLC to outsiders, your LLC might decide to use federal "Regulation D." Regulation D is really a formal, more complicated version of the private offering exemption, but it requires the filing of formal exemption paperwork. To use Regulation D, you must follow the specific requirements contained in the federal Regulation D statute, and file *Form D* with the Securities and Exchange Commission (SEC).

Generally, you stand a good chance of qualifying under Regulation D if you privately offer (without advertising or promotion) and sell membership interests to 35 or fewer people, and only to investors who, because of significant investment experience or personal net worth, can reasonably be assumed to be able to protect themselves. In addition, your membership interests must not be freely transferable—that is, you must place restrictions on the further transfer of your LLC memberships, as explained in the private offering exemption, above.

Example: Let's revisit the Value Added Ventures LLC. Assume that, instead of taking an investment from their friend Joe, the three original, active members cast a wider net looking for investment capital and find a venture capital group consisting of five affluent investors willing to invest $500,000 in their LLC. Their LLC lawyer again believes that the issuance of these membership interests will be exempt from securities registration, but for different reasons. This time, there are fewer than 35 investors, and all of them are sophisticated, professional investors with a lot of assets. While the issuance of these membership interests could probably still be eligible for the private offering exemption, their lawyer recommends filing for a federal Regulation D exemption to be on the safe side. The lawyer has each investor sign an investment letter that certifies she meets the accredited investor requirements of the Regulation D rules, is purchasing the investment for her own account, assumes the risk of the investment, has read and received all financial statements necessary to make an informed decision, and understands that the resale of memberships is restricted under the federal and state securities laws. A notice under Regulation D is filed with the SEC and the state securities agency, and copies of the investment letters and the notice form are placed in the LLC records binder.

Many states also recognize this exemption, meaning that if a securities transaction complies with federal Regulation D, it also meets state exemption rules.

c. One-State Sales

There is another exemption that is available under the federal securities laws but not under any state laws. Called the "intrastate offering exemption," contained in Section 3(a)(11) of the Securities Act, this one exempts the offer and sale of securities made within one state only. So if you privately offer and sell memberships within your state and only to residents of your state, you probably qualify for this federal exemption. But since state securities laws do not contain an exemption like this one, it may not be too helpful to you if you don't also meet the requirements of either the private placement or the Regulation D exemption set out above. Even though you wouldn't need to make a filing with the federal SEC if you qualify for this exemption, you *would* need to file with the securities agency in your state.

You'll have to look into state securities law exemptions too. In some states, you may need to file a form to qualify for an exemption from state securities requirements, often along with a filing fee. To learn about state securities rules that may affect you, you can check your state securities laws online. The state of Wyoming hosts a Web page that has links to the state securities for most states. The Web address for this page is http://soswy.state.wy.us/sos/sos2.htm. Then click on the link to your state's security agency website, and you should be able to quickly link to a security exemption page on the site that lists any exemptions that apply to private security offerings in your state. Normally, it takes just a few minutes to locate your state's private placement exemption (or a similar "small" or "limited" offering) exemption and to read the section of the law that contains its requirements. As an alternative, you can call your state's securities board or similar agency and ask for a copy of the state laws and regulations that deal with the sale of LLC membership interests. Of course, you may not be able to decipher the legalese, in which case I suggest spending an hour or so with a lawyer to clear up any state securities issues.

After finding out about the exemptions available, for both the feds and the state, you must decide whether to rely on the private placement exemption or file for a formal exemption. This decision should be a legal and practical one that you make based upon your own personal comfort level in this area of law and the particular facts of your LLC.

Talking to a lawyer may be your best bet. As I mentioned above, you can do your own research in this area, but the securities laws are murky, and the newness of the LLC throws a little extra mud in the water. If you're not sure whether you're required by law to either qualify for an exemption or register your membership interests as securities, consider spending some time with a lawyer to get her take on your situation—brainstorming with an LLC lawyer to come up with a safe securities law approach should be well worth the estimated one to five hours worth of legal fees necessary to put this technical legal issue to rest. Not an inexpensive solution, but one that can save you money in legal fees and court costs later.

3. Securities Registration

If your membership interests are in fact securities and the sale of them doesn't fall under one the above exemptions, you may have to register them with federal and state securities agencies. This is a somewhat unlikely scenario for most smaller LLCs, but if it's necessary, it makes sense to hire a lawyer to help you register. Securities laws are very complex—there are numerous streamlined and full-blown federal and state registration procedures, meaning that it probably isn't worth your time and effort to do it yourself.

Getting Legal and Tax Help for Your LLC

Throughout this book, I've flagged several LLC legal and tax issues that go beyond the scope of this overview presentation. If you think that any of these more complex issues might apply to your situation, consider a consultation with an experienced small business lawyer or advisor. And even if you didn't identify any areas where additional help is essential, if you plan to start an LLC of any size or complexity—or convert a good-sized existing business to LLC status—you're likely to benefit from the advice of someone who has done it many times before. And this is true even if you sensibly plan to do much of the form preparation and filing work yourself. Although getting a few hours of professional help will cost several hundreds of dollars, it is likely to be money well spent.

A. Getting Legal Help for your LLC

Here are suggestions on finding a good small business lawyer. First things first. What kind of lawyer should you be looking for?

1. The "Legal Coach" Arrangement

Most small business people do not want—and can't afford—a lawyer who is programmed to try to take over all of your legal decision-making and paperwork. Instead, we suggest you find a small business lawyer who's willing to be your "legal coach"—a professional who is willing to work with you, not just for you—in establishing your LLC and helping with ongoing LLC legal formalities. Under this model, the lawyer helps you take care of many routine legal matters yourself, but also helps you educate yourself on the basics of small business and LLC law and is available for short consultations—and, if necessary, help with paperwork—as more complicated legal issues arise.

a. How to Find a Lawyer Who's Willing to Be Your Coach

Many lawyers are not yet comfortable with the "legal coach" model, which has only begun to become popular in the last decade. For example, some lawyers won't review documents you have drafted using self-help materials, claiming that there is not enough profit in it to justify the trouble and malpractice risk. So to save time, when you call a lawyer (see Section 2, below, for tips on getting referrals to lawyers), make it clear that you are looking for a lawyer who will help you help yourself (for example, review a contract that you have prepared) or who can handle ongoing legal work from time to time. If the lawyer has a problem with this type of relationship, keep shopping—plenty of good local lawyers are anxious to find more business clients.

When you find a lawyer who seems agreeable to the arrangement you've proposed, ask if you can come in to meet for a half hour or so. At the in-person interview, discuss important issues such as the lawyer's customary charges for services, as explained in Section 3, below. Pay particular attention to the rapport between you and your lawyer. Remember, you are looking for a legal advisor who will work with you. Trust your instincts and seek a lawyer whose personality and business sense are compatible with your own.

b. When to Use a Legal Coach

People with simple small businesses who wish to form a basic LLC can very likely do this safely on their own. As I have mentioned earlier, Nolo publishes both a book (*Form Your Own LLC*) and a software program (*LLC Maker*) to allow you to do this at a very reasonable cost. So where might a small business coach come in? First, consider talking to your coach briefly about your conclusion that it makes sense for you to start an LLC or convert your existing business to an LLC. (And don't forget to ask your coach about the securities issues that I discussed in Chapter 6, Section C—your lawyer should be very familiar with your state securities law.) Most likely, she'll confirm your conclusion, and encourage you to take the next step.

With a reliable self-help resource, you should be able to draft and file your articles of organization on your own. Your next step will be to draft your longer and more complicated operating agreement. It's possible you may want to run your draft past your legal coach for a review and any suggestions on how you should fine tune it to fit your situation.

Later, your coach will be best employed to look over and help draft important documents such as contracts and leases and to be available to talk to you should you experience a dispute with an employee, customer, supplier or competitor. Obviously, the amount of work you hand over to a legal coach is up to you. Again, many small business owners find that it makes sense to gain a good working knowledge of legal basics (employment law, for example) and talk to their lawyer only when really needed. Fortunately, legal information and resources are becoming even easier to find on the Internet (see Section 5, below). And many small business publications and trade associations regularly publish very helpful materials.

2. Finding a Lawyer

When looking for a small business lawyer, the best approach is to ask someone you trust to be able to make an informed referral. If you can't think of an obvious person, talk to people who own or operate efficiently run businesses of comparable size and scope to yours. Obviously you are looking for someone who highly recommends a helpful, knowledgeable and reasonably priced lawyer specializing in small business issues. If the business person you talk to has successfully formed an LLC with the help of the lawyer, so much the better. If you talk to several business people, chances are you'll come away with some good leads. And, of course, other knowledgeable people in your network, such as

your banker, accountant, insurance agent or real estate broker, may also
be able to provide the names of lawyers they trust to help them with
business matters.

How shouldn't you search for a lawyer? Don't just pick a name out
of a phone book, legal directory or advertisement—you really have no
idea what you are getting. Lawyer referral services operated by bar
associations are usually equally unhelpful. Often, these simply supply
the names of lawyers who have signed onto the service, often accepting
the lawyer's word for what types of skills she has. Many successful
lawyers who already have more than enough business don't sign up for
these services.

What about looking for a lawyer online? Obviously many lawyers
have their own websites, and there are a number of online lawyer
directories. Although none of these can replace the knowledgeable
recommendation of a savvy business person, some of the better websites
have the potential to become useful places to collect information about
lawyers. While none of the online directories currently do a great job of
providing practical information about lawyers, keep your eye out for
sites that do two things:

- provide in-depth biographical information about a lawyer. You want
  to know where the lawyer went to school, how long she has been in
  practice, what her specialties are and whether she has advanced
  training in small business law, has published articles or books on the
  subject or is a member of relevant trade organizations.

- provide helpful information about how a lawyer likes to practice.
  For example, if a lawyer uses her site to explain that she enjoys
  helping small business people understand the legal information they
  need to actively participate in solving their own legal problems, you
  may wish to set up an appointment.

3. Paying for a Lawyer

Few small business people can afford to buy all the legal information they need at upwards of $200 per hour. The fact that you are reading this book is good evidence that you understand the need to obtain as much legal information on your own as possible—using a lawyer only when you really require his negotiating, drafting or litigating skills. For most day-to-day legal concerns, you only need a legal coach or mentor adept at helping you help yourself, not someone who wants to mail you a bill every Friday.

When you approach a lawyer, it's important to be up-front about money and to get a clear understanding about how and when you'll be charged. For example, if you call the lawyer from time to time for general advice or to be steered to a good information source, how will you be billed? Some lawyers bill a flat amount for a call or a conference; others bill to the nearest 6-, 10- or 20-minute interval. Whatever the lawyer's system, you need to understand it.

Especially at the beginning of your working relationship, when you are still a little unsure about how the lawyer operates, ask specifically about what a particular job, such as forming a limited liability company, will cost. If you feel it's too much, say so. You should be able to do some of the routine work yourself, thus reducing the fee. Even if you have the money to pay, it is usually unwise to pay the lawyer a hefty retainer up-front—if you are not satisfied with the lawyer's work, you'll have a tough time getting even a partial refund. Far better to pay for a few hours of the lawyer's time and go from there.

Especially if you will hire a lawyer to help with a significant legal problem (for example, defend a lawsuit), it's a good idea to get your arrangement in writing. In several states, fee agreements between lawyers and clients must be in writing only if the expected fee is $1,000 or more or is contingent on the outcome of a lawsuit. But whether required or not, it's a good idea to get a written agreement.

4. Using Nonlawyer Professionals

Using other types of professionals can cut down on legal costs when appropriate. Often, nonlawyer professionals perform some tasks better and at less cost than lawyers. For example, look to management consultants for strategic business planning, real estate brokers or appraisers for valuation of property, financial planners for investment advice, an experienced bookkeeper for routine financial recordkeeping, independent paralegals for routine form-drafting and CPAs for the preparation of LLC tax returns (partnership or corporate returns, depending on your LLC's tax classification). Each of these matters is likely to have a legal aspect, and eventually it's possible you'll want to consult your lawyer. But at the very least you'll use a lot less lawyer time and probably save some money if you get as much information as possible from nonlawyer professionals.

Because it is a relatively new profession, a few words about the "independent paralegal" are in order. Sometimes called legal document preparers, these nonlawyer professionals specialize in helping nonlawyers prepare routine legal forms such as those needed for divorce, bankruptcy and organizing a business. In a number of states, including California, Florida and Arizona, these services are readily available for a fraction of what lawyers charge. In others, such as Texas, where lawyers are intent on limiting competition by prosecuting paralegals for the unauthorized practice of law, they are harder to find. Working with an independent paralegal to form an LLC can make sense when you are conversant with all of the legal issues and are looking for reasonably priced help with form preparation. But since independent paralegals are not in business to provide in-depth legal information, they are not a good substitute for lawyers. And, of course, if you are willing to do the form preparation yourself, you can save even the paralegal's fee.

5. Doing Self-Help Legal Research

Law is information, not magic. If you can look up necessary information yourself, you need not purchase it from a lawyer. Finding basic LLC law is not difficult. Much of the research necessary to understand your state's LLC act can be done without a lawyer by using the Internet. For instance, by going to Nolo's Legal Research Center at www.nolo.com/research/index.html, you can access the LLC statutes of all 50 states. Of course, interpreting typically obtuse legal language can be difficult, so if important issues are involved, it can make sense to check your conclusions with a lawyer. Or if you have the energy and time, you can read one of the professional practice manuals lawyers often rely on.

In doing broad legal research for your business, there are a number of sources for legal rules, procedures and issues that you may wish to examine. Here are a few:

- *State limited liability company statutes.* These state laws—your state's LLC act—should be your primary focus for finding the rules for organizing and operating your LLC.

- *Other state laws, such as the Corporations, Partnerships, Securities, Commercial, Civil, Labor and Revenue Codes.* These and other laws govern the operation of other types of businesses or specific business transactions; the content, approval and enforcement of commercial contracts; employment practices and procedures, employment tax requirements, and other aspects of doing business in your state. Depending on the type of business operations you engage in, you also may want to research statutes and regulations dealing with legal topics such as environmental law, products liability, real estate, copyrights and so on. Again, go to Nolo's Legal Research Center to find your state laws, then search for the particular law you want to read.

- *Federal laws.* These include the tax laws and procedures found in the Internal Revenue Code and the Treasury Regulations that implement these code sections; regulations dealing with advertising, warranties and other consumer matters adopted by the Federal Trade Commission; and equal opportunity statutes such as Title VII of the Civil Rights Act administered by the Justice Department and Equal Employment Opportunities Commission. You can find these laws by going to the federal section of Nolo's Legal Research Center, at www.nolo.com/federal/codes/findlaw.html, and using the U.S. Code search box or the Code of Federal Regulations search box.

- *Administrative rules and regulations (issued by federal and state administrative agencies charged with implementing statutes).* State and federal statutes are often supplemented with regulations that clarify specific statutes and contain rules for an agency to follow in implementing and enforcing them. For example, most states have enacted special administrative regulations under their securities statutes that provide exemptions for businesses registering the offer and sale of interests to others within the state. Most federal administrative rules can be found in the Code of Federal Regulations, which, again, you can search in Nolo's Legal Research Center at www.nolo.com/federal/codes/findlaw.html. A good way to locate the state rules and regulations that apply to LLCs is to go to the website of your state's LLC filing office, which normally is part of the Secretary of State or another office that handles corporate filings. A link to other state agencies often is provided that can lead you to specific state regulations that govern the particular business your LLC will engage in.

- *Secondary sources.* Also important in researching business law are sources that provide background information on particular areas of law. One example is this book. Others are commonly found in the business, legal or reference section of your local library or bookstore (for example, see the Nolo small business titles in the next section).

6. Nolo Small Business Legal Resources

A good place to start when you have a legal question is always Nolo's Online Legal Encyclopedia (www.nolo.com/encyclopedia/index.html). It contains lots of free, helpful information on all sorts of business tasks. For instance, in the small business section of the encyclopedia, you'll find information on limited liability, financing, accounting and contracts. Also on Nolo's website you can check our answers to Frequently Asked Questions (FAQs)—a collection of answers to over 1,000 of the questions our customers ask most often.

For further learning, below are several titles published by Nolo that offer valuable business information for LLC owners:

- *LLC Maker™*, by Anthony Mancuso. Windows 95 software that assembles LLC articles of organization (or certificate of formation or organization) according to each state's legal requirements, plus an operating agreement and other LLC formation paperwork. Includes extensive legal and program help, plus state-by-state information screens—it also launches your web browser to go to your state's LLC filing office website and LLC act automatically.

- *Form Your Own Limited Liability Company,* by Anthony Mancuso. This book with CD provides a full treatment of LLC laws and legalities. It contains step-by-step instructions for preparing articles and an LLC operating agreement to form an LLC in your state. Comes with tear-out and computer disk forms.

- *Your Limited Liability Company: An Operating Manual,* by Anthony Mancuso. Provides ready-to-use minute forms for holding formal LLC meetings and contains forms and information for formally approving legal, tax and other important business decisions that arise in the course of operating an LLC. All forms as tear-outs and on disk.

- *How to Create a Buy-Sell Agreement*, by Anthony Mancuso and Bethany K. Laurence. This book shows you how to adopt comprehensive buy-sell provisions to handle the purchase and sale of ownership interests in an LLC when an owner withdraws, dies, becomes disabled or wishes to sell an interest to an outsider. Comes with an easy-to-use agreement—simply check the appropriate options, then fill in the blanks. Buy-sell agreement included as a tear-out and on disk.

- *Tax Savvy for Small Business*, by Frederick Daily. This book gives business owners information about federal taxes and explains how to make the best tax decisions for business, maximize profits and stay out of trouble with the IRS.

- *The Employer's Legal Handbook*, by Fred Steingold. Here's a comprehensive resource that compiles all the basics of employment law in one place. It covers safe hiring practices, wages, hours, tips and commissions, employee benefits, taxes and liability, insurance, discrimination, sexual harassment and termination.

- *Legal Guide for Starting and Running a Small Business*, by Fred Steingold. This book is an essential resource for every small business owner, whether just starting out or already established. Find out the basics about forming a business, negotiating a favorable lease, hiring and firing employees, writing contracts and resolving business disputes.

B. Getting Tax Help

As I discuss in detail in Chapter 4, forming an LLC involves understanding and choosing among various tax options. One of these issues is to determine if you want your LLC to be taxed on a pass-through basis or if it might make sense—now or later—to elect corporate tax treatment with the IRS by filing *IRS Form 8832, Entity Classification Election*. Other LLC business decisions involve run-of-the-mill, but important, tax-related issues: selecting a tax year and accounting period, setting up appropriate bookkeeping procedures, withholding and reporting payroll taxes, preparing tax returns and scheduling distributions of profits and losses to LLC members. To accomplish these tasks and make informed decisions in these and other tax areas may require help from a tax advisor. How do you find one?

1. Finding an LLC Tax Advisor

As with locating a knowledgeable small business lawyer, the best way to find an excellent tax advisor is to shop around for someone recommended by small business people whose judgment you trust. In addition to thoroughly knowing what she is doing, your tax person should be available over the phone to answer routine questions, or by mail or fax to handle paperwork and correspondence, with a minimum of formality. It is likely that you will spend much more time dealing with your tax advisor than your legal advisor, so be particularly attentive to the personal side of this relationship.

LLC tax issues are often cloudy and subject to a range of interpretations and strategies, so it is absolutely essential that you discuss and agree to the level of tax-aggressiveness you expect from your advisor. Some LLC owners prefer to live on the tax edge, saving every possible tax dollar. Others are content to steer a more middle course—foregoing the most aggressive tax strategies in exchange for an extra measure of peace of mind. Whatever your tax strategy, make sure you find a tax advisor who feels the same way you do, or is willing to defer to your more aggressive or conservative tax tendencies.

2. Other LLC Tax Resources

Your tax advisor isn't your only tax and financial resource. For example, banks can be an excellent source of general financial advice. After all, if they are a creditor of your LLC, they have a stake in the success of your business. The Small Business Administration's website (www.sba.gov) can be an ideal source of financial and tax information and resources.

The IRS publishes a number of helpful publications. You can pick these up at your local IRS office or order by phone; download them from the IRS website (http://www.irs.ustreas.gov/prod/bus_info/index.html) or call the toll-free IRS forms and publications request telephone number at 1-800-TAX-FORM. Here are several I recommend:

- *IRS Publication 509, Tax Calendars.* This pamphlet contains a tax calendar showing important dates for business and employer filings during the year.

- *IRS Publication 15, Circular E, Employer's Tax Guide*, and the *Publication 15 Supplement, IRS Publication 937, Business Reporting*, and *IRS Publication 334, Tax Guide for Small Business.* You can find further information on withholding, depositing, reporting and paying federal employment taxes in these publications.

- *IRS Publication 538, Accounting Period and Methods*, and *IRS Publication 583, Information for Business Taxpayers.* These publications provide helpful information on accounting methods and bookkeeping procedures.

Self-Help Tax Resource. Unfortunately, many books and articles that cover LLCs and LLC taxation are not written in plain English, and do a poor job of explaining the basic terms and concepts necessary to fully appreciate the material they cover. One exception (which I mentioned earlier) is Prentice-Hall's *Comprehensive Federal Taxation* book, updated annually (the current edition is called *Federal Taxation 2000, Comprehensive*). It is used primarily as a text for business students, and may be available at a local business or law library. Although this book is rather advanced (and it's not cheap), it should give you a good handle on small business accounting and taxes in general.

■

State Information

ALABAMA

Filing Office

Secretary of State
Corporate Section
Box 5616
Montgomery, AL 36103
Telephone: 334-242-5324

Filing Office URL

http://www.sos.state.al.us/business/corporations.cfm

LLC Statutes

The Alabama LLC Act is contained in Title 10, Chapter 12, of the Alabama statutes, and is browsable from the following Web page (select Title 10, then Chapter 12):

http://www.legislature.state.al.us/CodeofAlabama/1975/coatoc.htm

LLC Name Requirements

The name of an Alabama LLC must contain the words "Limited Liability Company" or the abbreviation "LLC" or "L.L.C."

Call the filing office to check name availability. An available LLC name may be reserved for 120 days for $10.

Note: You must reserve your name with the filing office before preparing and bringing your articles to the county probate judge for filing (the probate judge forwards your articles to the filing office).

Name of LLC Organizational Document

Articles of organization

State-Provided Articles of Organization

The filing office provides an LLC formation summary sheet together with a fill-in-the-blanks articles of organization form and a "Report of Domestic Limited Liability Company" form.

Internet Forms: Guidelines for creating Alabama articles, along with various forms, can be downloaded from the state website.

Filing Fees

$40, payable to the "Secretary of State," plus a separate check for $35 for the "Probate Court Judge," who receives and records the original articles.

Special Forms and Procedures

Make sure you have reserved your name with the filing office before preparing your articles. You can check name availability at the filing office website or by calling the filing office. Include a copy of the name reservation certificate with your articles.

Submit an original plus two copies of signed articles and your name reservation certificate to the nearest county probate court judge (check local governmental telephone listing and call for address). The judge will record the original articles of organization and forward a copy with the fees to the Secretary of State.

After filing articles of organization, fill in the Report of Domestic LLC form and send the original plus two copies of the completed form, together with a check for $5, to the Secretary of State.

State Tax Status

An LLC is treated by the state as a partnership, unless it is treated otherwise by the IRS, in which case it is treated by the state as it is treated by the IRS. [Section 10-12-8(b)] If treated as a partnership, you'll file Alabama Department of Revenue Form 65, Partnership/Limited Liability Company Return of Income.

ALASKA

Filing Office

Department of Commerce & Economic Development
Division of Banking, Securities & Corporations
Corporations Section
Box 110808
Juneau, AK 99811-0808
Telephone: 907-465-2530

Filing Office URL

http://www.dced.state.ak.us/bsc/corps.htm

LLC Statutes

The Alaska LLC Act is contained in Title 10, Chapter 10.50, of the Alaska statutes, starting at Section 10.50.010, and is browsable from the following Web page:

http://www.dced.state.ak.us/bsc/corps.htm

LLC Name Requirements

The name of an Alaska LLC must contain the words "Limited Liability Company" or the abbreviations "LLC" or "L.L.C." The word "Limited" may be abbreviated as "Ltd." and the word "Company" as "Co." The name may not contain the words "city," "borough" or "village" or otherwise imply that the company is a municipality.

Names already in use can be searched on the filing office website (or call 907-465-2530). An available LLC name may be reserved for 120 days for

$25. A proposed LLC name may be registered (kept on the rolls of the filing office) by paying an annual fee of $25.

Name of LLC Organizational Document
Articles of organization

State-Provided Articles of Organization
The filing office provides a fill-in-the-blanks articles of organization form form, with instructions, plus an information booklet with requirements for organizing and operating an Alaska LLC.

Internet Forms: Alaska LLC articles and other forms can be downloaded from the state website.

Filing Fees
$250 fee (includes $100 biennial license fee—due every two years), payable to the "State of Alaska."

Special Forms and Procedures
If you are converting an existing partnership to an LLC, prepare and attach Form 08-431, "Application for Certificate of Conversion," to your LLC articles. This is a simple form, available for downloading from the filing office website, that contains general information on the prior partnership.

State Tax Status
Follows IRS classification.

ARIZONA

Filing Office
Arizona Corporation Commission
Corporation Filing Section
1300 West Washington
Phoenix, AZ 85007-2996
Telephone: 800-345-5819 (in AZ only) or 602-542-3135
Tucson Branch Office: 520-628-6560 (accepts LLC filings)

Filing Office URL
http://www.cc.state.az.us/corp/index.htm

LLC Statutes
The Arizona LLC Act is contained in Title 29, Chapter 4, of the Arizona Statutes, starting at Section 29.601, and is browsable from the following Web page:
http://www.azleg.state.az.us/ars/29/601.htm

The filing office will provide a copy of the Arizona LLC Act upon request, at no charge.

LLC Name Requirements
The name of an Arizona LLC must end with the words "Limited Liability Company" or "Limited Company" or the abbreviations "LLC," "LC," "L.L.C." or "L.C." If your LLC name is also a trademark, attach a Declaration of Trademark Holder (available from the filing office or its website) to your articles.

Call the filing office to check name availability (602-542-3230). An available LLC name may be reserved for 120 days for $10.

Name of LLC Organizational Document
Articles of organization

State-Provided Articles of Organization

The filing office provides a fill-in-the-blanks articles of organization form, plus a "Notice of Filing" form, which must be published after the filing of articles.

Internet Forms: The latest Arizona LLC articles of organization form, with instructions, plus other Arizona LLC forms (Notice of Filing, Application for Reservation of LLC Name and others) can be downloaded from the filing office website. General instructions for forming an LLC plus a checklist of steps to take to form an Arizona LLC also are available for downloading.

Filing Fees

$50, payable to the "Arizona Corporation Commission." $35 extra for expedited services.

Special Forms and Procedures

Post-Filing Formalities: Within 60 days of filing your articles, publish a "Notice of Filing" form (available from the filing office) three times in a newspaper of general circulation that publishes legal notices in the county where the LLC has its place of business (approved newspapers of general circulation are listed on the filing office website). The information supplied in the notice can be copied from your articles. Within 90 days of filing articles, you must file an "Affidavit of Publication," supplied by the newspaper that verifies the notice was published, with the Corporation Commission (no fee).

State Tax Status

Follows IRS classification.

ARKANSAS

Filing Office

Arkansas Secretary of State
Corporations Division
State Capitol
Little Rock, AR 72201-1094
Telephone: 501-682-5151

Filing Office URL

http://www.sosweb.state.ar.us/
corp_forms.html

LLC Statutes

The Arkansas LLC Act (called the "Small Business Entity Tax Pass Through Act"), is located in Title 4 (Business and Commercial Law), Subtitle 3 (Corporations and Associations), Chapter 32, starting with Section 4-32-101, and is browsable from the following Web page:

http://www.arkleg.state.ar.us/
newsdcode/lpext.dll?f=templates&fn=
default.htm

LLC Name Requirements

An Arkansas LLC name must contain the words "Limited Liability Company," "Limited Company," or the abbreviations "LLC," "LC," "L.L.C." or "L.C."

Names of LLCs that perform professional services must instead include the words "Professional Limited Liability Company," "Professional Limited Company," or the abbreviations "PLLC,"

"PLC," "P.L.L.C." or "P.L.C." For any type of Arkansas LLC, the word "Limited" may be abbreviated as "Ltd." and the word "Company" may be abbreviated as "Co."

An Arkansas LLC name may be reserved for 120 days for $25.

Name of LLC Organizational Document

Articles of organization

State-Provided Articles of Organization

The filing office provides a fill-in-the-blanks articles of organization form (Form LL-01), with instructions.

Internet Forms: The latest LLC articles of organization form, with instructions, plus other Arkansas LLC forms (Application for Reservation of LLC Name and others) can be downloaded from the filing office website.

Filing Fees

$50 fee, payable to the "Arkansas Secretary of State."

Special Forms and Procedures

If you are converting an existing partnership into an LLC, obtain a "Form for Conversion of Partnership to an LLC," available for downloading from the state website. Complete the form and attach it to your completed articles.

State Tax Status

An LLC with two or more members will be treated as a partnership for state tax purposes. An LLC with only one member will be treated as a sole proprietorship. [Section 4-32-1313] This state

classification conforms to federal default classification rules for LLCs. Presumably, an Arkansas LLC that elects corporate tax treatment with the IRS will be treated as a corporation for state tax purposes as well.

CALIFORNIA

Filing Office

California Secretary of State
Limited Liability Company Unit
P.O. Box 944228
Sacramento, CA 94244-2280
Telephone: 916-653-3795

Branch offices of the Secretary of State are located in Fresno, Los Angeles, San Francisco and San Diego. Currently, branch offices provide LLC forms over-the-counter only. They do not mail out forms or accept LLC filings.

Filing Office URL

http://www.ss.ca.gov/business/business.htm

LLC Statutes

The California Beverly-Killea Limited Liability Company Act is contained in the California Corporations Code, Title 2.5 (Limited Liability Companies), starting with Section 17000, and is browsable from the following Web page:

http://www.leginfo.ca.gov/calaw.html

The filing office will provide a summary of the California LLC Act (called the Beverly-Killea LLC Act) upon request.

LLC Name Requirements

The name of a California LLC must end with the words "Limited Liability Company" or the abbreviation "LLC" or "L.L.C." The word "Limited" may also be abbreviated as "Ltd." and the word "Company" as "Co." The LLC name may contain the names of one or more members, but may not include the words "bank," "insurance," "trust," "trustee," "incorporated" or "corporation," or the abbreviations "inc." or "corp."

An available LLC name may be reserved for 60 days for a $10 fee. The best way to secure a name is to reserve it by mail with the filing office. You can download a name reservation form from the LLC office website. (List one or more alternate names in case your first choice for an LLC name is not available for reservation.) To find out if a name is already in use online, you can search LLC and corporate records at the filing office website, but this won't tell you if your proposed name is *available*, since it may have been reserved by someone else for later use.

Name of LLC Organizational Document

Articles of organization

State-Provided Articles of Organization

The filing office provides a fill-in-the-blanks articles of organization form (Form LLC-1), with instructions. The basic articles form is all that is legally needed, although you may attach extra provisions to the state-provided form if you wish. The filing office also provides an annual LLC Statement of Information form, which must be filed within 90 days of forming the LLC.

If you are converting an existing partnership to an LLC, the state may soon publish a form for special conversion articles that you would use to set up your LLC instead of standard California LLC articles. Check the filing office website for the availability of this form.

Internet Forms: The latest California LLC articles of organization, with instructions, plus other California LLC forms (Reservation of LLC Name and others) can be downloaded from the Secretary of State's website.

Filing Fees

$70, payable to the "Secretary of State."

Initial LLC Fees: You must pay the FTB a minimum annual LLC tax of $800 within three months after forming your LLC (this annual minimum fee also applies to C and S corporations and limited partnerships, except new corporations are exempt from making the minimum payment for their first two tax years). The FTB should mail your LLC a notice to pay this amount after you form your LLC, but mark your calendar in case the state forgets to send out this notice.

Annual Fees: If your LLC will be treated and taxed as a partnership in California (most small LLCs), you must pay the FTB a minimum LLC fee of $800 each year. The FTB should mail your LLC a notice to pay this amount each year, but mark your calendar in case the board forgets to send out this notice. LLCs with total annual incomes of $250,000 or more must also pay the following additional annual fee amounts:

Annual Total California Income Additional Fee

(fees for the year 2001; expect future adjustments)

Income	Additional Fee
$250,000-$499,999:	$979
$500,000-$999,999:	$2,938
$1,000,000-$4,999,999:	$5,876
$5,000,000 or more	$8,814

Special Forms and Procedures

Note for Professionals: Currently, the more than 60 professions licensed by the state cannot form a California LLC. (Lawyers, accountants and architects, however, may form a Registered Limited Liability Partnership—ask the Secretary of State for RLLP forms and instructions if you are interested.) Also note that a California LLC may not engage in the business of issuing insurance policies or assuming insurance

risks (although an LLC can sell insurance as an agent or a broker). If you are unsure whether you can form a California LLC to render professional services, call your state licensing board.

Note: Expect the California LLC law to change soon to allow the formation of professional service LLCs. Call the filing office to ask about the status of pending legislation to allow the formation of professional LLCs in your area of practice.

State Tax Status

Follows IRS classification. As mentioned above, California LLCs must pay a minimum $800 tax each year, and an additional fee if annual LLC total income equals or exceeds $250,000 (see Annual Fees, above). These additional annual fee amounts are slated to be adjusted each year (expect future increases).

COLORADO

Filing Office

Secretary of State
1560 Broadway, Suite 200
Denver, CO 80202
Telephone: 303-894-2251

Filing Office URL

http://www.sos.state.co.us/pubs/business/main.htm

LLC Statutes

The Colorado LLC Act is contained in Title 7, Chapter 80, of the Colorado

Statutes, starting with Section 7-80-101, and is browsable from the following Web page:

http://www.leg.state.co.us/ inetcrs.nsf?OpenDatabase

LLC Name Requirements

The name of a Colorado LLC must end with the words "Limited Liability Company" or the abbreviation "LLC". The word "Limited" may be abbreviated as "Ltd." and the word "Company" as "Co."

For name availability, call the filing office. An available LLC name may be reserved for 120 days for $10.

Name of LLC Organizational Document

Articles of organization

State-Provided Articles of Organization

The filing office provides a fill-in-the-blanks articles of organization form, with instructions for new businesses. Provides special articles of organization to convert existing general or limited partnership to a Colorado LLC.

Internet Forms: The latest LLC articles of organization, with instructions, plus other Colorado LLC forms (Reservation of LLC Name and others) can be downloaded from the filing office website. Forms are provided in WordPerfect and Adobe Acrobat format. A "Filing Guide" is also browsable and downloadable, and includes helpful information on forming LLCs in Colorado.

Filing Fees

$50, payable to "Secretary of State." Expedited filing costs $50 extra. Papers returned to you by fax cost $7 more.

Special Forms and Procedures

If you are converting a partnership to an LLC, use the special form available for this purpose (Form 033, articles for conversion of a partnership to an LLC), which can be downloaded from the filing office website.

State Tax Status

Follows IRS classification.

CONNECTICUT

Filing Office

Connecticut Secretary of State
30 Trinity Street
P.O. Box 150470
Hartford, CT 06115-0470
Telephone: 860-509-6002

Filing Office URL

http://www.sots.state.ct.us

LLC Statutes

The Connecticut LLC Act is contained in Title 34, Chapter 613, of the Connecticut Statutes, starting with Section 34-100, and is browsable from the following Web page:

http://www.cslib.org/psaindex.htm

LLC Name Requirements

The name of a Connecticut LLC must contain the words "Limited Liability Company" or the abbreviations "LLC" or "L.L.C." The word "Limited" may be abbreviated as "Ltd." and the word "Company" as "Co."

An available LLC name can be reserved for 120 days for a $30 fee.

Name of LLC Organizational Document
Articles of organization

State-Provided Articles of Organization
The filing office provides a fill-in-the-blanks articles of organization form. A bank, trust, insurance, building and loan, utility (except telephone) or cemetery company cannot be formed as an LLC.

LLC forms requests: 860-509-6079.

Internet Forms: The latest LLC articles of organization, with instructions, plus other Connecticut LLC forms (Reservation of LLC Name and others) can be downloaded from the filing office website.

Filing Fees
$60, payable to "Secretary of State." Include $20 extra to receive a filed copy of the articles ($25 extra for a certified copy).

State Tax Status
Follows IRS classification. [Section 34-113]

DELAWARE

Filing Office
Department of State
Division of Corporations

P.O. Box 898
Dover, DE 19903
Telephone: 302-739-3073

Filing Office URL
http://www.state.de.us/corp/index.htm

LLC Statutes
The Delaware LLC Act is contained in Title 6 (Commerce and Trade), Chapter 18, of the Delaware Statutes, starting with Section 18-101, and is browsable from the following Web page:
http://www.michie.com/resources1.html

LLC Name Requirements
The name of a Delaware LLC must contain the words "Limited Liability Company" or the abbreviation "L.L.C." or "LLC" (with or without periods). The name may contain the names of members, or the words "Club," "Foundation," "Fund," "Institute," "Society," "Union," "Syndicate" or "Trust."

Name availability may be checked by calling 302-727-7283. An available LLC name may be reserved for 120 days for $10. (Currently, Delaware LLCs cannot use the Division of Corporations' 900-line to reserve a name.)

Name of LLC Organizational Document
Certificate of formation

State-Provided Certificate of Formation
When you ask for LLC information, Delaware will send you its forms pack-

age called "Incorporating Forms and Certificates." Included in this package is a fill-in-the-blanks certificate of formation for LLCs.

Internet Forms: The latest LLC certificate of formation, plus other LLC forms (Reservation of LLC Name and others) can be downloaded from the filing office website (under "Incorporating Forms and Certificates").

Filing Fees

$70, payable to the "Delaware Department of State" (includes $20 certified copy fee). The Department of State, Division of Corporations, also accepts major credit cards.

Annual Fees: A Delaware LLC must pay a flat annual franchise tax of $100. Contact the Franchise Tax Office of the Division of Corporations for more information and for tax forms; telephone 302-739-4225.

State Tax Status

Follows IRS classification.

DISTRICT OF COLUMBIA

Filing Office

Department of Consumer & Regulatory Affairs
Business Regulation Administration
Corporations Division
941 North Capitol Street, NE
Washington, DC 20002
Telephone: 202-442-8947

Filing Office URL

http://www.dcra.org

LLC Statutes

The District of Columbia LLC Act is contained in Title 29 (Corporations), Chapter 13, of the DC Code, starting with Section 29-1301, and is browsable from the following Web page:

http://www.michie.com.resources 1.html

Prentice-Hall Legal & Financial Services Publishing (212-373-7808) publishes a small booklet containing the corporation laws of Maryland and the District of Columbia (includes the limited liability company statutes) for approximately $20.

LLC Name Requirements

The name of a District of Columbia LLC must contain the words "Limited Liability Company" or the abbreviation "LLC" or "L.L.C." Names of LLCs that perform professional services must include the words "Professional Limited Liability Company" or the abbreviation "PLLC" or "P.L.L.C."

Name availability may be checked by calling the filing office. Available LLC names may be reserved for 60 days for $25.

Name of LLC Organizational Document

Articles of organization

State-Provided Articles of Organization

The district provides guidelines and a sample form for articles of organization.

Internet Forms: The latest District of Columbia LLC forms are available for viewing and downloading at the filing office website.

Filing Fees

$100, payable to the "D.C. Treasurer."

Special Forms and Procedures

One-member LLCs are not allowed in the District of Columbia at present.

Include a signed "Written Consent of Registered Agent," available from the filing office website, with your articles.

Don't be confused if you read the instructions on the website that mention filing a copy of your LLC operating agreement; you do not have to submit a copy of this agreement when you file articles of organization.

State Tax Status

Follows IRS classification. Also note: District of Columbia LLCs are subject to 14.5% tax on income earned in the District of Columbia.

FLORIDA

Filing Office

Florida Department of State
Registration Section
Division of Corporations
P.O. Box 6327
Tallahassee, FL 32314
Telephone: 850-487-6051

Filing Office URL

http://www.dos.state.fl.us/doc/index.html

LLC Statutes

The Florida LLC Act is contained in Title XXXVI (Business Organizations), Chapter 608, of the Florida Statutes, starting with Section 608.401, and is browsable from the following Web page:

http://www.leg.state.fl.us/Welcome/index.cfm

LLC Name Requirements

The name of a Florida LLC must end with the words "Limited Liability Company," "Limited Company" or the abbreviation "LLC," "LC," "L.L.C." or "L.C." The word "limited" may be abbreviated as "Ltd."; the word "Company" may be abbreviated as "Co."

You cannot reserve a name for your LLC. You can search name availability at the Department of State's website (go to http://ccfcorp.dos.state.fl.us/corpweb/inquiry/corinam.html, and enter your proposed LLC name. Or you can check name availability by calling the Department of State (telephone: 850-487-6051). Once you have determined that a name is available, quickly submit your proposed articles for filing. If the name is not still available, you will be notified by the filing office.

Name of LLC Organizational Document
Articles of organization

State-Provided Articles of Organization

The filing office provides a fill-in-the-blanks articles of organization form, with instructions. Also provides an LLC booklet, titled "Florida Limited Liability Company Act," which contains the Florida LLC Act and a tear-out articles form. The separately supplied form and the tear-out fill-in-the-blanks form are identical.

Internet Forms: LLC forms, including articles and other forms, are available for downloading from the Division of Corporations' website.

Filing Fees

$100 for filing articles, plus $25 for filing the Designation of Registered Agent form (included in articles), for a total of $125, payable to the "Florida Department of State." The Department will send you a letter of acknowledgment upon filing.

Optional: You can add $52.50 to receive a certified copy of your articles from the filing office, and/or add $8.75 for a Certificate of Status certifying that your LLC is an active Florida LLC as of its filing date.

Special Forms and Procedures

Conversion of partnership: If you are converting an existing general or limited partnership to an LLC, you will need to attach a "certificate of conversion" form, available from the filing office website, to your articles and pay $100 extra for the conversion.

Optional Transmittal Letter: The filing office website has a special cover letter you can send with your articles. This official form helps you compute the filing fees, shows the proposed name of your LLC, and allows you to add a return name and address so you can receive the filing receipt and any certified copies of the articles after the original articles are filed.

State Tax Status

LLCs are currently treated as corporations under state tax law, regardless of their federal income tax classification or treatment (Florida has no personal income tax). Each year, you must file Form F-1120, Corporate Income/Franchise Tax Return, with the state, and make estimated tax payments if your expected annual tax exceeds specified limits. Florida LLCs pay an annual 5.5% artificial entity (corporate) tax on net taxable profits. Emergency Excise taxes are also assessed and paid with regular corporate/franchise taxes.

GEORGIA

Filing Office
Secretary of State
Corporations Division
Suite 315, West Tower
2 Martin Luther King Jr. Drive
Atlanta, GA 30334
Telephone: 404-656-2817

Filing Office URL

http://www.sos.state.ga.us/corporations

LLC Statutes

The Georgia LLC Act starts with Section 14-11-100 of the Georgia Code, and is browsable from the following Web page:

http://www.ganet.org/cgi-bin/pub/ocode/ocgsearch?docname=OCode/G/14/11/100

LLC Name Requirements

The name of a Georgia LLC must contain the words "Limited Liability Company" or "Limited Company" or one of the following abbreviations "LC," "LLC," "L.C." or "L.L.C." The word "Limited" may be abbreviated as "Ltd." and the word "Company" may be abbreviated as "Co." The name must not exceed 80 characters, including spaces and punctuation.

Important: You must reserve your proposed LLC name before you file your articles. Call the filing office at the above telephone number to check name availability and reserve your LLC name over the phone (there is no fee for an LLC name reservation). You can also check the availability of a name and reserve a name online at the filing office website.

If name reservation approval is given, you will be mailed a name reservation certificate, which contains your name reservation number. The name reservation is valid for 90 days.

Name of LLC Organizational Document

Articles of organization

State-Provided Articles of Organization

The filing office provides sample articles of organization, plus a transmittal form, which must be mailed with the articles for filing.

Internet Forms: LLC forms, including sample articles, transmittal form and other forms, are available for downloading from the filing office website.

Filing Fees

$75, payable to "Secretary of State." Attach check to completed transmittal form.

Special Forms and Procedures

Reserve your LLC name prior to filing your articles by calling the filing office (or reserve your name online at the LLC office website). If name reservation approval is given, you will be mailed a name reservation certificate. The LLC organizer must sign and submit a transmittal form (from the filing office website) with the check attached, along with the articles of organization. File the original and one copy of the articles. Include the original name reservation certificate with your papers.

Note: The Transmittal Form should be completed to show your name reservation number and the other requested information.

State Tax Status

Follows IRS classification.

HAWAII

Filing Office

Department of Commerce and
Consumer Affairs
Business Registration Division
P.O. Box 40
Honolulu, HI 96810
Telephone: 808-586-2727

Filing Office URL

http://www.businessregistrations
.com

LLC Statutes

The Hawaii LLC Act is contained in
Chapter 428 of the Hawaii Statutes,
starting with Section 428-101, and is
browsable from the following Web page:
http://www.businessregistrations
.com/legal/Statutes428.html

LLC Name Requirements

The name of a Hawaii LLC must
contain the words "Limited Liability
Company" or the abbreviation "LLC" or
"L.L.C." The word "Limited" may be
abbreviated as "Ltd." and the word
"Company" may be abbreviated as "Co."

An available LLC name may be
reserved for 120 days for $25.

Name of LLC Organizational Document

Articles of organization

State-Provided Articles of Organization

The filing office provides fill-in
articles of organization, plus a separate
instructions file.

Internet Forms: LLC forms, including sample articles with separate instructions, are available for downloading from
the filing office website.

Filing Fees

$100 fee, payable to the "Depart-
ment of Commerce and Consumer
Affairs."

Special Forms and Procedures

If you are converting an existing
partnership to an LLC, check the box
above Article I in the articles (the second
check box) to show you are converting
to an LLC; then complete Article VIII.
You must publish a notice of conversion
in a local newspaper prior to filing your
articles (as stated in Article VIII(d)). The
notice must be published once a week
for three successive weeks in a newspaper of general circulation in Hawaii. List
all three dates of publication and name
of the newspaper in Article VIII (d).

State Tax Status

Follows IRS classification.

IDAHO

Filing Office

Idaho Secretary of State
Corporations Division
700 West Jefferson
P.O. Box 83720
Boise, ID 83720-0080
Telephone: 208-334-2301

Filing Office URL

http://www.idsos.state.id.us/corp/corindex.htm

LLC Statutes

The Idaho LLC Act is contained in Title 53 (Partnership), Chapter 6, of the Idaho Statutes, starting with Section 53-601, and is browsable from the following Web page:

http://www3.state.id.us/idstat/TOC/53006KTOC.html

The filing office also distributes a free handbook containing the Idaho Limited Liability Company Act.

LLC Name Requirements

The name must contain the words "Limited Liability Company," "Limited Company" or the abbreviation "L.L.C." or "L.C." The word "Limited" may be abbreviated as "Ltd." and the word "Company" may be abbreviated as "Co." The name of a professional services LLC must end with the words "Professional Company" or the abbreviation "P.L.L.C."

An LLC name may be reserved for four months for $20.

Name of LLC Organizational Document

Articles of organization

State-Provided Articles of Organization

The filing office provides a fill-in-the-blanks articles of organization form, with instructions. For professional LLCs, the filing office provides a special articles form (Form LLC3).

Internet Forms: LLC forms, including regular and professional articles and other forms, are available for downloading from the filing office website.

Filing Fees

$100 fee, payable to the "Idaho Secretary of State." If the articles are not typed, if attachments are included, or if expedited filing is requested in the cover letter that accompanies the articles, the filing fee is $120.

Special Forms and Procedures

Note for Professionals: The filing office provides a special articles form for organizing a professional limited liability company (under Section 53-615 of the Idaho LLC Act). This special professional form (Form LLC3), available online or by calling the state office, should be used instead of regular Idaho articles if your LLC will perform licensed professional services in the fields of architecture, chiropractic, dentistry, engineering, landscape architecture, law, medicine, nursing, occupational therapy, optometry, physical therapy, podiatry, professional geology, psychology, certified or licensed public accountancy, social work, surveying or veterinary medicine.

State Tax Status

Follows IRS classification.

ILLINOIS

Filing Office

Illinois Secretary of State
Department of Business Services
Limited Liability Company Division
Room 359, Howlett Building
Springfield, IL 62756
Telephone: 217-524-8008
Branch Office: 17 North State Street, Suite 1137, Chicago, IL 60602 (for questions and information only; does not do LLC filings).

Filing Office URL

http://www.sos.state.il.us/depts/bus_serv/feature.html

LLC Statutes

The Illinois LLC Act is contained in Chapter 805 (Business Organizations), starting with Section 180/1-1, and is browsable from the following Web page:

http://www.legis.state.il.us/ilcs/ch805/ch805act180articles/ch805act180artstoc.htm

The filing office also provides a copy of the Illinois LLC Act, plus a pamphlet summarizing the legal and tax requirements and features of Illinois LLCs.

LLC Name Requirements

An Illinois LLC name must contain the words "Limited Liability Company" or the abbreviation "LLC" or "L.L.C." The abbreviations "Ltd." and "Co." are not allowed in Illinois LLC names.

Call 217-782-9520 to check availability of up to three proposed LLC names. LLC name availability may also be checked online.

A name reservation costs a whopping $300 so you probably will wish to simply check the availability of your proposed name before filing your articles, rather than reserving it. Or, call the LLC office to see if the reservation fee has been reduced to a more modest level.

Name of LLC Organizational Document

Articles of organization

State-Provided Articles of Organization

The filing office provides a fill-in-the-blanks articles of organization form (Form LLC-5.5), and a pamphlet summarizing the legal and tax requirements and features of Illinois LLCs.

Internet Forms: The latest LLC articles of organization form, plus other Illinois LLC forms (Reservation of LLC Name and others), can be downloaded from the filing office website.

Filing Fees

$400, payable to the "Secretary of State." Payment must be made by certified check, cashier's check, money order or an Illinois attorney's or CPA's check (do not send a personal check).

Annual Fees: LLCs do not pay state franchise taxes, but must pay an annual LLC renewal fee of $300.

Special Forms and Procedures

Note to Article 2: If you will do business under a name other than the one stated in the articles (you'll do business under an "assumed business name"), attach Form LLC-1.20, available from the LLC Division or its website, to your articles.

Medical Practice LLCs: The LLC organizer (the person who signs the articles) of an Illinois medical practice LLC must be a licensed Illinois physician.

Conversion of partnership: If you are converting an existing general or limited Illinois partnership to an LLC, you must follow some additional requirements, posted on the filing office website. You will need to include an attachment page with your articles and pay $100 extra for the conversion.

State Tax Status
Follows IRS classification.

INDIANA

Filing Office
Indiana Secretary of State
Corporations Division
302 W. Washington, Room E018
Indianapolis, IN 46204
Telephone: 317-232-6576

Filing Office URL
http://www.state.in.us/sos/
bus_service

LLC Statutes
The Indiana LLC Act (also called the "Indiana Business Flexibility Act") is contained in Title 23 (Business and Other Associations), Article 18, of the Indiana Code, starting with Section 23-18-1-1, and is browsable from the following Web page:

http://www.state.in.us/legislative/ic/code/title23/ar18/ch1.html

LLC Name Requirements
The name of an Indiana LLC must end with the words "Limited Liability Company" or the abbreviation "LLC."

Name availability can be checked by phone or online at the filing office's website. An available name may be reserved for 120 days for $20.

Name of LLC Organizational Document
Articles of organization

State-Provided Articles of Organization
Articles of organization forms are not provided, but the office sends out a Limited Liability Company Guide pamphlet, which summarizes LLC formation procedures and legal requirements in Indiana.

Internet Forms: The Limited Liability Company Guide, including guidelines for preparing LLC articles, plus standard forms (such as a request to reserve a name), are downloadable from the filing office website.

Filing Fees
$90, payable to "Secretary of State" (staple check to articles).

State Tax Status
Follows IRS classification.

IOWA

Filing Office

Iowa Secretary of State
Corporations Division
Hoover Building, 2nd Floor
Des Moines, IA 50319
Telephone: 515-281-5204

Filing Office URL

http://www.sos.state.ia.us/business/
services.html

LLC Statutes

The Iowa LLC Act is contained in
Title XII (Business Entities), Chapter
490A, of the Iowa Code, starting with
Section 490A.100, and is browsable
from the following Web page:

http://www.legis.state.ia.us/
IACODE/1999SUPPLEMENT/490A/

The filing office also provides a copy
of the LLC Act.

LLC Name Requirements

The name of an Iowa LLC must
contain the words "Limited Liability
Company" or "Limited Company" or the
abbreviation "L.L.C." or "L.C."

An available LLC name may be
reserved for 120 days for $10.

Name of LLC Organizational Document

Articles of organization

State-Provided Articles of Organization

The filing office does not provide a
fill-in-the-blanks articles of organization
form.

Internet Forms: The filing office
provides a reservation of name form and
other forms on its website.

Filing Fees

$50, payable to the "Iowa Secretary
of State."

Special Forms and Procedures

Additional information must be
provided in your articles if you are
converting an existing partnership to an
LLC. See the state website or call the
filing office for instructions on adding
this additional information to your
articles.

State Tax Status

Follows IRS classification.

KANSAS

Filing Office

Kansas Secretary of State
Corporation Division
First Floor, Memorial Hall
120 SW 10th Ave.
Topeka, KS 66612-1594
Telephone: 913-296-4564

Filing Office URL

http://www.kssos.org

LLC Statutes

The Kansas LLC Act is browsable
from the Web page listed below. The
LLC Act is contained in Chapter 17 of
the Kansas Statutes, Article 76, starting
with Section 17-7662 (ignore Sections
17-7601 to 17-76661). To locate it, in

the box near the bottom of the Web page titled, "Find a Statute Using the Statute Table of Contents," select Chapter 17, then select Article 76.

http://www.ink.org/public/legislative/statutes/statutes.cgi

The filing office may provide a photocopy of the Kansas Limited Liability Act upon request.

LLC Name Requirements

A Kansas LLC name MUST contain the words "Limited Liability Company" or "Limited Company" or the abbreviation "LLC," "L.L.C.," "LC" or "L.C." Omission of one of these terms in an LLC name may subject the LLC members to personal liability for claims made against the LLC.

An available LLC name may be reserved for 120 days for $20.

Name of LLC Organizational Document

Articles of organization

State-Provided Articles of Organization

The filing office provides a fill-in-the-blanks articles form (Form DL), with instructions.

Internet Forms: An LLC articles form (Form DL), instructions for the articles, plus other forms, can be downloaded from the filing office website.

Filing Fees

$150 fee, payable to the "Kansas Secretary of State."

Special Forms and Procedures

If you are forming a professional LLC, make sure to fill in the professional purpose of your LLC in the designated blank in the articles (for example, "surgical practice" or " practice of accountancy"). Also, see instruction 2 on the second page of the articles form for additional filing requirements that apply to professional LLCs.

If you are converting a partnership to an LLC, prepare and attach Kansas Form CV, Certificate of Conversion, to your articles. This is a simple form to prepare, and is available for downloading from the filing office website. Note that the total fee is $170 for filing both the LLC articles plus Form CV.

State Tax Status

Kansas LLCs are subject to the state's franchise tax on their net capital accounts.

KENTUCKY

Filing Office

Kentucky Secretary of State
Business Filings
P.O. Box 718
Frankfort, KY 40602
Telephone: 502-564-2848

Filing Office URL

http://www.sos.state.ky.us

LLC Statutes

The Kentucky LLC Act is contained in Title XXIII (Private Corporations and Associations), Chapter 275, of the Kentucky Statutes, starting with Section 275.001, and is browsable from the following Web page:

http://162.114.4.13/krs/275-00/CHAPTER.HTM

A copy of the Kentucky LLC Act can be obtained upon request from the Secretary of State for $10.

LLC Name Requirements

A Kentucky LLC name must contain the words "Limited Liability Company" or "Limited Company" or the abbreviation "LLC" or "LC." The word "Limited" may be abbreviated as "Ltd." and the word "Company" may be abbreviated as "Co."

A professional LLC name must contain the words "Professional Limited Liability Company" or "Professional Limited Company" or "PLLC" or "PLC." Professional LLCs are those whose members will practice one of the following professions: certified public or public accountant, architect or landscape architect, attorney, chiropractor, dentist, engineer, nurse, occupational therapist, optometrist, osteopath, pharmacist, physical therapist, physician, podiatrist, psychologist or veterinarian.

Name availability may be checked online at the filing office website. An available LLC name can be reserved for 120 days for $15.

Name of LLC Organizational Document

Articles of organization

State-Provided Articles of Organization

The filing office does not provide a fill-in form for articles, but does provide other forms for LLCs (Amendment of Articles, Change of Registered Agent or Office, Certificate of Existence or Authorization, Articles of Dissolution, etc.).

Internet Forms: LLC forms (such as Application for Reservation of Name) can be downloaded from the filing office website.

Filing Fees

$40, payable to the "Secretary of State."

Special Forms and Procedures

After filing your articles, you must file a copy of the file-stamped articles with the county clerk of the county where your LLC's registered office is located.

State Tax Status

Follows IRS classification.

LOUISIANA

Filing Office

Louisiana Secretary of State
Corporations Division
P.O. Box 94125
Baton Rouge, LA 70804-9125
Telephone: 504-925-4704

Filing Office URL

http://www.sec.state.la.us/comm/corp-index.htm

LLC Statutes

The Louisiana LLC Law is contained in Title XXIII (Private Corporations and Associations), Chapter 275, of the Louisiana Statutes, starting with Section 12:1301.

The following website currently does not contain the Louisiana statutes, just information on current and prior legislative bills and a browsable state constitution.

http://www.legis.state.la.us

The filing office publishes a "Corporation Law Book," which includes Limited Liability Company, Partnership, Trademark and Trade Name Laws of the state. The fee for a copy is $10.

LLC Name Requirements

The name of a Louisiana LLC must contain the words "Limited Liability Company" or the abbreviation "L.L.C." or "L.C."

Check LLC name availability by calling the filing office or by checking the name online at the filing office website.

LLC names may be reserved for 60 days for $20.

Name of LLC Organizational Document

Articles of organization

State-Provided Articles of Organization

The filing office provides a fill-in-the-blanks articles of organization form (Form 365), with instructions. The filing office also provides a "Limited Liability Company Initial Report," which must be filed with articles.

Internet Forms: The above forms, plus other forms, such as a Reservation of LLC Name form, can be downloaded from the filing office website.

Filing Fees

$60, payable to "Secretary of State."

Special Forms and Procedures

Attach a completed LLC Initial Report Form, available from the filing office website, to your articles. The LLC's registered agent, who must be named in the initial report, must sign the bottom of the report form in the presence of a notary.

Note: If your articles are filed within five working days of the date of notarization of the initial report form, which is submitted with your articles, the legal date of your LLC's existence begins on the date of notarization (prior to the actual date the articles are filed).

State Tax Status

Follows IRS classification.

MAINE

Filing Office
Secretary of State
Bureau of Corporations, Elections
& Commissions
101 State House Station
Augusta, ME 04333-0101
ATTN: Corporate Examining Section
Telephone: 207-287-3676

Filing Office URL
http://www.state.me.us/sos/cec/
cec.htm

LLC Statutes
The Maine LLC Act is contained in
Title 31 (Partnerships and Associations),
Chapter 13, of the Maine Statutes,
starting with Section 601, and is
browsable from the following Web page:
http://janus.state.me.us/legis/
statutes/31/title31sec601.html

LLC Name Requirements
The name of a Maine LLC must
contain the words "Limited Liability
Company" or the abbreviation "LLC" or
"L.L.C."
The name of a professional LLC
must also contain the words "chartered,"
"Professional Association" or abbrevia-
tion "P.A." For example, "Nesbitt &
Olsen, a chartered limited liability
company"; "Gregory & Wilson, Profes-
sional Association, Limited Liability
Company"; or "The Northbrae Dental
Clinic P.A., limited liability company."

Available LLC names may be
checked online at the filing office
website. An LLC name can be reserved
for 120 days for $20.

Name of LLC Organizational Document
Articles of organization

State-Provided Articles of Organization
The filing office provides fill-in-the-
blanks forms for most LLC filings,
including the articles of organization
(Form MLLC-6). The filing office also
mails WordPerfect 5.1 versions of its
forms, including LLC articles of organization, on disk, at no charge.
Internet Forms: The latest Maine
LLC articles of organization, with
instructions, plus other Maine LLC
forms (Reservation of LLC Name and
others) can be downloaded from the
filing office website.

Filing Fees
$125, payable to the "Secretary of
State."

State Tax Status
Follows IRS classification.

MARYLAND

Filing Office
Maryland Department of
Assessments & Taxation
Corporate Charter Division
Room 809
301 West Preston Street
Baltimore, MD 21201-2392
Telephone: 410-767-1184

Filing Office URL

http://www.dat.state.md.us/sdatweb/charter.html

LLC Statutes

The Maryland LLC Act is contained in the Corporations and Associations heading, Title 4A, starting with Section 4A-101, and is browsable from the following Web page:

http://mgasearch.state.md.us/verity.asp

Call the filing office to request a copy of the Maryland LLC Act. Selected provisions of the Maryland LLC Act are also available online. Also, Prentice-Hall Legal & Financial Services Publishing (212-373-7808) publishes a booklet containing the corporation laws of Maryland and the District of Columbia (includes the LLC statutes) for approximately $20.

LLC Name Requirements

The name of a Maryland LLC must contain the words "Limited Liability Company" or one of the following abbreviations: "LLC," "LC," "L.L.C." or "L.C."

Call the filing office at 410-225-1350 to check name availability. An available name may be reserved for 30 days for a $7 fee.

Note: Every five years, your LLC must file a state-provided form (by September 15) that affirms that the LLC is actively engaged in the business for which it was formed. If you fail to file

this form on time, your LLC can lose its right to use its name.

Name of LLC Organizational Document

Articles of organization

State-Provided Articles of Organization

The filing office provides a fill-in-the-blanks articles of organization form, with instructions.

Internet Forms: The latest Maryland LLC articles of organization form and guidelines for preparing this form, plus other Maryland LLC forms (such as Reservation of LLC Name), can be downloaded from the filing office website. First go to instructions for forming an LLC, then click "Get Form" to download articles.

Filing Fees

$50, payable to "SDAT" (this is the acronym for the State Department of Assessments & Taxation). A certified copy is $6 plus $1 per page extra.

Annual Filing: Every five years, your LLC must file a statement (by September 15) affirming that it is still actively engaged in the business for which it was formed. (Presumably, you may change or expand the original line of business as stated in your articles.)

State Tax Status

Follows IRS classification.

MASSACHUSETTS

Filing Office

Commonwealth of Massachusetts
Corporations Division
One Ashburton Place, 17th Floor
Boston, MA 02108
Telephone: 617-727-9640

Filing Office URL

http://www.state.ma.us/sec/cor

LLC Statutes

The Massachusetts LLC Act is
contained in Title XXII (Corporations),
Chapter 156C, of the Massachusetts
General Laws, starting with Section 1,
and is browsable from the following
Web page:

http://www.magnet.state.ma.us/legis/
laws/mgl/156C-1.htm

The filing office provides a copy of
the LLC Regulations, which contains the
requirements for forming and operating
a Massachusetts LLC.

LLC Name Requirements

The name of a Massachusetts LLC
must contain the words "Limited Liability Company," "Limited Company" or
the abbreviation "LLC," "LC," "L.L.C." or
"L.C." Available LLC names may be
reserved for 30 days for $15.

Name of LLC Organizational Document

Certificate of organization

State-Provided Certificate of Organization

The filing office does not provide a
fill-in-the-blanks form for the "certificate
of organization," but it does provide a
copy of the LLC Regulations, which
contains the requirements for forming
and operating a Massachusetts LLC,
which can help you prepare a Certificate
of Organization.

Internet Forms: Instructions for
preparing the Certificate as well as other
forms (not including the Certificate
itself) are available from the state's
website.

Filing Fees

$500 fee, payable to the "Common-
wealth of Massachusetts."

Annual Fees: You must file an
annual report and pay a fee of $500 per
year.

Special Forms and Procedures

One-member LLCs are not allowed
in Massachusetts at present.

A professional service LLC must
obtain a certificate from the state board
that regulates the profession that states
that each member or manager who will
render a professional service is duly
licensed. Your state professional board
should be able to provide this statement
and help you prepare a certificate of
organization for your professional LLC.

Note for Professionals: Existing
Massachusetts general partnerships that
operate professional practices can
register as Registered Limited Liability
Partnerships instead of converting their
general partnerships to LLCs (the

registration process is simple and provides limited liability protection to the LLP partners). For more information, see the Massachusetts Secretary of the Commonwealth LLP regulations, available upon request.

State Tax Status

Follows IRS classification.

MICHIGAN

Filing Office

Department of Consumer & Industry Services
Bureau of Commercial Services
Corporation Division
7150 Harris Drive
P.O. Box 30054
Lansing, MI 48909
Telephone: 517-241-6400

Filing Office URL

http://www.cis.state.mi.us/bcs/corp

LLC Statutes

The Michigan LLC Act is contained in Chapter 450 (Corporations) of the Michigan Compiled Laws, Act 23 of 1993, starting with Section 450.4101, and is browsable from the following Web page:

http://www.michiganlegislature.org/law/getObject.asp?objName=450-4102&relation=previous

The filing office will send out copy of the Michigan Limited Liability Company Act upon request at no charge.

LLC Name Requirements

The name of a Michigan LLC must contain the words "Limited Liability Company" or the abbreviation "LLC," "LC," "L.L.C." or "L.C."

The name of a professional service LLC must instead include one of the following words or abbreviations: "Professional Limited Liability Company," "PLLC," "P.L.L.C.," "PLC." or "P.L.C."

An available LLC name can be reserved for six months for $25.

Name of LLC Organizational Document

Articles of organization

State-Provided Articles of Organization

The filing office provides a fill-in-the-blanks articles of organization form (Form C & S 700), with instructions. If you are converting a partnership to an LLC, use Form C & S 753 instead. If you are forming a professional LLC, use Form C & S 701 (if your LLC will perform licensed services in the professions of public accountant, dentist, osteopathic physician, physician, surgeon, doctor of divinity or other clergy, or attorney). Or if you are converting a professional partnership to a professional LLC, use Form C & S 753p.

Internet Forms: The latest versions of all of Michigan LLC forms, plus instructions and the state's guidelines for approving each form, can be found on the filing office website.

Note: Articles can be filed electronically after filling out a "Mich-Elf" application to get a filer number. Call 517-214-6400 for more information or read about the Mich-Elf system on the filing office website.

Filing Fees

$50 nonrefundable fee, payable to the "State of Michigan."

Special Forms and Procedures

Use Form C & S 753 instead of the standard articles if converting a partnership to an LLC.

Use Form C & S 701 instead to file articles for a professional LLC—if your LLC will perform licensed services in the professions of public accountant, dentist, osteopathic physician, physician, surgeon, doctor of divinity or other clergy, or attorney. Or use Form C & S 753p if converting a professional partnership to a professional LLC.

State Tax Status

Michigan imposes a 2.3% tax on the LLC's tax base.

MINNESOTA

Filing Office

Minnesota Secretary of State
Business Services Division
180 State Office Building
100 Constitution Avenue
St. Paul, MN 55155-1299
Telephone: 612-297-1455

Filing Office URL

http://www.sos.state.mn.us/business/index.html

LLC Statutes

The Minnesota LLC Act is contained in Chapter 322B of the Minnesota Statutes, starting with Section 322B.01, and is browsable from the following Web page:
http://www.revisor.leg.state.mn.us/stats/322B/

LLC Name Requirements

The name of a Minnesota LLC must contain the words "Limited Liability Company" or the abbreviation "LLC." LLC names cannot include the words "incorporated" or "corporation" or their abbreviations.

Professional LLCs must, instead, choose a name which ends with one of the following words or abbreviations: "Professional Limited Liability Company," "Limited Liability Company," "PLC" or "P.L.L.C."

You can check name availability by calling 612-296-2803. An LLC name may be reserved for $35.

Name of LLC Organizational Document

Articles of organization
(Managers are called Governors)

State-Provided Articles of Organization

The filing office provides a fill-in-the-blanks articles of organization form, with instructions.

Internet Forms: articles and other forms are available for downloading from the filing office website.

Filing Fees

$135, payable to the "Minnesota Secretary of State."

State Tax Status

Follows IRS classification.

MISSISSIPPI

Filing Office

Mississippi Secretary of State
Corporate Division
P.O. Box 136
Jackson, MS 39205-0136
Telephone: 601-359-1333

Filing Office URL

http://www.sos.state.ms.us

LLC Statutes

The Mississippi LLC Act is contained in Title 79 (Corporations, Associations and Partnerships) of the Mississippi Code, Chapter 29, starting with Section 79-29-101, and is browsable from the following Web page:

http://www.michie.com/resources1.html

LLC Name Requirements

The name of a Mississippi LLC must contain the words "Limited Liability Company" or the abbreviation "LLC" or "L.L.C."

Professional service LLCs must instead choose a name which includes one of the following words or abbreviations: "Professional Limited Liability Company," "Limited Liability Company," "PLLC" or "P.L.L.C."

Your LLC name must fit on the two lines of the name field on the state certificate of formation form, with no more than 60 characters per line.

An available LLC name can be reserved for 180 days for $25.

Name of LLC Organizational Document

Certificate of formation

State-Provided Certificate of Formation

The filing office provides a fill-in certificate of formation (Form 0100).

Internet Forms: The latest version of the Mississippi LLC certificate of formation (Form F100) can be downloaded from the filing office website (you also can fill in the form online as explained below). It is provided in Microsoft Word document format—the state website also provides a link to allow you to download the Microsoft Word viewer program (a free download) to view and fill in the Word version of the certificate of formation offline.

If you have installed the OmniForm program on your computer, or installed the OmniForm Internet Filler Plug-in available free from the filing office website, you can view, fill in and print this certificate of formation online. You also must install the barcode font on your system as explained on the filing office website. (The barcode font is available for downloading from the website, and is named "3of9.TTF." It should be copied to your system folder as explained in the website instructions.) Before printing the articles, make sure a barcode appears in the upper-left corner of pages 1 and 2 of the form.

Filing Fees
$50, payable to the "Secretary of State."

State Tax Status
Follows IRS classification. [Section 79-29-112 of the MS LLC Act]

MISSOURI

Filing Office
Secretary of State
Corporation Division
P.O. Box 778
Jefferson City, MO 65102
Telephone: 573-751-4153

Filing Office URL
http://mosl.sos.state.mo.us/bus-ser/soscor.html

LLC Statutes
The Missouri LLC Act is contained in Title XXIII (Corporations, Associations and Partnerships) of the Missouri Statutes, Chapter 347, starting with Section 347.010, and is browsable from the following Web page:

http://www.moga.state.mo.us/STATUTES/C347.HTM

The filing office will send out a copy of the Missouri Limited Liability Company Act upon request at no charge.

LLC Name Requirements
The name of a Missouri LLC must contain the words "Limited Liability Company," "Limited Company" or the abbreviations "LLC," "LC," "L.L.C." or "L.C." It may not contain the abbreviation "Ltd."

An available LLC name can be reserved for $25.

Name of LLC Organizational Document
Articles of organization

State-Provided Articles of Organization
The filing office provides a fill-in-the-blanks articles of organization form (LLC-1), with instructions.

Internet Forms: The Missouri articles of organization form, plus other forms, are available for downloading from the filing office website.

Filing Fees
$105, payable to the "Director of Revenue."

Special Forms and Procedures
Professionals should form a Limited Liability Partnership (LLP) instead of an LLC. Ask the filing office for the LLP organization form.

State Tax Status
Follows IRS classification.

MONTANA

Filing Office
Montana Secretary of State
Corporation Bureau
P.O. Box 202801
Helena, MT 59620-2801
Telephone: 406-444-3665

Filing Office URL
http://www.state.mt.us/sos/
Business_Services/business_services
.html

LLC Statutes
The Montana LLC Act is contained in Title 35 (Corporations, Partnerships and Associations) of the Montana Code, Chapter 8, starting with Section 35-8-101, and is browsable from the following Web page (first expand Title 35 in the table of contents pane, then expand Chapter 8):

http://statedocs.msl.state.mt.us/cgi-bin/om_isapi.dll?clientID=19210 &infobase =mca_99.nfo&softpage= Browse_Frame_Pg

LLC Name Requirements
The name of a Montana LLC must contain the words "Limited Liability Company" or "Limited Company" or the abbreviations "LLC," "LC," "L.L.C." or "L.C."

If you are forming a professional liability company, the LLC name must instead contain the words "Professional Limited Liability Company," "Professional L.L.C." or the abbreviation "P.L.L.C."

An available LLC name may be reserved for $10.

Name of LLC Organizational Document
Articles of organization

State-Provided Articles of Organization
The filing office provides a fill-in-the-blanks articles of organization form (Form dlc-1), plus an LLC fact sheet booklet containing instructions on forming a Montana LLC. The filing office also provides an annual limited liability company report form.

Internet Forms: The latest version of the Montana LLC articles of organization, plus other forms, can be downloaded from the filing office website.

Filing Fees
$70 fee, payable to the "Montana Secretary of State."

Special Forms and Procedures
If you are forming a professional LLC, on the articles of organization form, check the box in the First Article that reads "Professional Limited Liability Company." Also, insert the type of professional services in the blank in the Seventh Article.

State Tax Status
Follows IRS classification.

NEBRASKA

Filing Office

Nebraska Secretary of State
Corporate Division
P.O. Box 94608
Lincoln, NE 68509-4608
Telephone: 402-471-4079

Filing Office URL

http://www.nol.org/home/SOS/
corps/corpform.htm

LLC Statutes

The Nebraska LLC Act is contained in Chapter 21 (Corporations and Other Companies) of the Nebraska Statutes, starting with Section 21-2601, and is browsable from the Web page listed below. The quickest way to get to the LLC Act is to type "LLC" (include the quotes) in the search box and press enter. A list of statutes appears in the found box. Among the found statutes you should see Section 21-2604, close to the start of the first section of the LLC Act. Select this section, then navigate forward and back through the various sections of the act. (It takes too long to go to the LLC Act by expanding Chapter 21 in the table of contents pane.)

http://statutes.unicam.state.ne.us/
Statutes

LLC Name Requirements

The name of a Nebraska LLC must end with the words "Limited Liability Company," or the abbreviation "LLC" or "L.L.C."

Note: Identification of your company as an LLC (by including the above words or abbreviation in your LLC name) must appear on all correspondence, stationery, checks, invoices and documents executed by the LLC. Failure to comply can result in personal liability for LLC members and managers (see Nebraska LLC Act, Section 21-2604).

An available LLC name may be reserved for 120 days for $20.

Name of LLC Organizational Document

Articles of organization

State-Provided Articles of Organization

The filing office provides a fill-in-the-blanks articles of organization form (Form 2606).

Internet Forms: The latest version of the Nebraska LLC articles of organization form, plus other LLC forms, can be downloaded from the filing office website.

Filing Fees

$100, payable to the "Secretary of State," plus $5 per page of articles. Add $10 to receive a certificate of organization from the Secretary of State after filing.

Special Forms and Procedures

Professional LLCs should use "Application for Registration as a Professional Limited Liability Company" instead of the standard articles. This form is available on the filing office website.

State Tax Status
Follows IRS classification.

NEVADA

Filing Office
Secretary of State
New Filings Section
101 N. Carson Street, Suite 3
Carson City, NV 89701-4786
Telephone: 775-684-5708
Filings may also be made at the
Secretary of State's Satellite Office in Las
Vegas (702-486-2880).

Filing Office URL
http://sos.state.nv.us/comm_rec/
index.htm

LLC Statutes
The Nevada LLC Act is contained in
Title 7 (Business Associations; Securities; Commodities), Chapter 86, of the
Nevada Statutes, starting with Section
86.011, and is browsable from the
following Web page:
http://www.leg.state.nv.us
The filing office sends out a copy of
Nevada's LLC statutes at no charge. A
copy of the Nevada LLC law also can be
obtained upon request from the Legislative Counsel Bureau, Publications
Division, at 702-687-6800.

LLC Name Requirements
The name of a Nevada LLC must
contain the words "Limited Liability
Company," "Limited Company" or
"Limited" or the abbreviations "LLC,"
"LC," or "L.L.C." The word "Company"
may be abbreviated as "Co."
To check name availability, call the
filing office. An available LLC name may
be reserved for 90 days for $20.

Name of LLC Organizational Document
Articles of organization

State-Provided Articles of Organization
The filing office provides a fill-in-
the-blanks articles of organization form
(CORPART1999.01), with instructions.
Internet Forms: The latest version of
the Nebraska LLC articles of organization form, plus other LLC forms, can be
downloaded from the filing office
website.

Filing Fees
$125, plus $10 for the certification
of one copy of the articles, payable to the
"Secretary of State."

State Tax Status
Nevada does not have a state income
tax scheme, and there is no special state
entity tax levied on LLCs.

NEW HAMPSHIRE

Filing Office
New Hampshire Secretary of State
State House, Room 204
107 North Main Street
Concord, NH 03301-4989
Telephone: 603-271-3244

Filing Office URL
http://www.state.nh.us/sos/corpo-
rate/index.htm

LLC Statutes

The New Hampshire LLC Act is contained in Title 28 (Partnerships), Chapter 304C, of the New Hampshire Statutes, starting with Section 304-C:1, and is browsable from the Web page listed below. Click the heading for Chapter 304C to go to the index of sections of the LLC Act.

http://sudoc.nhsl.lib.nh.us/rsa/default.htm

You can order a copy of the New Hampshire LLC Law for approximately $20 by calling the New Hampshire State Library at 603-271-2144 (it will cost approximately $10 if you go to the library and make copies yourself). As an alternative, a copy of New Hampshire's Corporations, Partnerships and Associations law, which includes the LLC statutes, is available from Butterworth Legal Publishers in Oxford, New Hampshire, for $30 (603-353-4223), or from the Mitchie Company, Charlottesville, Virginia (800-446-3410).

LLC Name Requirements

The name of a New Hampshire LLC must contain the words "Limited Liability Company" or the abbreviations "LLC" or "L.L.C." The state specifically says that an additional space may be inserted between the letters or periods in either of these two abbreviations. The name may contain the words "company," "association," "club," "foundation," "fund," "institute," "society," "union,"

"syndicate," "limited" or "trust" or abbreviations of these words.

If you are forming a professional LLC, the LLC name must instead end with the words "Professional Limited Liability Company" or the abbreviation "P.L.L.C."

An available LLC name may be reserved for 120 days for $15.

Name of LLC Organizational Document

Certificate of formation

State-Provided Certificate of Formation

The filing office provides a fill-in-the-blanks certificate of formation form (Form LLC 1), with instructions, and an addendum to certificate of formation (Form LLC-1-A).

Internet Forms: The New Hampshire LLC certificate of formation and other forms are available on the filing office website.

Filing Fees

$85, payable to the "Secretary of State." This fee includes $50 for filing the Addendum form.

Annual Fees: LLCs must pay an annual report fee of $100.

Special Forms and Procedures

Attach a completed "addendum to certificate of formation" (Form LLC 1-A), available from the filing office website, to your certificate of formation. The Addendum states that the offer and sale of interests in the LLC will be made according to specific New Hampshire security law requirements. Most smaller

LLCs will be able to check Item 1, which certifies that the LLC is eligible for the New Hampshire small offering exemption for securities interests sold without advertising, to ten or fewer persons, within 60 days after the date of formation of the business (the date the LLC articles are filed). Otherwise, you must complete Item 2 or 3 on the form. If you have questions, call the New Hampshire Division of Securities Regulation (613-271-3244) or ask a small business lawyer for help in preparing this form and meeting the requirements of state securities law.

State Tax Status
Follows IRS classification.

NEW JERSEY

Filing Office
New Jersey Department of Treasury
Division of Revenue
Corporate Filings
P.O. Box 308
Trenton, NJ 08625-0308
Telephone: 609-292-9292

Filing Office URL
http://www.state.nj.us/njbgs

LLC Statutes
The New Jersey LLC Act is contained in Title 42 (Partnerships and Partnership Associations), Chapter 2B, of the New Jersey Statutes, starting with Section 42:2B-1, and is browsable from the following Web page:

http://www.njleg.state.nj.us

LLC Name Requirements
The name of a New Jersey LLC must include the words "Limited Liability Company" or the abbreviation "L.L.C."

Name availability can be checked by phone by calling 609-530-8312. Dial-in direct-access of name availability also can be used; for sign up information, call 609-530-6400.

An available LLC name may be reserved for 120 days for $50.

Name of LLC Organizational Document
Certificate of formation

State-Provided Certificate of Formation
New Jersey does not provide a standard Certificate of Formation form. Instead, New Jersey provides an online LLC formation and business registration service. (Go to the home page of the LLC filing office and click on "Services/ Online Services," then scroll to the list of Online Services and select "One-Stop Business Filing and Registration.")

If you do not have an Internet connection or prefer to file paperwork to form your LLC, complete the New Jersey Business Registration Package (Form NJ-REG), which includes a two-page Public Record Filing for New Business Entity portion that can be used to form an LLC. (Form NJ-REG is available by calling the filing office at the number above.) Unless you do not have an Internet connection, we recommend you form your LLC online rather than by completing and mailing the NJ-REG form.

Filing Fees
Check or money order for $100, payable to "Secretary of State." Expedited filing is $10 extra.

State Tax Status
Follows IRS classification.

NEW MEXICO

Filing Office
State Corporation Commission
Corporation Department
Chartered Documents Bureau
P.O. Drawer 1269
Santa Fe, NM 87504-1269
Telephone: 1-800-947-4722

Filing Office URL
http://www.nmprc.state.nm.us

LLC Statutes
The New Mexico LLC Act is contained in Chapter 53 (Corporations), Article 19, of the New Mexico Statutes, starting with Section 53-19-1, and is browsable from the following Web page:
http://www.michie.com/resources1.html

LLC Name Requirements
The name of a New Mexico LLC must contain the words "Limited Liability Company" or "Limited Company" or one of the following abbreviations: "LLC," "LC," "L.L.C." or "L.C." The word "Limited" may be abbreviated as "Ltd."

and the word "Company" may be abbreviated as "Co."

An available LLC name may be reserved for 120 days for $20.

Name of LLC Organizational Document
Articles of organization

State-Provided Articles of Organization
The filing office provides a fill-in-the-blanks articles of organization form (Form NMSCC DLLC-CD), with instructions, which includes an Affidavit of Acceptance of Appointment of Registered Agent (which must be completed and filed with the articles).

Internet Forms: New Mexico LLC articles, with instructions, plus other forms, are available for downloading from the filing office website.

Filing Fees
$50, payable to the "State Corporation Commission."

State Tax Status
Follows IRS classification.

NEW YORK

Filing Office
Department of State
Division of Corporations
State Records and Uniform
Commercial Code
41 State Street
Albany, NY 12231
Telephone: 518-473-2492

Filing Office URL

http://www.dos.state.ny.us/corp/
corpspub.html

LLC Statutes

The New York LLC Law is contained
in Chapter 34 of the New York Consoli-
dated Laws, starting with Section 101,
and is browsable from the following
Web page:

http://assembly.state.ny.us/leg

The filing office provides a copy of
the New York Limited Liability Company Law at no charge.

LLC Name Requirements

The name of a New York LLC must
contain the words "Limited Liability
Company" or the abbreviations "LLC" or
"L.L.C."

Professional Service LLCs: If you are
forming a professional LLC, your LLC
name must instead end with the words
"Professional Limited Liability Company" or "Limited Liability Company" or
the abbreviation "P.L.L.C.," "PLLC,"
"LLC" or "L.L.C." Your LLC name may
have to conform to additional rules
enforced by the state board that regulates your profession.

Certain words may not be contained
in a New York LLC name unless special
permission is obtained from the state.
These prohibited or restricted words
include the following: community
renewal, tenant relocation, urban
development, urban relocation, acceptance, guaranty, annuity, indemnity,
assurance, insurance, investment,
benefit, loan, bond, mortgage, casualty,
savings, surety, endowment, title,
fidelity, trust, finance and underwriter.
The names of professions, such as
"doctor," "lawyer" and the like should
not be used except with the permission
of the state board that regulates the
particular profession.

The availability of proposed LLC
names cannot be checked over the
phone. Instead, mail a letter to the filing
office, by snail mail or email, to ask if a
name is currently available ($5 per name
for checking LLC name availability). The
email address is
corporations@dos.state.ny.us. An
available LLC name may be reserved for
60 days for $20.

Name of LLC Organizational Document

Articles of organization

State-Provided Articles of Organization

The filing office provides a fill-in-
the-blanks articles of organization (Form
DOS-1336), with instructions. To file
articles for a professional LLC, use Form
DOS-1374 instead. If you are converting
your partnership to an LLC, use Form
DOS-1363.

Internet Forms: The filing office
offers its forms for downloading on its
website, including standard LLC articles
of organization, articles of Conversion of
a Partnership to an LLC, and articles of
organization for a Professional Service
LLC. The state office also provides a

booklet titled "Forming a Limited Liability Company in NY," which can be downloaded from the site. I recommend you obtain this guide—it contains specific instructions to the state articles forms, plus useful LLC legal and tax information.

Filing Fees

$200, payable to the "Department of State." Fees may be paid by check or money order (but if over $500, must be paid by certified check).

Special Forms and Procedures

Within 120 days of filing your articles, you must publish a copy of the information in your articles for six successive weeks in two newspapers in the county where your LLC principal office is located. A local newspaper can help you make this filing (the county clerk in your area has a list of approved newspapers to use when making this publication). After publication, an affidavit of publication must be mailed to the filing office. The newspapers you use should be able to help you meet this affidavit filing requirement (the filing fee for each affidavit is $25).

If you wish to convert a general or limited partnership to a New York LLC, the filing office provides a special Certificate of Conversion form (Form DOS-1363). If you are converting an existing New York limited partnership to an LLC, the conversion does not become effective until a Certificate of Cancellation form (available from the filing office) is filed with the filing office.

Note: there is also a Certificate of Conversion form (Form DOS-1364) posted on the state website for use by LLCs that first file standard articles, then file a Certificate of Conversion. We suggest you use Form 1363 instead, rather than using this alternate, two-step procedure. The two procedures are contained in Section 1006 of the NY LLC Act, which can be browsed through a link on the filing office website.

If your LLC will provide licensed professional services, use the state-provided articles of organization for a professional service company (Form DOS-1374) instead of the standard articles. The state website proves a link to the list of professions that must use this special form to form a professional LLC. You must also obtain a certificate from the New York licensing board that regulates your profession, stating that all LLC members and managers hold valid licenses to practice the professional service rendered through the LLC. A copy of this certificate must be attached to your original articles filed with the filing office. Also, a certified copy of the articles must be filed with the New York licensing board for the profession within 30 days after filing with the Department of State.

State Tax Status

Follows IRS classification, but the state levies a tax on the LLC based upon the number of LLC members.

NORTH CAROLINA

Filing Office

North Carolina Department of the Secretary of State
Corporations Division
P.O. Box 29622
Raleigh, NC 27626-0622
Telephone: 919-807-2225
Toll Free: 888-246-7636

Filing Office URL

http://www.secretary.state.nc.us/corporations

LLC Statutes

The North Carolina LLC Act is contained in Chapter 57C of the North Carolina Statutes, starting with Section 57C-1-01, and is browsable from the following Web page:

http://www.secstate.state.nc.us

LLC Name Requirements

The name of a North Carolina LLC must end with the words "Limited Liability Company" or the abbreviation "L.L.C." The words "Limited" and "Company" may be abbreviated to "Ltd." and "Co."

If you are forming a professional LLC, your LLC name must instead end with the words "Professional Limited Liability Company" or the abbreviation "P.L.L.C." Your professional LLC name may have to conform to additional rules enforced by the state board that regulates your profession.

You can check the availability of a name for your LLC on the filing office website. An available LLC name may be reserved for $10.

Name of LLC Organizational Document

Articles of organization

State-Provided Articles of Organization

The filing office provides a fill-in-the-blanks articles of organization form (Form L-01). If you are forming a professional LLC, use Form PLLC-02 instead of the standard articles. If you are converting an existing general or limited partnership to an LLC, use Form L-01A instead of the standard articles.

Internet Forms: The articles of organization form, with instructions, plus other forms, are available for downloading from the Corporations Division website (follow the links to the corporations section; it contains the LLC forms). A guide to incorporating, which includes helpful name, trademark and securities law information applicable to LLCs, plus state business and licensing office listings, is also available for downloading.

Filing Fees

$125, payable to "Secretary of State."

Special Forms and Procedures

Professional articles (Form PLLC-02), available from the state's website, should be used to form a professional LLC.

Conversion articles (Form L-01A), available from the state's website, should be used to convert an existing general or limited partnership to an LLC.

State Tax Status

Follows IRS classification.

NORTH DAKOTA

Filing Office

North Dakota Secretary of State
Corporations Division
600 East Boulevard Avenue
Bismarck, ND 58505-0500
Telephone: 701-328-4284

Filing Office URL

http://www.state.nd.us/sec/Business/businessinforegmnu.htm

LLC Statutes

The North Dakota LLC Act is contained in Title 10-32 of the North Dakota Century Code, starting with Section 10-32-01, and is browsable from the Web page listed below. Select Chapter 10-32 in the table of contents pane to go to the start of the LLC Act.

http://www.state.nd.us/lr

You may order the North Dakota LLC Act from the filing office for $27.

LLC Name Requirements

The name of a North Dakota LLC must contain the words "Limited Liability Company" or the abbreviation "LLC" or "L.L.C." It cannot contain the words "bank," "banker" or "banking."

An available LLC name may be reserved for 12 months for $10.

Name of LLC Organizational Document

Articles of organization
(Managers are called Governors)

State-Provided Articles of Organization

The filing office provides a fill-in-the-blanks articles of organization form (Form 115-LCA), with instructions. The last page of this form is an "original appointment of agent," which must be filed with the articles.

Internet Forms: The filing office website provides a brochure summarizing state LLC requirements that includes a sample articles of organization form that you can use to prepare your own form. The website also offers a Registered Agent Consent to Serve form.

Filing Fees

$135 ($125 for filing articles, plus $10 for filing Registered Agent Consent to Serve form), payable to the "Secretary of State."

Special Forms and Procedures

LLCs created to perform licensed professional services should file articles of organization for a Professional Limited

Liability Company; a sample form is available from the filing office together with a separate brochure summarizing the requirements. (This is not yet available online.)

State Tax Status
Follows IRS classification.

OHIO

Filing Office
Ohio Secretary of State
Business Services Division
P.O. Box 1329
Columbus, OH 43216
Telephone: 614-466-3910
Toll Free: 877-SOS-FILE (877-767-3453)

Filing Office URL
http://www.state.oh.us/sos

LLC Statutes
The Ohio LLC Act is contained in Title XVII (Corporations-Partnerships), Chapter 1705, of the Ohio Statutes, starting with Section 1705.01, and is browsable from the following Web page:
http://onlinedocs.anderson
publishing.com

LLC Name Requirements
The name of the limited liability company must include the words

"limited liability company," "LLC," "L.L.C.," "limited," "Ltd" or "Ltd."
Call the filing office for name availability (or email your name availability request to busserv@sos.state.oh.us). Names may be reserved for 60 days for a $5 fee.

Name of LLC Organizational Document
Articles of organization

State-Provided Articles of Organization
The filing office provides a fill-in-the-blanks articles of organization form (Form 115-LCA), with instructions, along with an original appointment of agent (Form LCO), which must be filed with the articles.
Internet Forms: The Secretary of State's website provides downloadable LLC forms. Click the link to Corporate Filing Forms that appears under the Business Services Information heading on the main SOS page.
The One Stop Business Permit Center (800-248-4040), operated by the Ohio Department of Development, also provides some state LLC forms.

Filing Fees
$85 fee, payable to the "Ohio Secretary of State."

State Tax Status
Follows IRS classification.

OKLAHOMA

Filing Office

Oklahoma Secretary of State
2300 N. Lincoln Blvd.
Room 101
State Capitol Building
Oklahoma City, OK 73105-4897
Telephone: 405-522-4560

Filing Office URL

http://www.sos.state.ok.us/business/
business%20information.htm

LLC Statutes

The Oklahoma LLC Act is contained in Title 18 (Corporations) of the Oklahoma Statutes, starting with Section 18-2000, and is browsable from the Web page listed below. It's best to restrict your search of Oklahoma statutes to Title 18 (Corporations). Type "2000" (without quotes) in the "Search Oklahoma Statutes Database" box to find Section 18-2000 (the start of the LLC Act). Note that the text of each statute is provided in rtf format, and you must download rtf files section by section.

http://www2.lsb.state.ok.us/tsrs/
os_oc.htm

LLC Name Requirements

The name of an Oklahoma LLC must contain the words "Limited Liability Company" or "Limited Company" or the abbreviations "LLC," "LC," "L.L.C." or "L.C." The word "Limited" may be abbreviated as "Ltd." and "Company" may be abbreviated as "Co."

Call the filing office to check name availability. An available LLC name may be reserved for 60 days for $10.

Name of LLC Organizational Document

Articles of organization

State-Provided Articles of Organization

The filing office provides a sample articles of organization form (SOS Form 0073), with instructions.

Licensed professionals should use SOS Form 01, professional articles of organization, instead of the standard articles.

Internet Forms: LLC forms, including the latest articles of organization forms, are available for downloading from the filing office website.

Filing Fees

$100, payable to the "Secretary of State."

Special Forms and Procedures

Licensed professionals should use SOS Form 01, professional articles of organization, instead of the standard articles. A downloadable form is available from the filing office website.

State Tax Status

Follows IRS classification.

OREGON

Filing Office

Oregon Secretary of State
Corporation Division
255 Capitol Street, NE, Suite 151

Salem, OR 97310-1327
Telephone: 503-986-2200

Filing Office URL

http://www.sos.state.or.us/corpora-
tion/bizreg/bizreg.htm

LLC Statutes

The Oregon LLC Act is contained in
Chapter 63 of the Oregon Statutes,
starting with Section 63.001, and is
browsable from the following Web page:

http://www.leg.state.or.us/ors/
063.html

The filing office may provide a copy
of the Oregon Limited Liability Company Act upon request (free or for a $5
fee).

LLC Name Requirements

The name of an Oregon LLC must
contain the words "Limited Liability
Company" or the abbreviation "LLC" or
"L.L.C." May not contain the words
"Cooperative," "Limited Partnership" or
the abbreviation "L.P."

Call the filing office to check name
availability. An available LLC name may
be reserved for 120 days for $10.

Name of LLC Organizational Document

Articles of organization

State-Provided Articles of Organization

The filing office provides a sample
articles of organization form (Form
CR151), with instructions.

Internet Forms: The articles form,
with instructions, plus other forms, are
available on the filing office website (see
Business Registry Forms).

Filing Fees

$40, payable by check to the "Cor-
poration Division." (Credit cards can
also be used; the card number and
expiration date should be submitted on a
separate sheet of paper.)

Special Forms and Procedures

If you are forming an LLC to practice
one of a number of special professions
(such as law, accounting or medicine),
Article 8 of your articles of organization
must specify the type of professional
services your LLC will perform. The state
licensing board that regulates your
profession can tell you if your profession
must comply with this requirement (as
well as other requirements relating to
Oregon professional LLCs).

State Tax Status

Follows IRS classification.

PENNSYLVANIA

Filing Office

Commonwealth of Pennsylvania
Department of State
Corporation Bureau
P.O. Box 8722
Harrisburg, PA 17105-8722
Telephone: 717-787-1057

Filing Office URL

http://www.dos.state.pa.us/corp/
index.htm

LLC Statutes

The Pennsylvania LLC Act is contained in Title 19 (Corporations and Business Associations), Chapter 89, of the Pennsylvania Statutes, starting with Section 8901. The LLC Act (Chapter 89) had not been added to the browsable chapter lists in Title 19 at the time of our research. Please check the following Web page to see if it has been added to Title 19:

http://www.pacode.com/secure/data/019/019toc.html

LLC Name Requirements

The name of a Pennsylvania LLC must contain the words "Company," "Limited" or "Limited Liability Company" or the abbreviation "LLC." The word "Limited" can be abbreviated as "Ltd.," and the word "Company" as "Co."

The availability of up to three names can be checked per phone call by calling the filing office. An available name can be reserved for 120 days for $52.

Name of LLC Organizational Document

Certificate of organization

State-Provided Certificate of Organization

The filing office provides a fill-in-the-blanks certificate of organization form, with instructions, as well as an "LLC docketing statement," which must be filed with the certificate.

Internet Forms: Pennsylvania LLC articles, with instructions, plus other forms, are available on the filing office website. LLC forms on disk are also available from the filing office (Microsoft Word and WordPerfect versions) for $52 each.

Filing Fees

$100 fee, payable to the "Department of State."

Annual Fees: An annual registration fee of at least $330 is payable to the Department of State.

Special Forms and Procedures

Submit an original certificate of organization form and three copies of the LLC docketing statement (available from the state website). Also enclose a stamped, self-addressed postcard (or an envelope with an additional copy of the articles enclosed) to obtain a receipt (or a file-stamped copy of your articles) from the filing office.

If you are forming one of the special, restricted professional LLCs, you may be required to attach a consent form to your articles, which shows board approval of the formation of your LLC (the board first checks to make sure all members/managers are licensed). If a professional association is being converted to an LLC, you may be required to file a "certificate of election by professional association of LLC," available for downloading from the filing office website. Check with the Corporation Bureau or your professional association board for more information.

State Tax Status

The state generally taxes LLCs as corporations (except for certain professional service LLCs). One consequence of this treatment is that a Pennsylvania LLC may make a state S corporation tax election. [Section 8925 of the PA LLC Act]

RHODE ISLAND

Filing Office

Rhode Island Secretary of State
Corporations Division
100 North Main Street
Providence, RI 02903-1335
Telephone: 401-222-3040

Filing Office URL

http://155.212.254.78/corporations.htm

LLC Statutes

The Rhode Island LLC Act is contained in Title 7 (Corporations, Associations and Partnerships), Chapter 7-16, of the Rhode Island General Laws, starting with Section 7-16-1, and is browsable from the following Web page:

http://www.rilin.state.ri.us/Statutes/TITLE7/7-16/INDEX.HTM

LLC Name Requirements

The name of a Rhode Island LLC must end with the words "Limited Liability Company" or the abbreviations "LLC" or "L.L.C." Upper and lower case abbreviations are specifically permitted.

Call the filing office to check name availability. An available name may be reserved for 120 days for a fee of $50.

Name of LLC Organizational Document

Articles of organization

State-Provided Articles of Organization

The filing office provides a fill-in-the-blanks articles of organization form (Form 400).

Internet Forms: LLC articles plus other forms can be downloaded from the filing office website.

Filing Fees

$150, payable to the "Rhode Island Secretary of State."

State Tax Status

Follows IRS classification.

SOUTH CAROLINA

Filing Office

South Carolina Secretary of State
Corporations Department
P.O. Box 11350
Columbia, SC 29211
Telephone: 803-734-2158

Filing Office URL

http://www.scsos.com/Corporations.htm

LLC Statutes

The new South Carolina LLC Act, effective as of January 1, 2001, is contained in Title 33 (Corporations, Partnerships and Associations), Chapter 44, of the South Carolina Code, starting with Section 33-44-101, and is browsable from the following Web page:

http://www.lpitr.state.sc.us/code/t33c044.htm

The prior LLC Act (Title 33, Chapter 43—repealed as of January 1, 2001) is browsable from the following Web page:

http://www.lpitr.state.sc.us/code/t33c043.htm

LLC Name Requirements

The name of a South Carolina LLC must contain the words "Limited Liability Company" or "Limited Company" or the abbreviations "L.L.C.," "LLC," "LC," or "L.C." The word "Limited" may be abbreviated as "Ltd." and the word "Company" may be abbreviated as "Co."

If you are creating an LLC to perform professional services, such as accounting, medicine or law, you may need to comply with special professional LLC name requirements. Call your state licensing board for further information.

An LLC name may be reserved for 120 days by filing two copies of the "Application to Reserve an LLC Name" form along with a $25 fee.

Name of LLC Organizational Document

Articles of organization

State-Provided Articles of Organization

The filing office provides a fill-in-the-blanks articles of organization form, and an articles of organization form for professional LLCs. Here are a few ways to order forms:

Call Kitco, a legal forms supplier, at 800-351-1244. Kitco provides printed fill-in-the-blanks articles for a fee.

Send a check to the filing office for $2 and ask for LLC forms on an IBM PC compatible computer disk (WordPerfect 5.1 format). Articles of organization, with instructions, are in the ARTICLES.LLC file. Forms for LLC name reservation as well as articles of organization of Professional Service LLC are also included on the disk.

Internet Forms: Not available at present time. May be available in the future as the filing office develops its website.

Filing Fees

$110 fee, payable to the "South Carolina Secretary of State."

Special Forms and Procedures

If you are converting an existing partnership to an LLC, obtain a special articles form from the filing office to use to convert an existing partnership to an LLC. This form is not currently available for downloading from the filing office website.

State Tax Status

Follows IRS classification, except: Under Section 12-2-25 of the South Carolina statutes, a one-member LLC that is not taxed by South Carolina for income tax purposes as a corporation is ignored for all South Carolina tax purposes.

SOUTH DAKOTA

Filing Office

South Dakota Secretary of State
State Capitol
500 East Capitol
Pierre, SD 57501-5070
Telephone: 605-773-4845

Filing Office URL

http://www.state.sd.us/sos/Duties/
CORPADMN.HTM

LLC Statutes

The South Dakota LLC Act is
contained in Title 47 (Corporations),
Chapter 34, of the South Dakota Codified Laws, starting with Section 47-34-1,
and is browsable from the following
Web page:

http://www.michie.com/
resources1.html

LLC Name Requirements

The name of a South Dakota LLC
must contain the words "Limited
Liability Company" or "Limited Company" or the abbreviations "L.L.C.,"
"LLC," "LC," or "L.C." The word "Limited" may be abbreviated as "Ltd." and
the word "Company" may be abbreviated as "Co."

An available LLC name can be
reserved for 120 days for $15.

Name of LLC Organizational Document

Articles of organization
(Managers are called governors.)

State-Provided Articles of Organization

The filing office provides a fill-in-
the-blanks articles of organization form,
with instructions, plus a copy of the
South Dakota Limited Liability Company
Act (Chapter 47-34 of the South Dakota
Codified Laws), upon request, at no
charge.

Internet Forms: LLC articles, plus
other forms, are available for downloading online at the filing office website.

A South Dakota "Business Startup
Package" is available from: http://
www.state.sd.us/state/executive/oed/
doingb.htm.

Special Forms and Procedures

The articles must be accompanied by
the LLC's first annual report. This form
is available at the filing office website.

Filing Fees

Payable to the "Secretary of State," as
follows:

LLCs with less than $50,000 of capital:	$90
LLCs with $50,001–$100,000 of capital:	$150
LLCs with more than $100,000 of capital:	$150 plus 50 cents for each additional $1,000 of capital over the first $100,000.

State Tax Status

South Dakota does not impose a
state income tax.

TENNESSEE

Filing Office

Tennessee Department of State
Division of Business Services
Corporations Section
312 Eighth Avenue North
6th Floor, William R. Snodgrass
Tower
Nashville, TN 37243
Telephone: 615-741-2286

Filing Office URL

http://www.state.tn.us/sos/
service.htm#corporations

LLC Statutes

The Tennessee LLC Act is contained
in Title 48 (Corporations and Associations), Chapters 201-248, of the Tennessee Code, starting with Section 48-201-
101, and is browsable from the following Web page:

http://www.michie.com/
resources1.html

The filing office will provide a copy
of the Tennessee Limited Liability
Company Act upon request.

LLC Name Requirements

The name of a Tennessee LLC must
contain the words "Limited Liability
Company" or the abbreviations "LLC" or
"L.L.C."

If you are forming a professional
LLC, your LLC name must instead
contain the words "Professional Limited
Liability Company" or "Professional
LLC," "Professional Limited Company,"
or "Limited Liability Professional Com-
pany" or the abbreviations "PLLC,"
"PLC," "P.L.L.C.," "P.L.C." or "L.L.P.C."

The availability of a proposed LLC
name may be checked over the phone by
calling the filing office. An available LLC
name may be reserved for four months
for $20.

Name of LLC Organizational Document

Articles of organization
(Managers are called governors.)

State-Provided Articles of Organization

The filing office provides a fill-in-
the-blanks articles of organization form
(Form SS-4248), with instructions.

Existing general or limited partnerships must convert to a Tennessee LLC
by filing special Form SS-4248, "Articles
of Conversion."

Internet Forms: The standard
articles, with instructions, articles of
conversion, plus other forms, are from
the filing office website. A Limited
Liability Companies Filing Guide is also
available for downloading.

Note: You can ignore the "Certificate
of Formation" form listed in the index to
downloadable forms. It is an optional
form that can be filed to show that the
LLC began its legal existence on a date
after filing of the articles (if you request a
delayed effective date for your articles).

Filing Fees

Minimum fee is $300, payable to the
"Tennessee Secretary of State." (Actual
fee is $50 per LLC member, so, for LLCs

with more than six initial members, the fee will go up by $50 per member.)

Special Forms and Procedures

Existing general or limited partnerships must convert to a Tennessee LLC by filing special Form SS-4248, "Articles of Conversion."

If you are converting an existing partnership to an LLC, use the special state-provided articles instead of standard articles (articles of conversion are available for downloading from the filing office website).

Note: Section 48-205-101(10) of the Tennessee LLC Act requires LLC articles to indicate that the LLC has the power to expel a member if you want your LLC to have this power. If you want your LLC to have this power, you must add a provision to your articles that says the LLC has the power to expel a member (insert this additional provision in Article 9 or on an attachment page to the articles).

There are additional types of provisions that must be included in the articles if you want them to apply to your LLC. For example, if you want to allow some members to have a first right to make additional contributions to the LLC (preemptive rights) or if you want your managers ("governors") to be able to approve transfers of memberships or be able to trigger a dissolution of the LLC, you must add appropriate provisions to your articles.

State Tax Status

Follows IRS classification.

TEXAS

Filing Office

Texas Secretary of State
Filings Division
Corporations Section
P.O. Box 13697
Austin, TX 78711-3697
Telephone: 512-463-5583

Filing Office URL

http://www.sos.state.tx.us/corp/index.shtml

LLC Statutes

The Texas LLC Act is contained in Title 32 (Corporations), Part 3, of the Vernon's Texas Civil Statutes, starting with Article 1.01, and is browsable from the following Web page:

http://www.capitol.state.tx.us/statutes/statutes.html

LLC Name Requirements

The name of a Texas LLC must contain the words "Limited Liability Company" or "Limited Company" or the abbreviations "L.L.C.," "LLC," "LC," "L.C." or "Ltd. Co."

If you are forming a professional LLC, your LLC name must instead contain the words "Professional Limited Liability Company" or the abbreviations "PLLC" or "P.L.L.C."

Name availability may be checked over the phone by calling 512-463-5555 (for a $5 fee) or by emailing corpinfo@sos.state.tx.us (free).

An available LLC name may be reserved for 120 days for $25.

Name of LLC Organizational Document
Articles of organization

State-Provided Articles of Organization
The filing office provides guidelines, or summaries, to draft your own regular or professional articles of organization, but does not provide a blank form. These summaries simply list the requirements for contents of the articles, and do not include the form itself.

For $35, you can order the "Filing Guide for Business Organizations & Nonprofit Associations," which contains instructions and other forms (not articles of organization) for Texas LLCs.

Internet Forms: LLC forms (such as a reservation of name form) are available from the filing office website. Again, the Texas site provides only summaries of the requirements for articles of organization (download Form 205) and for professional articles of organization (Form 206).

Faxed Forms: All forms promulgated by the Corporations Section may be obtained by calling 900-263-0060 (there is a fee of $1 per minute for using the 900 number). A caller may choose to have a form faxed instantaneously or may leave his or her name and mailing address, and the form will be mailed within three business days.

Filing Fees
$200, payable to the "Secretary of State."

Special Forms and Procedures
If you are forming a professional LLC, special requirements apply to the contents of your articles. Guidelines for preparing professional LLC articles can be downloaded from the filing office website.

State Tax Status
Texas LLCs, like Texas corporations, are subject to the payment of state franchise taxes.

UTAH

Filing Office
Utah Division of Corporations & Commercial Code
160 East 300 South, 2nd Floor
Box 146705
Salt Lake City, UT 84114-6705
Telephone: 801-530-4849

Filing Office URL
http://www.commerce.state.ut.us/corporat/corpcoc.htm

LLC Statutes
The Utah LLC Act is contained in Title 48 (Partnership), Chapter 2b, of the Utah Code, starting with Section 48-2b-101, and is browsable from the Web

page listed below. Expand Title 48 in the table of contents pane, then select Title 48-Chapter 02b to go to the start of the LLC Act.

http://www.le.state.ut.us/ Documents/code_const.htm

The filing office provides a photocopy of the Utah Limited Liability Company Act on request (typically at no charge).

LLC Name Requirements

The name of a Utah LLC must contain the words "Limited Liability Company," "Limited Company" or the abbreviations "L.L.C." or "L.C."

An available LLC name may be reserved for 120 days for $20.

Name of LLC Organizational Document
Articles of organization

State-Provided Articles of Organization

The filing office provides sample articles of organization for member-managed LLCs (if you specifically ask for one by phone).

Internet Forms: The filing office website provides a guideline and a sample articles of organization that you can use to draft your own articles of organization, but does not provide a blank form. The site does provide a wealth of information on doing business in the state. Other forms can be downloaded from the filing office website, such as a reservation of business name form.

Filing Fees
$50, payable to "State of Utah."

State Tax Status
Follows IRS classification.

VERMONT

Filing Office
Vermont Secretary of State
81 River Street, Drawer 09
Montpelier, VT 05609-1104
Telephone: 802-828-2386

Filing Office URL
http://www.sec.state.vt.us/corps/ corpindex.htm

LLC Statutes

The Vermont LLC Act is contained in Title 11 (Corporations, Partnerships and Associations), Chapter 21, of the Vermont Statutes, starting with Section 3001, and is browsable from the following Web page:

http://www.leg.state.vt.us/statutes/ title11/chap021.htm#03001

LLC Name Requirements

The name of a Vermont LLC must contain the words "Limited Liability Company" or "Limited Company" or the abbreviations "LLC," "LC," "L.L.C." or "L.C." The word "Limited" may be abbreviated as "Ltd." and the word "Company" may be abbreviated as "Co."

If you are forming a professional LLC, your LLC name must instead include the words "Professional Limited

Liability Company" or "Professional Limited Company" or the abbreviations "PLC," "P.L.C." (presumably, the abbreviations "P.L.L.C." and "PLLC" are also permitted, but these are not specifically mentioned in the professional LLC name statute—Section 3012(c)(5)). Again, the word "Limited" may be abbreviated as "Ltd." and the word "Company" may be abbreviated as "Co."

An LLC name, if available, may be reserved for 120 days for a $20 fee.

Name of LLC Organizational Document
Articles of organization

State-Provided Articles of Organization
The filing office provides a fill-in-the-blanks articles of organization form, with instructions, and background information on forming and running Vermont LLCs.

Internet Forms: Vermont LLC forms, including articles of organization, are available for downloading from the filing office website. It may soon be possible to fill out LLC articles of organization online. Check the website for details.

Filing Fees
$75, payable to "Vermont Secretary of State."

State Tax Status
Follows IRS classification.

VIRGINIA

Filing Office
Clerk of the State Corporation Commission
P.O. Box 1197
First Floor
Richmond, VA 23218-1197
Telephone: 804-371-9733

Filing Office URL
http://www.state.va.us/scc/division/clk/corp.htm

LLC Statutes
The Virginia LLC Act is contained in Title 13 (Corporations) of the Virginia Code, starting with Section 13.1-1000, and is browsable from the following Web page:

http://legis.state.va.us/codecomm/codehome.htm

A copy of the Virginia Corporation Law, which includes Virginia's limited liability company statutes, is available from the State Corporation Commission for $25.

LLC Name Requirements
The name of a Virginia LLC must contain the words "Limited Liability Company" or "Limited Company" or the abbreviations "LLC," "LC," "L.L.C." or "L.C."

If you are forming a professional LLC, your LLC name may instead include the words "Professional Limited Liability Company" or "Professional Limited Company" or the abbreviations

"PLC," "P.L.C.," "PLLC" or "P.L.L.C."
Use of these alternate words or abbreviations is optional—you can stick with the standard LLC designators listed in the first paragraph if you wish.

An available LLC name can be reserved for 120 days for $10.

Name of LLC Organizational Document
Articles of organization

State-Provided Articles of Organization
The filing office provides a fill-in-the-blanks articles of organization form (Form 1011), articles of organization to convert an existing partnership to an LLC (Form 1010.1) and articles of organization for a professional LLC (Form 1103), with instructions for each form.

Persons forming an LLC practice in medicine, law, dentistry, accounting, pharmacy, optometry, behavioral sciences, veterinary medicine or insurance consulting should form a professional LLC. All others should form a regular LLC.

Internet Forms: Virginia LLC forms, including articles of organization forms (Forms 1011, 1010.1 and 1103) are available for downloading from the filing office website. A helpful Business Registration Guide, which contains forms, plus tax, licensing and other state information, is available for downloading.

Filing Fees
$100, payable to "State Corporation Commission."

Special Forms and Procedures
To form a professional LLC, download and use Form 1103 from the filing office website. To convert an existing partnership into a new LLC, use Form 1010.1 (also available from the state website).

State Tax Status
Follows IRS classification.

WASHINGTON

Filing Office
Washington Secretary of State
Corporations Division
P.O. Box 40234
Olympia, WA 98504-0234
Telephone: 360-753-7115

Filing Office URL
http://www.secstate.wa.gov/corps/default.htm

LLC Statutes
The Washington LLC Act is contained in Title 25.15 of the Washington Code, starting with Section 25.15.005, and is browsable from the following Web page:

http://search.leg.wa.gov/wslrcw/
RCW%20%2025%20%20TITLE/
RCW%20%2025%20.%2015%20%20
CHAPTER/RCW%20%2025%20.%
2015%20%20chapter.htm

LLC Name Requirements

The name of a Washington LLC must contain the words "Limited Liability Company," "Limited Liability Co." or the abbreviation "LLC" or "L.L.C."

If you are forming a professional LLC, your LLC name must instead include the words "Professional Limited Liability Company" or "Professional Limited Liability Co." or the abbreviations "PLLC" or "P.L.L.C." Dental service LLCs and others may have additional name requirements and restrictions (for example, the LLC name may need to list the surnames of all members). Check with your state professional licensing board for further information.

Available names can be checked online from the filing office website. The fee to reserve an available LLC name for 180 days is $30.

Name of LLC Organizational Document

Certificate of formation

State-Provided Certificate of Formation

The filing office provides a fill-in-the-blanks certificate of formation form.

Internet Forms: Washington LLC forms, including the certificate of formation form, are available for downloading from the filing office website.

Filing Fees

$175, payable to "Secretary of State."

State Tax Status

State applies a gross income tax on LLCs (which also applies to partnerships). State has no personal income tax.

WEST VIRGINIA

Filing Office

West Virginia Secretary of State
Corporations Division
Bldg. 1, Suite 157-K
1900 Kanawha Blvd. East
Charleston, WV 25305-0770
Telephone: 304-558-8000

Filing Office URL

http://www.state.wv.us/sos/corp/
startup.htm

LLC Statutes

The West Virginia LLC Act is contained in Chapter 31B of the West Virginia Code, starting with Section 31B-1-101, and is browsable from the following Web page:

http://www.state.wv.us/sos/corp/
wvcode31B.htm

The filing office provides a copy of the West Virginia LLC Act upon request.

LLC Name Requirements

The name of a West Virginia LLC must contain the words "Limited Liability Company" or "Limited Company" or the abbreviations "L.L.C.," "LLC," "LC," or "L.C." The word "Limited" may be abbreviated as "Ltd." and the word "Company" may be abbreviated as "Co."

If you are forming a professional LLC, your name must instead include the words "Professional Limited Liability Company" or the abbreviations "Professional L.L.C.," "Professional LLC," "PLLC" or "P.L.L.C."

An available LLC name may be reserved for 120 days for $15.

Name of LLC Organizational Document
Articles of organization

State-Provided Articles of Organization
The filing office provides a standard fill-in articles of organization form (Form LLD-1).

If you are converting a general or limited partnership to an LLC, you'll need to attach a completed Form LLD/F-6, Statement of Conversion (available from the filing office), to your Form LLD-1.

Internet Forms: Articles plus other forms, such as an application to reserve an LLC name, are available for downloading from the filing office website.

Filing Fees
$100, payable to the "Secretary of State."

Special Forms and Procedures
Your organizer must sign the articles of organization in the presence of a Notary Public.

If you are forming a professional LLC (one engaged in the practice of

accounting, architecture, law, chiropody, chiropractic, dentistry, osteopathy, medicine, podiatry or veterinary medicine), check the box in the blank immediately following Article 2. Professional LLCs must attach a list of the names and addresses of all members to their articles (see Article 8). Articles for a professional LLC will not be filed until the filing office receives a confirmation from the state licensing board that all LLC members have current licenses and have met the professional requirements of the board. (The Secretary determines how this confirmation is to be made; it is the responsibility of the organizer(s) to obtain this confirmation.)

If you are converting a general or limited partnership to an LLC, attach a completed Form LLD/F-6, Statement of Conversion (available from the filing office), to your Form LLD-1.

State Tax Status
Follows IRS classification.

WISCONSIN

Filing Office
Department of Financial Institutions
P.O. Box 7846
Madison, WI 53707-7846
Telephone: 608-261-7577

Filing Office URL
http://www.wdfi.org/corporations/default.htm

LLC Statutes

The Wisconsin LLC Act is contained in Chapter 183 of the Wisconsin Statutes, starting with Section 183.0102, and is browsable from the following Web page:

http://folio.legis.state.wi.us/cgi-bin/ om_isapi.dll?clientID=435036&infobase= stats.nfo& jump=ch.%20183&softpage= Browse_Frame_Pg

Send $1.50 to the Department of Financial Institutions to request a copy of the Wisconsin LLC Act (ask for a copy of Chapter 183).

LLC Name Requirements

The name of a Wisconsin LLC must contain the words "Limited Liability Company" or "Limited Liability Co." or end with the abbreviation "LLC" or "L.L.C."

A proposed LLC name, if available, can be reserved by calling the filing office, for a $30 charge. A mailed name reservation request costs $15.

Name of LLC Organizational Document

Articles of organization

State-Provided Articles of Organization

The filing office provides a fill-in-the-blanks articles of organization form, with instructions, plus a free booklet titled, "Starting a Business? Here's Help."

Internet Forms: Wisconsin LLC forms, including articles of organization, are available for downloading from the state website.

Note: The state LLC filing office provides an online LLC formation service called "Quickstart LLC." We recommend you use this online service to form your LLC instead of mailing articles of organization to the state filing office because:

1) the online service costs less ($130 instead of the $170 charge for filing paper articles of organization), and

2) the online service is fast and easy to use and includes a name availability search prior to the acceptance of your online application.

Filing Fees

$170, payable to the "Department of Financial Institutions."

Note: You pay a lower fee ($130) to form your LLC online with the Wisconsin Quickstart LLC service.

State Tax Status

Follows IRS classification. Also note: If treated as partnership, an LLC is subject to a temporary state surcharge tax.

WYOMING

Filing Office

Secretary of State's Office
Corporations Division
The Capitol
Cheyenne, WY 82002-0020
Telephone: 307-777-7311

Filing Office URL

http://soswy.state.wy.us/corporat/corporat.htm

LLC Statutes

The Wyoming LLC Act is contained in Title 17 of the Wyoming Statutes, Chapter 15, starting with Section 17-15-101, and is browsable from the following Web page:

http://soswy.state.wy.us/corporat/statutes.htm

The filing office provides a copy of the Wyoming Limited Liability Company Act for free upon request.

LLC Name Requirements

The name of a Wyoming LLC must contain the words "Limited Liability Company," "Limited Company," the abbreviations "LLC," "L.L.C.," "LC" or "L.C." or one of the following combination forms: "Ltd. Liability Company," "Ltd. Liability Co." or "Limited Liability Co." (Any of these nine forms is acceptable.)

The availability of a proposed LLC name can be checked online at the filing office website. The fee to reserve an available LLC name for 120 days is $25.

Name of LLC Organizational Document

Articles of organization

State-Provided Articles of Organization

The filing office provides a fill-in-the-blanks articles of organization form.

(Note: the official form does not include a provision to elect "flexible LLC status," which allows an LLC to have just one member; if you use the official form to file articles, your LLC must have two members.)

Internet Forms: Wyoming LLC forms, including articles of organization and a name reservation form, are available for downloading from the filing office website.

Filing Fees

$100, payable to the "Secretary of State."

Annual Fees: Annual LLC tax is $100.

Special Forms and Procedures

The official Wyoming articles of organization form does not include a provision electing "flexible LLC status," which allows your LLC to have just one member. In other words, if you use the official form, without alteration, your LLC must have at least two members. For more information, see the state website or ask a business lawyer.

The written consent of the registered agent to his or her appointment in this capacity must accompany the articles. A written consent form is available from the state website.

State Tax Status

No state income tax.

Sample Operating Agreement

Operating Agreement

of

Otto's Oughto Shop L.L.C.,

a Member-Managed Limited Liability Company

A. Preliminary Provisions

1. Effective Date

This Operating Agreement of Otto's Oughto Shop L.L.C., effective on the date of signing, is adopted by the members whose signatures appear at the end of this agreement.

2. Formation

This limited liability company (LLC) was formed by filing Articles of Organization, a Certificate of Formation or a similar organizational document with the state of California's LLC filing office on January 1, 2002. Unless a delayed effective date was specified when the Articles, Certificate of Formation or similar document was filed, the legal existence of this LLC commenced on the date of such filing. A copy of this organizational document has been placed in the LLC's records book.

3. Name

The formal name of this LLC is as stated above. However, this LLC may do business under a different name by complying with the state's fictitious or assumed business name statutes and procedures.

4. Registered Office and Registered Agent

The registered office address of this LLC is:
55 El Portal Avenue
Portola, California 94567
The registered agent of this LLC is:
Otto Mann
The registered agent and/or office of this LLC may be changed from time to time as the members may see fit, by filing a change of registered agent or office statement with the state LLC filing office. It will not be necessary to amend this provision of the Operating Agreement if and when such changes are made.

5. Business Purpose

The specific business purposes and activities contemplated by the founders of this LLC at the time of initial signing of this agreement consist of the following: operate an automotive parts supply store.

It is understood that the foregoing statement of powers shall not serve as a limitation on the powers or abilities of this LLC, which shall be permitted to engage in any and all lawful business activities. If this LLC intends to engage in business activities outside the state of its formation that require the qualification of the LLC in other states, it shall obtain such qualification before engaging in such out-of-state activities.

6. Duration of LLC

The duration of this LLC shall be perpetual. This LLC shall terminate when a proposal to dissolve the LLC is adopted by the membership of this LLC or when this LLC is otherwise terminated in accordance with law.

B. Membership Provisions

1. Nonliability of Members

No member of this LLC shall be personally liable for the expenses, debts, obligations or liabilities of the LLC, or for claims made against it.

2. Reimbursement for Organizational Costs

Members shall be reimbursed by the LLC for organizational expenses paid by the members. The LLC shall be authorized to elect to deduct organizational expenses and start-up expenditures ratably over a period of time as permitted by the Internal Revenue Code and as may be advised by the LLC's tax advisor.

3. Management

This LLC shall be managed exclusively by all of its members.

4. Members' Capital Interests

A member's capital interest in this LLC shall be computed as a fraction, the numerator of which is the total of a member's capital account and the denominator of which is the total of all capital accounts of all members. This fraction shall be expressed in this agreement as a percentage, which shall be called each member's "capital interest" in this LLC.

5. Membership Voting

Except as otherwise may be required by the Articles of Organization, Certificate of Formation or a similar organizational document, other provisions of this Operating Agreement, or under the laws of this state, each member shall vote on any matter submitted to the membership for approval by the managers of this LLC in proportion to the member's capital interest in this LLC. Further, unless otherwise stated in another provision of this Operating Agreement, the phrase "majority of members" means a majority of members whose combined capital interests in this LLC represent more than 50% of the capital interests of all members in this LLC, and a majority of members, so defined, may approve any item of business brought before the membership for a vote.

6. Compensation

Members shall not be paid as members of the LLC for performing any duties associated with such membership, including management of the LLC. Members may be paid, however, for any services rendered in any other capacity for the LLC, whether as officers, employees, independent contractors or otherwise.

7. Members' Meetings

The LLC shall not provide for regular members' meetings. However, any member may call a meeting by communicating his or her wish to schedule a meeting to all other members. Such notification may be in person or in writing, or by telephone, facsimile machine, or other form of electronic communications reasonably expected to be received by a member, and the other members shall then agree, either personally, in writing, or by telephone, facsimile machine or other form of electronics communication to the member calling the meeting, to meet at a mutually acceptable time and place. Notice of the business to be transacted at the meeting need not be given to members by the member calling the meeting, and any business may be discussed and conducted at the meeting.

If all members cannot attend a meeting, it shall be postponed to a date and time when all members can attend, unless all members who do not attend have agreed in writing to the holding of the meeting without them. If a meeting is postponed, and the postponed meeting cannot be held either because all members do not attend the postponed meeting or the nonattending members have not signed a written consent to allow the postponed meeting to be held without them, a second postponed meeting may be held at a date and time announced at the first postponed meeting. The date and time of the second postponed meeting shall also be communicated to any members not attending the first postponed meeting. The second postponed meeting may be held without the attendance of all members as long as a majority of the capital interests of the membership of this LLC is in attendance at the second postponed meeting. Written notice of the decisions or approvals made at this second postponed meeting shall be mailed or delivered to each nonattending member promptly after the holding of the second postponed meeting.

Written minutes of the discussions and proposals presented at a members' meeting, and the votes taken and matters approved at such meeting, shall be taken by one of the members or a person designated at the meeting. A copy of the minutes of the meeting shall be placed in the LLC's records book after the meeting.

8. Membership Certificates

This LLC shall be authorized to obtain and issue certificates representing or certifying membership interests in this LLC. Each certificate shall show the name of the LLC and the name of the member, and shall state that the person named is a member of the LLC and is entitled to all the rights granted members of the LLC under the Articles of Organization, Certificate of Formation or a similar organizational document, this Operating Agreement, and provisions of law. Each membership certificate shall be consecutively numbered and signed by each of the current members of this LLC. The certificates shall include any additional information considered appropriate for inclusion by the members on membership certificates.

In addition to the above information, all membership certificates shall bear a prominent legend on their face or reverse side stating or summarizing any transfer restrictions that apply to memberships in this LLC under the Articles of Organization, Certificate of Formation or a similar organizational document and/or this Operating Agreement, and the address where a member may obtain a copy of these restrictions upon request from this LLC.

The records book of this LLC shall contain a list of the names and addresses of all persons to whom certificates have been issued, show the date of issuance of each certificate, and record the date of all cancellations or transfers of membership certificates by members or the LLC.

9. Other Business by Members

Each member shall agree not to own an interest in, manage or work for another business, enterprise or endeavor, if such ownership or activities would compete with this LLC's business goals, mission, profitability or productivity, or would diminish or impair the member's ability to provide maximum effort and performance in accomplishing the business objectives and, if applicable, managing the business of this LLC.

10. Admission of New Members

Except as otherwise provided in this agreement, a person or entity shall not be admitted into membership in this LLC unless each member consents in writing to the admission of the new member. The admission of new members into this LLC who have been transferred, or wish to be transferred, a membership interest in this LLC by an existing member of this LLC is covered by separate provisions in this Operating Agreement.

C. Tax and Financial Provisions

1. Tax Classification of LLC

The members of this LLC intend that this LLC be initially classified as a partnership for federal and, if applicable, state income tax purposes. It is understood that all members may agree to change the tax treatment of this LLC by signing, or authorizing the signature of, IRS Form 8832, Entity Classification Election, and filing it with the IRS and, if applicable, the state tax department within the prescribed time limits.

2. Tax Year and Accounting Method

The tax year of this LLC shall end on the last day of the month of December. The LLC shall use the cash method of accounting. Both the tax year and the accounting period of the LLC may be changed with the consent of all members if the LLC qualifies for such change, and may be effected by the filing of appropriate forms with the IRS and state tax offices.

3. Tax Matters Partner

If this LLC is required under Internal Revenue Code provisions or regulations, it shall designate from among its members a "tax matters partner" in accordance with Internal Revenue Code Section 6231(a)(7) and corresponding regulations, who will fulfill this role by being the spokesperson for the LLC in dealings with the IRS as required under the Internal Revenue Code and Regulations, and who will report to the members on the progress and outcome of these dealings.

4. Annual Income Tax Returns and Reports

Within 60 days after the end of each tax year of the LLC, a copy of the LLC's state and federal income tax returns for the preceding tax year shall be mailed or otherwise provided to each member of the LLC, together with any additional information and forms necessary for each member to complete his or her individual state and federal income tax returns. This additional information shall include a federal (and, if applicable, state) Form K-1 (Form 1065—Partner's Share of Income, Credits, Deductions) or equivalent income tax reporting form, as well as a financial report, which shall include a balance sheet and profit and loss statement for the prior tax year of the LLC.

5. Bank Accounts

The LLC shall designate one or more banks or other institutions for the deposit of the funds of the LLC, and shall establish savings, checking, investment and other such accounts as are reasonable and necessary for its business and investments. One or more members of the LLC shall be designated with the consent of all members to deposit and withdraw funds of the LLC, and to direct the investment of funds from, into and among such accounts. The funds of the LLC, however and wherever deposited or invested, shall not be commingled with the personal funds of any members of the LLC.

6. Title to Assets

All personal and real property of this LLC shall be held in the name of the LLC, not in the names of individual members.

D. Capital Provisions

1. Capital Contributions by Members

Members shall make the following contributions of cash, property or services to the LLC, on or by specified dates, as shown next to each member's name below. The fair market values of items of property or services as agreed between the LLC and the contributing member are also shown below.

Name of Member: Otto Mann
Description of Payment: Cash
Value of Capital Payment: $20,000
Date of Payment: January 15, 2002

Name of Member: Mike Maxwell
Description of Payment: Cash
Value of Capital Payment: $10,000
Date of Payment: January 15, 2002

2. Additional Contributions by Members

The members may agree, from time to time by unanimous vote, to require the payment of additional capital contributions by the members, on or by a mutually agreeable date.

3. Failure to Make Contributions

If a member fails to make a required capital contribution within the time agreed for a member's contribution, the remaining members may, by unanimous vote, agree to reschedule the time for payment of the capital contribution by the late-paying member, setting any additional repayment terms, such as a late payment penalty, rate of interest to be applied to the unpaid balance, or other monetary amount to be paid by the delinquent member, as the remaining members decide. Alternatively, the remaining members may, by unanimous vote, agree to cancel the membership of the delinquent member, provided any prior partial payments of capital made by the delinquent member are refunded promptly by the LLC to the member after the decision is made to terminate the membership of the delinquent member.

4. No Interest on Capital Contributions

No interest shall be paid on funds or property contributed as capital to this LLC, or on funds reflected in the capital accounts of the members.

5. Capital Account Bookkeeping

A capital account shall be set up and maintained on the books of the LLC for each member. It shall reflect each member's capital contribution to the LLC, increased by each member's share of profits in the LLC, decreased by each member's share of losses and expenses of the LLC, and adjusted as required in accordance with applicable provisions of the Internal Revenue Code and corresponding income tax regulations.

6. Consent to Capital Contribution Withdrawals and Distributions

Members shall not be allowed to withdraw any part of their capital contributions or to receive distributions, whether in property or cash, except as otherwise allowed by this agreement and, in any case, only if such withdrawal is made with the written consent of all members.

7. Allocations of Profits and Losses

Except as otherwise provided in the Articles of Organization, Certificate of Formation or a similar organizational document, or this Operating Agreement, no member shall be given priority or preference with respect to other members in obtaining a return of capital contributions, distributions or allocations of the income, gains, losses, deductions, credits or other items of the LLC. Except as otherwise provided in the Articles of Organization, Certificate of Formation or a similar organizational document, or this Operating Agreement, the profits and losses of the LLC, and all items of its income, gain, loss, deduction and credit shall be allocated to members according to each member's capital interest in this LLC.

8. Allocation and Distribution of Cash to Members

Cash from LLC business operations, as well as cash from a sale or other disposition of LLC capital assets, may be allocated and distributed from time to time to members in accordance with each member's capital interest in the LLC, as may be decided by a majority of the capital interests of the members.

9. Allocation of Noncash Distributions

If proceeds consist of property other than cash, the members shall decide the value of the property and allocate such value among the members in accordance with each member's capital interest in the LLC. If such noncash proceeds are later reduced to cash, such cash may be distributed among the members according to the distribution cash allocations provisions in this agreement.

10. Allocation and Distribution of Liquidation Proceeds

Regardless of any other provision in this agreement, if there is a distribution in liquidation of this LLC, or when any member's interest is liquidated, all items of income and loss shall be allocated to the members' capital accounts, and all appropriate credits and deductions shall then be made to these capital accounts before any final distribution is made. A final distribution shall be made to members only to the extent of, and in proportion to, any positive balance in each member's capital account.

E. Membership Withdrawal and Transfer Provisions

1. Withdrawal of Members

A member may withdraw from this LLC by giving written notice to all other members at least 90 days before the date the withdrawal is to be effective. In the event of such withdrawal, the LLC shall pay the departing member the fair value of his or her LLC interest, less any amounts owed by the member to the LLC. The departing and remaining members shall agree at the time of departure on the fair value of the departing member's interest and the schedule of payments to be made by the LLC to the departing member, who shall receive payment for his or her interest within a reasonable time after departure from the LLC. If the departing and remaining members cannot agree on the value of departing member's interest, they shall select an appraiser, who shall determine the current value of the departing member's interest. This appraised amount shall be the fair value of the departing member's interest, and shall form the basis of the amount to be paid to the departing member.

2. Restrictions on the Transfer of Membership

Notwithstanding any other provision of this agreement, a member shall not transfer his or her membership in the LLC unless all of the nontransferring LLC members first agree in writing to approve the admission of the transferee into this LLC. Further, no member may encumber a part or all of his or her membership in the LLC by mortgage, pledge, granting of a security interest, lien or otherwise, unless the encumbrance has first been approved in writing by all other members of the LLC.

Notwithstanding the above provision, any member shall be allowed to assign an economic interest in his or her membership to another person without the approval of the other members. Such an assignment shall not include a transfer of the member's voting or management rights in this LLC, and the assignee shall not become a member of the LLC.

F. Dissolution Provisions

1. Events That Trigger Dissolution of the LLC

The following events shall trigger a dissolution of the LLC, except as provided:

a. Dissociation of a Member. The dissociation of a member, which means the death, incapacity, bankruptcy, retirement, resignation or expulsion of a member, or any other event that terminates the continued membership of a member shall cause a dissolution of this LLC only if and as provided below:

1. If a vote must be taken under state law to avoid dissolution. If, under provisions of state law, a vote of the remaining LLC members is required to continue the existence of this LLC after the dissociation of a member, the remaining members shall affirmatively vote to continue the existence of this LLC within the period, and by the number of votes of remaining members, that may be required under such provisions. If such a vote is required, but the period or number of votes requirement is not specified under such provisions, all remaining members must affirmatively vote to a continuation of this LLC within 90 days from the date of the date of dissociation of the member. If the affirmative vote of the remaining members is not obtained under this provision, this LLC shall dissolve under the appropriate procedures specified under state law.

2. If a vote is not required under state law to avoid dissolution. If provisions of state law do not require such a vote of remaining members to continue the existence and/or business of the LLC after the dissociation of a member, and/or allow the provisions of this Operating Agreement to take precedence over state law provisions relating to the continuance of the LLC following the dissociation of a member, then this LLC shall continue its existence and business following such dissociation of a member without the necessity of taking a vote of the remaining members. Notwithstanding the above, if the LLC is left with fewer members than required under state law for the operation of an LLC following the dissociation of a member of this LLC, the LLC shall elect or appoint a member in accordance with any provisions of state law regarding such election or appointment. If such election or appointment is not made within the time period specified under state law, or, if no time period is specified under state law and the LLC makes no election or appointment within 90 days following the date of dissociation of the member, this LLC shall dissolve under the appropriate procedures specified under state law.

b.   **Expiration of LLC Term.** The expiration of the term of existence of the LLC if such term is specified in the Articles of Organization, Certificate of Formation or a similar organizational document, or this Operating Agreement, shall cause the dissolution of this LLC.

c.   **Written Agreement to Dissolve.** The written agreement of all members to dissolve the LLC shall cause a dissolution of this LLC.

d.   **Entry of Decree.** The entry of a decree of dissolution of the LLC under state law shall cause a dissolution of this LLC.

If the LLC is to dissolve according to any of the above provisions, the members and, if applicable, managers, shall wind up the affairs of the LLC, and take other actions appropriate to complete a dissolution of the LLC in accordance with applicable provisions of state law.

G. General Provisions

1. Officers

The LLC may designate one or more officers, such as a President, Vice President, Secretary and Treasurer. Persons who fill these positions need not be members of the LLC. Such positions may be compensated or noncompensated according to the nature and extent of the services rendered for the LLC as a part of the duties of each office. Ministerial services only as a part of any officer position will normally not be compensated, such as the performance of officer duties specified in this agreement, but any officer may be reimbursed by the LLC for out-of-pocket expenses paid by the officer in carrying out the duties of his or her office.

2. Records

The LLC shall keep at its principal business address a copy of all proceedings of membership meetings, as well as books of account of the LLC's financial transactions. A list of the names and addresses of the current membership of the LLC also shall be maintained at this address, with notations on any transfers of members' interests to nonmembers or persons being admitted into membership in the LLC.

Copies of the LLC's Articles of Organization, Certificate of Formation or a similar organizational document, a signed copy of this Operating Agreement, and the LLC's tax returns for the preceding three tax years shall be kept at the principal business address of the LLC. A statement also shall be kept at this address containing any of the following information that is applicable to this LLC:

- the amount of cash or a description and value of property contributed or agreed to be contributed as capital to the LLC by each member;
- a schedule showing when any additional capital contributions are to be made by members to this LLC;
- a statement or schedule, if appropriate, showing the rights of members to receive distributions representing a return of part or all of members' capital contributions; and
- a description of events, or the date, when the legal existence of the LLC will terminate under provisions in the LLC's Articles of Organization, Certificate of Formation or a similar organizational document, or this Operating Agreement.

If one or more of the above items is included or listed in this Operating Agreement, it will be sufficient to keep a copy of this agreement at the principal business address of the LLC without having to prepare and keep a separate record of such item or items at this address.

Any member may inspect any and all records maintained by the LLC upon reasonable notice to the LLC. Copying of the LLC's records by members is allowed, but copying costs shall be paid for by the requesting member.

3. All Necessary Acts

The members and officers of this LLC are authorized to perform all acts necessary to perfect the organization of this LLC and to carry out its business operations expeditiously and efficiently. The Secretary of the LLC, or other officers, or all members of the LLC, may certify to other businesses, financial institutions and individuals as to the authority of one or more members or officers of this LLC to transact specific items of business on behalf of the LLC.

4. Mediation and Arbitration of Disputes Among Members

In any dispute over the provisions of this Operating Agreement and in other disputes among the members, if the members cannot resolve the dispute to their mutual satisfaction, the matter shall be submitted to mediation. The terms and procedure for mediation shall be arranged by the parties to the dispute.

If good-faith mediation of a dispute proves impossible or if an agreed-upon mediation outcome cannot be obtained by the members who are parties to the dispute, the dispute may be submitted to arbitration in accordance with the rules of the American Arbitration Association. Any party may commence arbitration of the dispute by sending a written request for arbitration to all other parties to the dispute. The request shall state the nature of the dispute to be resolved by arbitration, and, if all parties to the dispute agree to arbitration, arbitration shall be commenced as soon as practical after such parties receive a copy of the written request.

All parties shall initially share the cost of arbitration, but the prevailing party or parties may be awarded attorney fees, costs and other expenses of arbitration. All arbitration decisions shall be final, binding and conclusive on all the parties to arbitration, and legal judgment may be entered based upon such decision in accordance with applicable law in any court having jurisdiction to do so.

5. Entire Agreement

This Operating Agreement represents the entire agreement among the members of this LLC, and it shall not be amended, modified or replaced except by a written instrument executed by all the parties to this agreement who are current members of this LLC as well as any and all additional parties who became members of this LLC after the adoption of this agreement. This agreement replaces and supersedes all prior written and oral agreements among any and all members of this LLC.

6. Severability

If any provision of this agreement is determined by a court or arbitrator to be invalid, unenforceable or otherwise ineffective, that provision shall be severed from the rest of this agreement, and the remaining provisions shall remain in effect and enforceable.

H. Signatures of Members and Spouses of Members

1. Execution of Agreement

In witness whereof, the members of this LLC sign and adopt this agreement as the Operating Agreement of this LLC.

Date: _____

Signature: _____
                 Otto Mann, Member

Date: _____

Signature: _____
                 Mike Maxwell, Member

2. Consent of Spouses

The undersigned, if any, are spouses of above-signed members of this LLC. These spouses have read this agreement and agree to be bound by its terms in any matter in which they have a financial interest, including restrictions on the transfer of memberships and the terms under which memberships in this LLC may be sold or otherwise transferred.

■

Checklist for Forming an LLC

Here in one place is a list of the factors that should inform your decision as to whether it makes sense to run your business as an LLC. And assuming the answer is yes, this checklist also explains what you need to do to actually create your LLC. Use this checklist in conjunction with the state-by-state LLC requirements listed in Appendix A. In addition, this list is not meant to be exhaustive. If yours is a brand new business, you'll obviously have to take many other steps that apply to all businesses, not just LLCs, including getting a business license and finding a location for your business.

I. Decide if an LLC is the right structure for my business

[√] Is my type of business one where business debts and claims could threaten my personal assets?

[√] Do I own sufficient personal assets that would be at risk (such as equity in a house) if a successful business-based lawsuit resulted in a judgment that could be collected from my personal assets?

[√] How much does my state charge for creating an LLC? Does my state also charge an annual fee?

[√] How are LLCs taxed in my state (do I have to pay an annual LLC entity franchise or income tax to my state)?

[√] Is my business or profession licensed by the state? If so, will I be required to set up a professional LLC or a professional corporation instead?

[√] Would I benefit more from the stock structure of a corporation because I plan to distribute stock options or "go public" with an IPO (initial public offering) in the future? (I discuss the benefits of corporations in Chapter 2.)

[√] (Optional.) Have I consulted with an accountant or lawyer on any complex tax and legal issues surrounding my business formation?

II. Name My Business

[√] Choose an appropriate name for my business.
[√] Do a state and federal trademark search if necessary.
[√] Check the availability of the name with the LLC filing office.
[√] Reserve the name with the LLC filing office (for a small fee).

III. Follow Steps Required by Your State

[√] File my articles of organization (or certificate of organization or formation)
with my state's LLC filing office, along with the required fee.
[√] Publish a notice of intention to form my LLC (required in only some states).
[√] File a notice of bulk sales (sometimes required when converting an existing
business to an LLC—see Chapter 6, Section A4b).

IV. Steps to Take After Formation

[√] Prepare my LLC operating agreement.
[√] Create my LLC recordkeeping binder.
[√] Hold the LLC's first organizational meeting to adopt the operating agreement
and elect officers (such as president, secretary). Place minutes of meeting in
my LLC records binder.
[√] File for a Tax I.D. Number (EIN) with the IRS.
[√] Open a bank account.
[√] Get liability insurance coverage.

V. On-Going Formalities

[√] Record other important ongoing decisions with minutes or written consent
forms.
[√] Sign lease agreements, contracts, loans in my LLC's name.
[√] File annual state LLC reports if required (typically for a minimum fee).
[√] For multi-member LLCs: File annual LLC informational returns (partnership
tax returns) with the IRS and my state.

■

Index

■

CATALOG

...more from nolo

	PRICE	CODE
BUSINESS		
Avoid Employee Lawsuits (Quick & Legal Series)	$24.95	AVEL
The CA Nonprofit Corporation Kit (Binder w/CD-ROM)	$59.95	CNP
Consultant & Independent Contractor Agreements (Book w/CD-ROM)	$29.95	CICA
The Corporate Minutes Book (Book w/CD-ROM)	$69.95	CORMI
The Employer's Legal Handbook	$39.95	EMPL
Firing Without Fear (Quick & Legal Series)	$29.95	FEAR
Form Your Own Limited Liability Company (Book w/CD-ROM)	$44.95	LIAB
Hiring Independent Contractors: The Employer's Legal Guide (Book w/CD-ROM)	$34.95	HICI
How to Create a Buy-Sell Agreement & Control the Destiny of your Small Business (Book w/Disk-PC)	$49.95	BSAG
How to Form a California Professional Corporation (Book w/CD-ROM)	$59.95	PROF
How to Form a Nonprofit Corporation (Book w/CD-ROM)—National Edition	$44.95	NNP
How to Form a Nonprofit Corporation in California (Book w/CD-ROM)	$44.95	NON
How to Form Your Own California Corporation (Binder w/CD-ROM)	$39.95	CACI
How to Form Your Own California Corporation (Book w/CD-ROM)	$34.95	CCOR
How to Form Your Own New York Corporation (Book w/Disk—PC)	$39.95	NYCO
How to Form Your Own Texas Corporation (Book w/CD-ROM)	$39.95	TCOR
How to Write a Business Plan	$29.95	SBS
The Independent Paralegal's Handbook	$29.95	PARA
Leasing Space for Your Small Business	$34.95	LESP
Legal Guide for Starting & Running a Small Business	$34.95	RUNS
Legal Forms for Starting & Running a Small Business (Book w/CD-ROM)	$29.95	RUNS2
Marketing Without Advertising	$22.00	MWAD
Music Law (Book w/Disk—PC)	$29.95	ML
Nolo's California Quick Corp (Quick & Legal Series)	$19.95	QINC
Nolo's Guide to Social Security Disability	$29.95	QSS
Nolo's Quick LLC (Quick & Legal Series)	$24.95	LLCQ
The Small Business Start-up Kit (Book w/CD-ROM)	$29.95	SMBU

	PRICE	CODE
The Small Business Start-up Kit for California (Book w/CD-ROM)	$29.95	OPEN
The Partnership Book: How to Write a Partnership Agreement (Book w/CD-ROM)	$39.95	PART
Sexual Harassment on the Job	$24.95	HARS
Starting & Running a Successful Newsletter or Magazine	$29.95	MAG
Tax Savvy for Small Business	$34.95	SAVVY
Working for Yourself: Law & Taxes for the Self-Employed	$39.95	WAGE
Your Limited Liability Company: An Operating Manual (Book w/Disk—PC)	$49.95	LOP
Your Rights in the Workplace	$29.95	YRW

CONSUMER

Fed Up with the Legal System: What's Wrong & How to Fix It	$9.95	LEG
How to Win Your Personal Injury Claim	$29.95	PICL
Nolo's Encyclopedia of Everyday Law	$28.95	EVL
Nolo's Pocket Guide to California Law	$15.95	CLAW
Trouble-Free Travel...And What to Do When Things Go Wrong	$14.95	TRAV

ESTATE PLANNING & PROBATE

8 Ways to Avoid Probate (Quick & Legal Series)	$16.95	PRO8
9 Ways to Avoid Estate Taxes (Quick & Legal Series)	$29.95	ESTX
Estate Planning Basics (Quick & Legal Series)	$18.95	ESPN
How to Probate an Estate in California	$49.95	PAE
Make Your Own Living Trust (Book w/CD-ROM)	$34.95	LITR
Nolo's Law Form Kit: Wills	$24.95	KWL
Nolo's Simple Will Book (Book w/CD-ROM)	$34.95	SWIL
Plan Your Estate	$39.95	NEST
Quick & Legal Will Book (Quick & Legal Series)	$15.95	QUIC

FAMILY MATTERS

Child Custody: Building Parenting Agreements That Work	$29.95	CUST
The Complete IEP Guide	$24.95	IEP
Divorce & Money: How to Make the Best Financial Decisions During Divorce	$34.95	DIMO
Do Your Own Divorce in Oregon	$29.95	ODIV
Get a Life: You Don't Need a Million to Retire Well	$24.95	LIFE
The Guardianship Book for California	$34.95	GB
How to Adopt Your Stepchild in California (Book w/CD-ROM)	$34.95	ADOP
A Legal Guide for Lesbian and Gay Couples	$25.95	LG
Living Together: A Legal Guide (Book w/CD-ROM)	$34.95	LTK
Using Divorce Mediation: Save Your Money & Your Sanity	$29.95	UDMD

	PRICE	CODE

GOING TO COURT

Beat Your Ticket: Go To Court and Win! (National Edition) .... $19.95 — BEYT

The Criminal Law Handbook: Know Your Rights, Survive the System .... $29.95 — KYR

Everybody's Guide to Small Claims Court (National Edition) .... $24.95 — NSCC

Everybody's Guide to Small Claims Court in California .... $24.95 — CSCC

Fight Your Ticket ... and Win! (California Edition) .... $24.95 — FYT

How to Change Your Name in California .... $34.95 — NAME

How to Collect When You Win a Lawsuit (California Edition) .... $29.95 — JUDG

How to Mediate Your Dispute .... $18.95 — MEDI

How to Seal Your Juvenile & Criminal Records (California Edition) .... $34.95 — CRIM

Nolo's Deposition Handbook .... $29.95 — DEP

Represent Yourself in Court: How to Prepare & Try a Winning Case .... $34.95 — RYC

HOMEOWNERS, LANDLORDS & TENANTS

California Tenants' Rights .... $27.95 — CTEN

Contractors' and Homeowners' Guide to Mechanics' Liens
(Book w/Disk—PC)—California Edition .... $39.95 — MIEN

The Deeds Book (California Edition) .... $24.95 — DEED

Dog Law .... $14.95 — DOG

Every Landlord's Legal Guide (National Edition, Book w/CD-ROM) .... $44.95 — ELLI

Every Tenant's Legal Guide .... $26.95 — EVTEN

For Sale by Owner in California .... $29.95 — FSBO

How to Buy a House in California .... $29.95 — BHCA

The Landlord's Law Book, Vol. 1: Rights & Responsibilities
   (California Edition) (Book w/CD-ROM) .... $44.95 — LBRT

The California Landlord's Law Book, Vol. 2: Evictions (Book w/CD-ROM) .... $44.95 — LBEV

Leases & Rental Agreements (Quick & Legal Series) .... $24.95 — LEAR

Neighbor Law: Fences, Trees, Boundaries & Noise .... $24.95 — NEI

The New York Landlord's Law Book (Book w/CD-ROM) .... $39.95 — NYLL

Renters' Rights (National Edition) .... $24.95 — RENT

Stop Foreclosure Now in California .... $29.95 — CLOS

HUMOR

29 Reasons Not to Go to Law School .... $12.95 — 29R

Poetic Justice .... $9.95 — PJ

IMMIGRATION

How to Get a Green Card .... $29.95 — GRN

U.S. Immigration Made Easy .... $44.95 — IMEZ

	PRICE	CODE

MONEY MATTERS

	PRICE	CODE
101 Law Forms for Personal Use (Book w/Disk—PC)	$29.95	SPOT
Bankruptcy: Is It the Right Solution to Your Debt Problems? (Quick & Legal Series)	$19.95	BRS
Chapter 13 Bankruptcy: Repay Your Debts	$34.95	CH13
Creating Your Own Retirement Plan	$29.95	YROP
Credit Repair (Quick & Legal Series, Book w/CD-ROM)	$19.95	CREP
How to File for Chapter 7 Bankruptcy	$34.95	HFB
IRAs, 401(k)s & Other Retirement Plans: Taking Your Money Out	$29.95	RET
Money Troubles: Legal Strategies to Cope With Your Debts	$29.95	MT
Nolo's Law Form Kit: Personal Bankruptcy	$24.95	KBNK
Stand Up to the IRS	$24.95	SIRS
Surviving an IRS Tax Audit (Quick & Legal Series)	$24.95	SAUD
Take Control of Your Student Loan Debt	$24.95	SLOAN

PATENTS AND COPYRIGHTS

	PRICE	CODE
The Copyright Handbook: How to Protect and Use Written Works (Book w/CD-ROM)	$34.95	COHA
Copyright Your Software	$24.95	CYS
Domain Names	$24.95	DOM
Getting Permission: How to License and Clear Copyrighted Materials Online and Off (Book w/Disk—PC)	$34.95	RIPER
How to Make Patent Drawings Yourself	$29.95	DRAW
The Inventor's Notebook	$24.95	INOT
Nolo's Patents for Beginners (Quick & Legal Series)	$29.95	QPAT
License Your Invention (Book w/Disk—PC)	$39.95	LICE
Patent, Copyright & Trademark	$34.95	PCTM
Patent It Yourself	$49.95	PAT
Patent Searching Made Easy	$29.95	PATSE
The Public Domain	$34.95	PUBL
Web and Software Development: A Legal Guide (Book w/ CD-ROM)	$44.95	SFT
Trademark: Legal Care for Your Business and Product Name	$39.95	TRD

RESEARCH & REFERENCE

	PRICE	CODE
Legal Research: How to Find & Understand the Law	$34.95	LRES

SENIORS

	PRICE	CODE
Beat the Nursing Home Trap: A Consumer's Guide to Assisted Living and Long-Term Care	$21.95	ELD
The Conservatorship Book for California	$44.95	CNSV
Social Security, Medicare & Pensions	$24.95	SOA

SOFTWARE

**Call or check our website at www.nolo.com
for special discounts on Software!**

	PRICE	CODE
LeaseWriter CD—Windows	$129.95	LWD1
Living Trust Maker CD—Windows	$89.95	LTD2
LLC Maker—Windows	$89.95	LLP1
Personal RecordKeeper 5.0 CD—Windows	$59.95	RKD5
Small Business Pro 4 CD—Windows	$89.95	SBCD4
WillMaker 8.0 CD—Windows	$69.95	WP8

Special Upgrade Offer

Get 35% off the latest edition off your Nolo book

It's important to have the most current legal information. Because laws and legal procedures change often, we update our books regularly. To help keep you up-to-date we are extending this special upgrade offer. Cut out and mail the title portion of the cover of your old Nolo book and we'll give you 35% off the retail price of the NEW EDITION of that book when you purchase directly from us. For more information call us at 1-800-992-6656. This offer is to individuals only.

Order Form

Name

Address

City

State, Zip

Daytime Phone

E-mail

Our "No-Hassle" Guarantee

Return anything you buy directly from Nolo for any reason and we'll cheerfully refund your purchase price. No ifs, ands or buts.

☐ Check here if you do not wish to receive mailings from other companies

Item Code	Quantity	Item	Unit Price	Total Price

Method of payment

☐ Check ☐ VISA ☐ MasterCard
☐ Discover Card ☐ American Express

Subtotal	
Add your local sales tax (California only)	
Shipping: RUSH $9, Basic $5 (See below)	
"I bought 3, ship it to me FREE!"(Ground shipping only)	
TOTAL	

Account Number

Expiration Date

Signature

Shipping and Handling

Rush Delivery—Only $9

We'll ship any order to any street address in the U.S. by UPS 2nd Day Air* for only $9!

* Order by noon Pacific Time and get your order in 2 business days. Orders placed after noon Pacific Time will arrive in 3 business days. P.O. boxes and S.F. Bay Area use basic shipping. Alaska and Hawaii use 2nd Day Air or Priority Mail.

Basic Shipping—$5

Use for P.O. Boxes, Northern California and Ground Service.

Allow 1-2 weeks for delivery. U.S. addresses only.

For faster service, use your credit card and our toll-free numbers

Order 24 hours a day

Online	www.nolo.com
Phone	1-800-992-6656
Fax	1-800-645-0895
Mail	Nolo
	950 Parker St.
	Berkeley, CA 94710

Visit us online at
www.nolo.com

Take 2 minutes & Give us your 2 cents

Your comments make a big difference in the development and revision of Nolo books and software. Please take a few minutes and register your Nolo product—and your comments—with us. Not only will your input make a difference, you'll receive special offers available only to registered owners of Nolo products on our newest books and software. Register now by:

PHONE
1-800-992-6656

FAX
1-800-645-0895

EMAIL
cs@nolo.com

or **MAIL** us
this registration card

REMEMBER:
Little publishers have big ears. We really listen to you.

fold here

NOLO REGISTRATION CARD

NAME _____ DATE _____

ADDRESS _____

_____

CITY _____ STATE _____ ZIP _____

PHONE _____ E-MAIL _____

WHERE DID YOU HEAR ABOUT THIS PRODUCT? _____

WHERE DID YOU PURCHASE THIS PRODUCT? _____

DID YOU CONSULT A LAWYER? (PLEASE CIRCLE ONE)   YES   NO   NOT APPLICABLE

DID YOU FIND THIS BOOK HELPFUL?   (VERY) 5   4   3   2   1   (NOT AT ALL)

COMMENTS _____

_____

_____

WAS IT EASY TO USE?   (VERY EASY) 5   4   3   2   1   (VERY DIFFICULT)

DO YOU OWN A COMPUTER? IF SO, WHICH FORMAT? (PLEASE CIRCLE ONE)   WINDOWS   DOS   MAC

We occasionally make our mailing list available to carefully selected companies whose products may be of interest to you.
❏ If you do not wish to receive mailings from these companies, please check this box.
❏ You can quote me in future Nolo promotional materials. Daytime phone number _____.

LLCQ 1.2

NOLO IN THE NEWS

"Nolo helps lay people perform legal tasks without the aid—or fees—of lawyers."

—USA TODAY

Nolo books are ..."written in plain language, free of legal mumbo jumbo, and spiced with witty personal observations."

—ASSOCIATED PRESS

"...Nolo publications...guide people simply through the how, when, where and why of law."

—WASHINGTON POST

"Increasingly, people who are not lawyers are performing tasks usually regarded as legal work... And consumers, using books like Nolo's, do routine legal work themselves."

—NEW YORK TIMES

"...All of [Nolo's] books are easy-to-understand, are updated regularly, provide pull-out forms...and are often quite moving in their sense of compassion for the struggles of the lay reader."

—SAN FRANCISCO CHRONICLE

fold here

- -

Place
stamp here

nolo
950 Parker Street
Berkeley, CA 94710-9867

Attn:  **LLCQ 1.2**